BIBLICAL ORIGINS OF MODERN SECULAR CULTURE

BIBLICAL ORIGINS OF MODERN SECULAR CULTURE

An Essay
in the Interpretation
of Western History

Willis B. Glover

MERCER

ISBN 0-86554-138-8

All books published by Mercer University Press are produced on acid-free paper that exceeds the minimum standards set by the National Historical Publications and
Records Commission.

Library of Congress Cataloging in Publication Data
Glover, Willis B., 1917–
    Biblical origins of modern secular culture.
    Includes bibliographical references and index
    1. Civilization, Christian. 2. Bible—Influence—
Civilization, Occidental. 3. Civilization, Secular.
I. Title.
BR115.C5G57   1984   909'.09821   84-14868
ISBN 0-86554-138-8 (alk. paper)

CONTENTS

PREFACE... ix

I
INTRODUCTION.. 1

II
THE MEDIEVAL BEGINNING 17

III
THE RENAISSANCE VIEW OF MAN............................. 47

IV
SCIENCE AND THEOLOGY 79

V
THE ENLIGHTENMENT: THE BEGINNING
OF THE MODERN WORLD... 107

VI
PROMETHEUS UNBOUND 141

VII
THE WESTERN SENSE OF HISTORY 179

VIII
THE NEW HUMANISM: FAITH AND CULTURE 213

IX
FAITHS IN CRISIS 239

EPILOGUE 273

INDEX 277

To Miriam

PREFACE

This study is a historical essay. It is not historical research in the strict and proper meaning of that term. It is frankly based on the researches of other people, most of whose contributions are recognized in the works cited. I did not discover Walker Percy until this book was in the hands of the publisher. I have added his name to lists of Christian writers, but I have not done justice to his anticipation of much that I have tried to say.

The title of this essay could hardly be called too short; it, nevertheless, might be misleading. The subject is largely confined to intellectual culture; and its considerable discussion of the Christian intellectual tradition is not confined to what has been secularized.

Although it has obviously had disadvantages as well as advantages, I appreciate having spent my career in small colleges in which there has been considerable liveliness of discourse. I particularly appreciate having had personal contact and meaningful conversation with interesting people in a wide variety of fields. In addition to my colleagues in history, I wish to express my special thanks for encouragement, information, and helpful criticism to Ray Brewster, Dan Metts, Ted Nordenhaug, Rex Stevens, and Tom

Trimble. I am also indebted to Miss Bessie Killebrew, who with
great patience and good humor typed the manuscript.

Willis B. Glover
Mercer University
January 1984

I INTRODUCTION

For the first time in history a single culture dominates the world. The culture that slowly arose in Western Europe after the collapse of the Roman Empire has expanded beyond the borders of Europe and has proved so far superior to other cultures in a wide range of important human activities that it can no longer be thought of as having any rival. Indigenous cultures will give it different flavors and tones in different regions, but none, not even that of Islam, shows the slightest promise of withstanding its onslaught. A recent history of human culture on the Afro-Eurasian land mass from pre-historic times to the present was entitled by its eminent American author simply *The Rise of the West*.[1] Yet this uniquely successful civilization is now in the most serious crisis of its existence, and the question of its survival is raised by thoughtful and informed people.

The problem is not merely international strife and other forms of internal dissension; that has always characterized the West. Nor

---

[1]William H. MacNeill, *The Rise of the West* (Chicago, 1963).

is it even that our powers for destruction are unprecedented and capable of annihilating the race, for it is obvious that if that danger were removed the crisis would continue. The crisis of Western civilization is an identity crisis, a loss of confidence, of belief in its own worth. At bottom the crisis is religious, religious in that it involves the question of meaning at the most profound level of human experience.

During the last great surge of Western imperialism, in the age of Teddy Roosevelt and Rudyard Kipling, Western men were confident of the superiority of their culture to those of non-European peoples. It was not hard for those who had moral scruples about the exploitation of the colonial world to soothe their consciences with the thought that in the long run the West offered more than it took. That has changed now. After the peace of 1919 colonies were for the most part in the hands of governments committed to principles of self-determination and liberal government. As soon as colonial people began to demand their independence by appeal to the basic political principles of the colonial powers, they were able to put the latter on the defensive morally. Anticolonial movements within the colonial powers grew strong; it was soon impossible morally and politically (not militarily) to take the kind of action that would have been necessary to defeat or contain sustained movements of colonial people for national independence. Whether tactics like those of Gandhi would have been successful against Nazi Germany or the U.S.S.R. is an interesting question. At any rate the pattern of Western withdrawal became so accepted an outcome of any colonial demand for independence that when the Congolese demanded immediate freedom from Belgium, they got their independence with embarrassing suddenness. The Belgians have been criticized for irresponsibility in acceding to the demand that independence be immediate; but this was a light burden compared to the abuse that would surely have been heaped on them had they tried to delay so as to make a smoother transfer of power.

The paradox is not only that Western power was retreating at the same time Western culture was spreading, but that the spread of Western ideas, ideals, and techniques is what produced the retrenchment of Western power. There is, indeed, a still deeper paradox: just when Westernization is enveloping the whole globe and even the most anti-Western politicians are introducing Western industry and science and political techniques into their countries, the West itself has lost confidence in the value of its own culture. It has become a mark of high moral sensibility in many Western circles to assert the superiority of non-Western culture to our own.

What has happened to the West is not invasion and criticism by some alien authority, nor is it a case of development into some new phase of culture that now stands in judgment on what has preceded. The West is experiencing a kind of malaise, a failure of nerve that results from the lack of any source of meaning capable of conferring authority on our judgments and justifying our actions. The superstructure of civilization continues and even continues to develop, but the structural elements no longer point beyond themselves to a reality that confers any significance on them. They are experienced as artificial, superficial, and meaningless.

Cultures develop when a human population sharing a common way of being aware of the world, a common sense of what is real and important, proceeds to deal with the myriad concerns of human life. The kind of solutions they find to problems, the kind of action that seems to them just and reasonable in concrete situations will reflect their shared sense of reality. That is why the functional school of sociologists of religion is able (not quite adequately, to be sure) to define religion as whatever integrates a given culture. The religious basis of the culture of Western Europe has been very complex, especially in modern times, but despite serious contradictions and the fact that some Western humanistic faiths or sub-faiths have not been identified as religious, there has been a Western mode of being aware of the world, a Western sense of reality, that has served as an integrating principle constituting Western civilization as an historical entity. At the present time many people, including some of the most sensitive and intelligent, no longer find convincing what have hitherto been common commitments in the West. We are experiencing a crisis of faith.

Matthew Arnold was one of the first to see that loss of faith, if it becomes general, threatens the existence of culture. In *Dover Beach*, published in 1867, he foresaw the emptiness and direction-

lessness that has now, a century later, overtaken us.[2] His prediction, made when only one volume of *Das Kapital* had been
published, can be seen now to be closer to the real situation of modern man than the so-often-erroneous predictions of Marx. One
must not, however, give Arnold too much credit, for he did not understand the strength or the religious nature of the humanistic
faiths that in his day were surrogates for the declining Christian
faith. Matthew Arnold was not the only person in the late nineteenth century who saw the emptiness that was afflicting culture
like a blight. Nietzsche was a far more vehement and sustained
critic. But such were rare and had few followers; at least few followed them in this regard. The social critics, including the utopians
and Marx, are a different phenomenon. They also were keen critics
of the contemporary society and showed profound insights in their
criticisms, but they had answers; they proposed humanistic nostrums and thus championed some aspects of their Western heritage
as promising salvation.

It was not until the twentieth century that the malaise reached
any significant portion even of the intelligentsia. There is a watershed between Kipling and the Wasteland poets. Since World War
I some of the best Western literature has been devastatingly critical
of Western culture. The absence of community, our desperate need
for it, and the difficulty or impossibility of establishing it is the
theme of novel after novel. The intense experience of alienation and
meaninglessness known to existentialists as despair, nausea, an-
guish, and so forth, has been a major theme in the literature of recent decades. In the period after World War II this theme was taken
to such an extreme in the theater of the absurd as to raise some
question as to the continued viability of serious drama.

A sense of spiritual crisis is characteristic of twentieth-century
literature; but it by no means describes the whole. Yeats retreated
from the wasteland into Celtic tradition. Robert Frost dealt with
homey subjects in a way that enhanced the meaning of ordinary experience. Conrad probed the depths of the human spirit, but not in
a way that exhibits the characteristic here discussed. Faulkner was

---

[2]This was also his chief concern in *Literature and Dogma* (New York, 1883).

a humanist whose works reveal the richness and worth of human experience. He did not despair of man; but however much he drew upon the humane and Christian traditions of the West, he did not present a very encouraging picture of contemporary culture. There have also been a surprising number of excellent poets and novelists writing from a consciously Christian perspective: Eliot, Auden, Graham Greene, Mauriac, Charles Williams, Tolkien, Thornton Wilder, Robert Penn Warren, Volkoff, Allen Tate, Flannery O'Connor, Walker Percy, and others. They illustrate the continued creativity of the Christian tradition, and from this perspective some of them have been acutely aware of the emptiness of contemporary culture and of its unrelatedness to any supporting reality.

What is strikingly absent from literature since World War I are major literary celebrations of the amazing achievements of twentieth-century culture. Radically new developments in mathematics and logic have led to completely new fields of study and profoundly transformed the theoretical ground of mathematics. Advances as impressive have also been made in physics, chemistry, and biology. Scientific advance has made possible a myriad of inventions in electronics, atomic power, computer science, and automated machinery. Increases in economic production have led to a higher material standard of living in industrial countries than was dreamed of in any previous age and give hope for a similar rise elsewhere. Accounting, managerial, and organizational techniques have developed to the point that rigorous graduate programs are devoted to exploring their essentials. Dramatic voyaging into space and revolutionary breakthroughs in medicine have become common topics in the news. The achievements of the age are incredible in the sense of being beyond the grasp of any one mind or imagination; yet they have not had the exhilarating effect of the explorations and discoveries of the sixteenth century or of the Newtonian climax of classical physics. That they can be the subject of poetry is seen in Auden's *For the Time Being*; but his treatment of them is to show their meaninglessness in the context of our culture as a whole. Our greatest and most novel achievements are dissociated from any shared source of value that could endow them with meaning and mystery and so makes them in a positive way the matter of poetry.

One would think that our enhanced sense of historical existence, including as it does an awesome awareness of our responsibility for the future, of the challenge and the danger of that future,
might inspire at least the equivalent of Shelley's *Prometheus Unbound*. On the contrary it is hard to imagine a really good poet of
our own day saying anything like Tennyson's "Better fifty years of
Europe than a cycle of Cathay." It has become almost a mark of vulgarity to express hope for the future of mankind or praise recent
cultural achievements.

An opposite form of vulgarity emerged in the 1960s. The nihilism and disillusionment previously experienced by a number of intellectuals became articulate in the masses. Student protest
movements were the most obvious example. One should not ignore
the fact that the strident, unqualified, and violent denunciations of
a whole civilization by student minorities found a surprisingly sym-
pathetic response from other students, university faculties, and
even the general public. Public opinion was, of course, divided; but
the significant point is the number whose own loss of faith in the
existing culture brought them to the position: "We deplore the violence, but . . . "[3]

When the New Left, as the protest movement was called, denounced "the system," "the Establishment," "the power structure," or "bourgeois culture," these terms were synonyms for
Western civilization. That was their appeal. No one could take seriously the "ideas" of the New Left, if, indeed, they can be said to
have had any. They developed no theory of society and had no alternatives to offer. Their eclectic vocabulary borrowed heavily from
the Marxists, but that no more indicated a commitment to Marxism
than their talk of love made them Christian. Their choice of heroes—Che Guevara, Ho Chi Minh, and Mao Tse-tung—was a
choice too far from the realities of their own situation to involve any
danger of commitment. Their demand for "participatory democ-

---

[3]*The Report of the President's Commission on Campus Unrest* (Washington, 1970) 26-
27, 30-31, 43-46, passim. The report of this commission appointed by a conservative Republican president and chaired by William W. Scranton, former governor of
Pennsylvania, is itself an illustration of the support the New Left movement got
from many who did not approve of violent tactics.

racy" was nothing more than a call for anarchy in which their whims, no matter how destructive, would suffer no restraint. Whatever the particular issues in a given outbreak, the underlying attitude was one that found the existing society, including the university, utterly without value. Their nihilism was not a tactic because they had no policy to promote; it was the way they experienced the contemporary culture. In their case it is more accurate to speak of the loss of authority than of its defiance. It was not this or that authority that was questioned but *all* authority. Authority is essentially moral in nature. If all values collapse, what was formerly experienced and accepted as authority becomes mere oppressive power and is experienced as an intolerable tyranny. That was how the New Left experienced the power of universities, governments, parents, and social mores. To those not caught up in the movement the rebellion of the protesters seemed an immoral defiance of proper authority; but to those who found the traditional values of the West false and hypocritical and the culture itself meaningless, rebellion was not only defensible, but some continuing sense of personal integrity might make it seem morally imperative.

The protest movement was international in scope and lasted more than a decade. Nothing peculiar to the United States can explain it because there were outbreaks in a number of Western European countries. It was everywhere a minority movement, but its extent is hard to judge. One of the most surprising things about the whole phenomenon was the large number of faculty and students who had shown little prior inclination to rebel but who joined the rebels against the authorities, civil and academic, even when the actions of the latter were such as would have gone unquestioned less than a generation before. A celebrated case is the refusal of the Harvard faculty to support President Pusey in his appeal to civil authority to recover the administration building and so stop the illicit publication of confidential files on individuals.[4]

---

[4]When this incident occurred in the Spring of 1970, President Pusey had already given notice that he would retire in June 1971; but other presidents, for example President Douglas M. Knight of Duke, were forced out by student pressure.

The mood passed, and universities and Western civilization still stand. Despite sporadic violence there was never a serious material or political threat. From the perspective of the 1980s the real interest of the movement is in the blight of meaninglessness it exposes in our society. There is no reason to believe that there has been any fundamental recovery of meaning—any significant revival of faith, either Christian or humanistic. Nothing is more futile than an energetic nihilism that by definition can have no positive goal. It is not surprising that the radical activism of the sixties has subsided. For most people at any time the values of a society are mediated through the general culture. They do not seek, and are only vaguely aware of, any ultimate ground of those values. Life goes on even though the moral and religious underpinning of civilization has been seriously weakened. The situation of which the New Left movement was symptomatic has not changed fundamentally.

The extent and depth of the present crisis are probably not knowable now; certainly no quantitative assessment of them is within the capacity of the present writer. The ubiquity and persistence of the question of meaning does, however, indicate the basically religious nature of the crisis; and there can be no doubt that it is widespread enough to cause serious misgiving. Because the problem is at bottom religious, no political, sociological, or psychological explanations, though they may reveal some of the mechanisms at work, can get to the root of the matter.

The religious crisis, which is also a crisis in the relationship of religion and culture, requires an analysis of the religious situation in the modern world. This study undertakes to make that analysis by a method essentially historical. In the past the religious history of the West has been too much restricted to the internal history of Western Christianity. That the Christian faith has been the dominant religious influence on Western culture there can be little doubt, but failure to recognize the degree of complexity in our religious background, and particularly a failure to recognize the religious nature of what is generally referred to as modern secular humanism, has seriously distorted our understanding of Western history.

The influence of the Christian faith on Western culture especially in its medieval origins is obvious, but it is also extremely complex and in some respects extremely subtle. The obviousness of this influence has, unfortunately, led to oversimplications in our efforts at historical self-understanding and to neglect of the serious and difficult analysis necessary for grasping what really has been going on in the West and what is going on at the present time. The difficulty is not merely that Christian faith has been adulterated in a variety of ways by other religious and cultural traditions that are also parts of our Western heritage; nor that, from a Christian point of view at any rate, the faith has always and everywhere been perverted in its cultural expression by the sinfulness of Christians. The very term *Christian* is used in a bewildering number of ways. Those who would identify themselves as Christian do not agree on what makes such an identification authentic. The historian of culture must also contend with the chronologically uneven development of the cultural implications of Christianity. It is interesting and puzzling, for example, that social contract political theories, though clearly foreshadowed in Augustine, should have had their mature development only in the seventeenth century; or that the nominalistic and empirical implications of the doctrine of creation should have been so clearly seen in the fourteenth century, whereas the historical scholarship which is a natural product of the biblical sense of history should have had such a long and uneven development. It is, indeed, very significant that Christian faith remains culturally creative in our own age when it is no longer a commonly accepted authority and among many who are not by any personal commitment or conscious belief Christian. Existentialism is perhaps the clearest example of a cultural product that is biblical and even Augustinian in its origin even though many of its strongest proponents have been ignorant of that source.

Since the conversion of Europe, which was almost complete by the twelfth century, the most serious religious crisis in our history was the beginning of the Enlightenment. Paul Hazard has argued convincingly that a major turning point in the history of the Western consciousness was experienced in the single generation between 1680 and 1715. In this period, for the first time in the history of Christian Europe, a sizable number of sensitive and educated people repudiated Christianity as having any unique and superior

truth and took their stand on other ground.[5] Though the immediate
political effects were not as striking as in the Reformation, the *religious* significance of the Enlightenment was greater. Something
radically new had entered European life. Just how radical the new
development was was obscured for a long time by the continuation
of inherited concepts and idiom. Even those who openly repudiated Christian faith in the eighteenth century were rarely so bold
as to deny God even to themselves. There were very few atheists,
but the Enlightenment as a movement of the human spirit was essentially an exuberant experience of being emancipated from God
and from the limitations of nature by Reason's capacity to know
and make use of the laws of nature. There was a real ambiguity
here: it was by the rational order of nature that nature was to be
transcended and man's salvation achieved.

A new form of humanism was born, a humanism in which man
himself was to control his destiny to the perfection of himself and
his society. Deism was hardly more than window-dressing for the
new humanism. The easy transition from the Enlightenment into
the various atheistic faiths into which humanism differentiated in
the nineteenth century revealed how little deism was ever a genuine religion and made clear that the real faith of modern non-Christian man is in man himself.

To comprehend just what has happened it is necessary to understand some aspects of the Christian faith out of which modern
humanism developed. The biblical doctrine of creation is unique;
no religion other than those developed out of the biblical tradition
contains anything like it. In the biblical doctrine God is in any ontological sense completely discontinuous with the world. The
world, on the other hand, is completely dependent on God; it continues to exist by his continuing will for it to exist. Its unity is in his
will or purpose and not an intrinsic property. Its order is, therefore,

---

[5]Paul Hazard, *Le crise de la conscience européenne* (Paris, 1935); translated into English as *The European Mind, 1680-1715*, trans. J. Lewis May (Cleveland, New York,
1963). The "parallels" which Hazard saw between the Renaissance and the Enlightenment have been undermined or shown to require a different interpretation
by later studies of the religious dimension of the Renaissance (see chapter 3). But
the main thrust of his study is to show that the early Enlightenment marks the real
division between modern times and an earlier Europe.

in no way binding on God. The complete freedom of God with respect to the whole creation was a fundamental influence on late medieval thought. Since God's creative acts are subject to no eternal truths, knowledge of the world could not be derived deductively from philosophy but must come through actual observation. It could not, moreover, be certain knowledge because no one could know for sure what God might do next. There thus entered into Western philosophy, especially into its empirical tradition, that kind of relative skepticism which recognizes that human knowledge is not without a kind of validity, but yet sees it as partial and only approximate. The doctrine of creation also, by its emphasis on the direct (that is, unmediated) relationship of God to each creature, produced that awareness of reality that corresponded to and supported nominalism in medieval thought. All of these things entered as basic elements into the structure of the modern Western mind.

The doctrine of creation also had important implications for man himself that transformed his very mode of consciousness. In the biblical faith man is a very special creature. He is made "in the image" of God. This involves a special relationship to God, or at least the possibility of such a relationship. Not only is man dependent upon God like any other creature; he also has the capacity to respond to God in a way that is personal and communal. In this relation to or knowledge of the transcendent God, man himself transcends the rest of creation and enjoys a kind of freedom in relation to it. In the Genesis story man is given a mandate to subdue the world and control it. His freedom is a capacity for creative action; and he is, in the Christian view, a subcreator under God. Man's freedom also involves his ability to oppose his will to the purposes of God, to act as though he were independent of God, that is, to sin. How man's sin in turn affects his freedom is a very abstruse question in Christian thought which we cannot in this study digress to explore.

The transcendence of God and man means that history is free from the limitations of a determined natural order and that the future is open to novelty. Cyclical explanations of the ultimate reality man confronts are, therefore, no longer adequate. As awareness of this historical reality permeated the Western consciousness, modern man achieved a radically new mode of self-consciousness and of being aware of the world. He experienced a new sense of responsibility for his own future and for the future of the world.

What happened in the Enlightenment was that transcendently free man achieved, at least in his own self-consciousness, an emancipation from the transcendent God. The process was complex and confused. The Enlightened, with a handful of exceptions, still believed in a God who had created the world, but creation was restricted to a past event, and God was no longer sovereign over it in any active sense. The world, once created, was conceived as existing and operating on its own. Mankind, however, was not correspondingly reduced to a fixed place in the cosmic order. There were, to be sure, frequent eighteenth-century attempts to understand man in terms of natural law, but the dynamic spirit of the Enlightenment, that which gives it its force and power in modern culture, was its confidence that man is free in his reason to understand the laws of nature and able through this knowledge to control his destiny. Contradictory as it may seem from some points of view, the Enlightenment reserved for mankind a transcendent freedom which it denied to God. There were a few consistent determinists as there were a few atheists, but the spirit of the age was not fatalistic. All of this was not apparent at the time. Deism was never a real religion; it was a set of oversimplified and distorted popular conceptions out of the imperfectly Christian past; but deism successfully masked and facilitated the transition that was taking place. Only after deism was sloughed off and Enlightenment humanism developed into the atheistic and historical forms of the nineteenth century, was its true nature discernible.

Modern humanism, even in its initial Enlightenment stage, is emphatically not a return to classical views of man. Peter Gay's interpretation of the Enlightenment as a repudiation of Christianity in favor of classical humanism is wide of the mark and fails to do justice to the novelty and creativity of modern humanism. The point is clearly seen once one considers how far from the spirit of the Enlightenment or of later humanistic faiths is any sense of hybris. Classical culture understood man as having a fixed place in an unchanging cosmic order.[6] For him to attempt to rise above that place was hybris and brought inevitable destruction. Modern man recognizes no such limitations. Even when he is cynical, he accepts responsibility for his own future and the future of mankind. More commonly man has believed in the possibility of overcoming natural obstacles, perfecting his society, and shaping his destiny by his own actions in history. The utopian hope that has been so pervasive in modern culture has no counterpart in classical paganism. Stoicism was capable of orienting people toward practical action, but Stoic philosophers were as lacking in any fundamental sense of history as other Greeks and Romans. They did not conceive of changing man's fundamental situation in any radical way. Modern man does have such ambitions.

The differentiation of humanism after the French Revolution into a variety of humanistic faiths did not destroy the underlying unity of the West—that which enables us to use a term like *Western Civilization* meaningfully. Some of the new faiths were mutually exclusive like nationalism, utopian socialism, and Marxism; others like Benthamite liberalism and scientific humanism were capable of supporting each other. Yet they were all distinctively Western and contributed to the rich variety of the culture while retaining enough common ground to participate in the same cultural community. Much of this common ground was also shared with the traditional Christian faith. It enabled Christian and humanist to achieve some understanding of each other and make common commitments on a wide variety of issues. It also strengthened the culture's ties with its own past. Exploration of what Christianity and humanistic faiths have in common takes one a long way in identifying basic structures of the Western mind.

Modern atheistic humanism is cut off from any understanding of man in terms of his relationship to God; it cannot, for example, know man as a sinner. The humanist, nevertheless, understands man's relation to the world in a way that is essentially biblical and

---

[6]An occasional exception among the skeptics or sophists (Protagoras, for example) illustrates the spirit of free inquiry that characterized Greek rationalism, but defines only by exception the view of man and the cosmos that was the ground of classical culture.

unlike that of any nonbiblical cultural tradition. Modern man is aware of himself as transcending the natural world in a way that opens the possibility of understanding and controlling nature in the shaping of his own destiny. Even thorough-going naturalists like B. F. Skinner commonly talk of using our knowlege of a completely determined nature in order to shape our destinies to our good purposes and, in fact, warn us against neglecting to do so! The consciousness of historical existence in modern man is deeper than theories he may hold which contradict it.

Except for traces of classical, especially Neoplatonic, influence in romantic traditions, modern secular man does not think of the world as sacred and recognizes no spiritual reality that is not human. Apart from mankind, the world for the humanist is the "dead" world of modern science. What the humanist frequently does not recognize, though Professor Mircea Eliade among others has pointed it out clearly enough, is that this view of the world as without purpose or meaning of its own is biblical in origin. In the biblical tradition the world was desacralized when purpose was transferred from the world to a transcendent God who is discontinuous with it. This denial of spiritual quality to the cosmos sharply distinguishes the biblical tradition from cosmological cultures; but far from degrading the created world, it had the effect of endowing the material world with reality and worth as God's good creation. Modern humanism has inherited this positive attitude toward the material world, which is another thing it has in common with traditional Christianity.

As for spiritual reality, modern non-Christian humanists are mostly atheists, but they have a large measure of agreement with Christians about man. The transcendent freedom of man has been actually enhanced in humanistic thought by the elimination of God. Man tends to become the sole source of meaning, value, and purpose. The strength of belief in natural law obscured this in the eighteenth century, but it has become quite explicit in a variety of more recent humanisms. Western man's sense of radical freedom and responsibility for his own future is the basis of his consciousness of himself as existing historically. No doubt all people have existed historically, but a developed self-consciousness of such existence is peculiar to the West. It derives out of the biblical tradition, but the fullest development of some of its implications has been in non-Christian humanism.

In the Christian view man is not of infinite worth, but his unique relationship to God gives him a value that is incalculable in the strict sense that it is not comparable to the worth of other things. Since God knows each unique person wholly and since God does not need to deal in generalities, it is even implied that comparisons of the worth of one person to the worth of another are hazardous and valid only when made by limited and explicit criteria. Many Christians would go so far as to assert that the purpose of God in creation itself is his purpose for mankind. Non-Christians arrive at a similar high regard for humanity without reference to God. This view of man as transcending the world in his historical existence is a distinguishing mark of Western culture. It is the basis of common humanitarian concerns that are general, if not universal, among Western men. These concerns are shared even by forms of humanism like Sartre's existentialism or Julian Huxley's scientism which offer very little theoretical justification for being concerned about people who are not useful to oneself or to the progress of mankind.

The empiricism, the nominalism, the relative skepticism that characterize the modern West have already been mentioned, and their Christian origin will be dealt with again in the next chapter. Altogether there is an impressive Western mode of being aware of the world that is shared by Christian and humanist alike and is, indeed, what we mean when we say "Western."

This present study is an effort to get the main outlines of the history of our Western religious and cultural heritage into clearer focus. It is particularly concerned to show the role religion has had and still has in shaping the general structure of Western culture, especially Western intellectual culture. The integrating function of the Christian faith in the origin of a new culture in medieval Europe will be dealt with briefly; but attention will be centered on the historical continuity of modern humanism with Christian faith and the contradictions that have developed between Christian and atheistic branches of a common Western tradition. What is distinctively Western will be seen again and again to result from the actualizing in history of cultural implications in the biblical tradition.

Certain corollary issues will also receive some share of attention; among them will be (1) the almost incredible weakness of formal Christian theology since Pascal; (2) the origin and influence of a mechanistic worldview; and (3) naturalistic tendencies to return to a cosmological worldview.

Throughout this study religion is understood to mean man's concern with the ultimate meaning of his existence. Modern man's claim to be irreligious is, in this meaning of the term *religion*, seen to be frivolous and unfounded. It would be hard to name a time when more people were so consciously concerned with the problem of meaning. The crisis of our time is basically religious, and it is hoped that this essay in the interpretation of Western history may throw some light on that crisis.

II THE MEDIEVAL BEGINNING

The medieval centuries were not a Middle Age at all but the period in which our own culture first arose; modern European culture is understandable in any depth only against its medieval background. But if it is important for the student of modern culture to see his subject in a context of which the "medieval" period of origins is a significant part, it is extremely difficult for him to do so. Medieval history is an esoteric study demanding a rich and extensive background of knowlege and special linguistic techniques. At the present time the problem of the non-specialist who would like to avail himself of the work of medievalists is particularly difficult because the general interpretive frameworks have been mostly called in question and adequate alternative interpretations of the broader sort have not been developed, or, at least, have not gained wide currency.

The problem of periodization in European history has, to be sure, attracted considerable attention in the past generation. Discussion has centered primarily on the Renaissance and the suggestions some have made for marking the distinction between modern times and an earlier Europe some time later than the Renaissance.[1] In addition, the medievalists have fought successfully to eliminate the term *Dark Ages* from serious historical writing, except that some will allow it as applicable to the early Middle Ages only. They have also, I think, won acceptance of the fact that the medieval centuries were a dynamic period of movement and change. Yet no new conventions of interpretation consistent with the established results of specialized research have developed to replace the old concept of ancient-medieval-modern or to dispel attitudes and ideas derivative from the outmoded conception that the Renaissance marked a clean break with the Middle Ages. It is curious that medievalists, who have played so large a part in attacking the classical concept of the Renaissance, should have been so much less sensitive to the term *Middle Ages*, which is at least as bad a misnomer.[2]

The continuity of cultural development between the Middle Ages and the Renaissance (the terms, at least, have become too much a part of the language to be abandoned) is no longer open to question, and the tendency to date the modern period from some later time is more and more widespread; but the new idea that the Renaissance is a period of transition between a Christian Middle Ages and a secular modern culture can be extremely misleading.[3] If it means merely that the fifteenth and sixteenth centuries come between the fourteenth and the seventeenth, the concept of a transitional Renaissance is hardly more than a harmless truism. But the idea involves more than that. It implies that there was a discrete medieval civilization that reached a high order of integration then rapidly disintegrated in a way that freed Europe for the brilliance of the Renaissance. This idea of a distinct medieval culture that came to an end before the Renaissance distorts not only our understanding

---

[1]For Paul Hazard's periodization see above, page 10, footnote 5. Dietrich Gerhard argues that the beginning of modern times is with the industrial revolution and the French Revolution. "Periodization in European History," *American Historical Review* 61 (July 1956): 900-13. Gerhard's view and Hazard's are not mutually exclusive, but for the emphasis of the present essay Hazard's interpretation is more significant.

[2]Wallace K. Ferguson, *The Renaissance in Historical Thought* (Cambridge MA, 1948) 393-94.

[3]Ferguson adopted this idea and it has been widely accepted, ibid., 396.

of Europe during those early centuries, but also our understanding of how our own times are related to them. The Middle Ages was not a "middle," and it was not a separate and distinct civilization; it was the beginning of the civilization that still flourishes in Europe and has spread throughout the world.

When we are concerned with the religious substructure of Western culture, it is particularly important that the continuity of the Middle Ages with the subsequent history of Europe be understood as the continuation of a single culture. The fallacy of conceiving of the Middle Ages as a discrete Christian civilization has frequently led historians to treat the Christian faith as an anachronism at any time since the sixteenth century or even before. In truth, as this study is designed to show, even the non-Christian humanism of our own time can be understood only superficially if we ignore the continuing influence of biblical and Christian structures in Western culture.

In two respects especially, recent scholarship has changed our understanding of the religious history of the Middle Ages, and both changes are significant for the question of the religious basis of modern Western culture. The first of these shifts of interpretation is the increasing realization that the medieval centuries were not a period in which Europe was uniformly Christian. On the contrary, this was a period when Europe was in process of becoming Christianized, and the process never reached anything like completion. For a long time no informed person has thought the Middle Ages a static period without movement or achievement, but too often the cultural achievement of the age has been considered as something occurring in a uniformly Christian society. The facts are quite otherwise. The educational task of the medieval church was pursued for centuries with impressive results, but it was never successful to the point of creating the integrated Christian society that is a myth produced by an outmoded, but still commonplace, interpretation of the age.

The second area of recent investigation with major implications for the kind of study here undertaken is in the area of theology. A generation ago, even a general knowledge of fourteenth-century intellectual history was confined to a very small number of specialists who were just opening the field. Even medievalists often

dismissed the late scholastics as merely decadent. Now William of
Ockham is widely recognized as one of the great seminal minds of
our culture, and undergraduates can learn something of the
achievement of Nicholas d'Autrecourt, John Buridan, Albert of Saxony, Nicholas d'Oresme, and other fourteenth-century scholars
from the paperbacks in an average college store.

Scholasticism was not a body of knowledge but a method of investigation and understanding. It produced some very great intellectual monuments, and it gave depth and direction to the Western
mind. As a method it had to be abandoned, but the most telling
criticisms leading to its abandonment were developed by the scholastics themselves and had a major role in defining basic issues of
modern thought with which we are still concerned.[4] Scholasticism
was undermined by the development of Christian intellectual culture. Its eclipse was a very significant and very complex part of the
Christianizing of Europe. Let us, therefore, consider first the general process by which Christian faith was molding European culture and return to scholasticism as a special case.

It is important to distinguish one's appreciation for the quality
of individual Christian lives from the question of the historical development of Christian culture. Saintly Christians with unusual insight into the meaning of their faith have existed in every
generation of the Christian era. Certainly there were many such in
the early Middle Ages, but this is not a good indication of the degree of Christian influence on the general culture. The conversion
of northern Europe brought a vast influx of pagans into the church.[5]
The conversions were sincere in that the new religious authority
was really accepted, but the content of the new faith was very
poorly understood. In the long run the superior intellectual culture
of the church prevailed and pagan influence on the Christian faith
was only superficial; but the immediate task of the church was pro-
digious. The general culture responded slowly to the new religion,
and the low level of education resulted in serious adulterating in-

---

[4]Ernest A. Moody, "Empiricism and Metaphysics in Medieval Philosophy,"
Philosophical Review 67 (1958): 146-47, passim.

[5]This was in addition to the paganism that remained strong in the rural pop-
ulations of what had been the Roman Empire in the West.

fluences among the clergy themselves. Admixtures of fragmentary paganism and development of cults around specific saints were likely to be of local origin and influence; the extent of these aberrations was, therefore, a serious threat to the unity of the faith. The inherited patristic tradition was a strong force making for unity, but its success in preserving unity in the church was for a long time problematic. The ecclesiastical organization that made eventual reform a possibility was faced with the initial problem of purifying itself and establishing effective control over the lower clergy and even bishops.

Monasticism was an effort to establish truly Christian communities as enclaves within the general society. Although the monks were by no means recruited only from those with a serious vocation to spiritual life, the monasteries were on the whole oases of a purer faith and a more consistent doctrine. In them were developed ideals and attitudes that characterized medieval Christianity. Perhaps most obvious here is the strong emphasis on asceticism. The monks were also the chief institutionalization of the virtue of charity; and their practice of humility, though a good deal short of perfection, had a primary role in fixing that Christian virtue in the Western consciousness as a basic part of the ethical substratum of culture. Both the forms and the spirit of lay piety show the influence of the monks. The slowness with which this influence developed is evidence of how much the concept of "the Christian Middle Ages" needs qualification. Ironically, one of the clearest examples of this monastic influence is in the anti-clerical piety of several early twelfth-century heresies. Their asceticism, their legalistic emphasis on poverty as an ideal, their tendency toward a rather self-centered development of the individual spiritual life—all of these reflect the influence of monasticism. In subsequent centuries the translation of "books of hours" into the vernacular was a part of the great upswell of lay piety in the late Middle Ages. Also in less obviously religious ways the monks were influencing the value system of society. Christopher Dawson credits them with the positive attitude toward work that has characterized the West. Here is involved some affirmation of the good creation and also a sense of the dignity of the lowliest man.

The monks should not, of course, be given all the credit. Other churchmen, especially the more conscientious bishops, were frequently the source of reform within the church and of efforts to influence the general society toward more Christian conduct. The pacifistic effort of the church in the eleventh century, for example, owed its leadership primarily to local councils of bishops.[6] The concern of many churchmen for the sufferings of the peasants as a result of war seems to have been the initial impulse behind the Peace of God and the Truce of God.

In the early Middle Ages, the secular institution that was most easily assimilated into Christian thought and endowed with Christian meanings and sanctions was the monarchy. The pagan Germanic kings had been religious authorities; upon their conversion it was easy for them and their subjects to see them in a similar role as Christians. A positive relationship between Christian faith and political authority was as old as the New Testament and had been considerably developed by the fathers of the ancient church. That development continued in the early Middle Ages. Charlemagne seems to have conceived himself in his kingly office as the leader of a Christian society with responsibility for the spiritual health of the people. The idea continued through the Middle Ages and into modern times as a conception of Christendom that competed with the alternate doctrine of the two keys. From the beginning the new Christian kingdoms in the West found in the Christian faith that mystique, that moral and religious ground of political authority, that is essential to the healthy state. The idea of the Christian king ordained by God to his task and his authority was an inheritance from the ancient world. Despite the weakness of the new territorial states, the persistence and development of this idea was a major step toward the concept of a Christian society. The states themselves, however, were very imperfectly Christianized and they had a very limited influence on the development of the society as a whole.

The importance of the monarchies and the empire to the central political narrative of European history has probably been a signif-

---

[6]Marc Bloch, *Feudal Society*, trans. L. A. Manyon (Chicago, 1961) 412-13.

icant factor in the creation of the myth of the Christian Middle Ages. Actually the Christian conceptions of kingship were hardly more than a foot in the door toward the development of a Christianized Europe.

Feudalism, unlike monarchy, was a new product of the early medieval situation and reflects more accurately how far the society was from being essentially Christian. There was no ancient tradition of Christian feudalism to build upon as there was for Christian monarchy. Nevertheless, if the society had been as pervasively influenced by Christian thought and a Christian structure of values as has been generally supposed, one might expect new institutions to exhibit a distinctively Christian orientation; on this supposition the new institutions should be more purely Christian than those related to ancient traditions. Actually, of course, the opposite was the case. Feudalism was an order of society that grew out of the needs of the times and reflected the orientation of the society toward its problems; yet it is hard to see any distinctively Christian influence in the basic feudal institutions.

Efforts of the church to penetrate this new order and bring it under the influence of the Christian religion began early, but results were frustratingly meager and sporadic and the very partial cumulative success of the effort was slow in coming.

Sidney Painter distinguishes three aspects of chivalry: feudal, religious, and courtly.[7] Of these the original, and throughout the medieval period the most basic, was feudal chivalry. Painter describes the feudal ethic in some detail. The two basic virtues were loyalty and prowess or effectiveness in battle. The other feudal virtues were generosity, courtesy, and love of glory. All of these except courtesy had premedieval pagan origins, and courtesy was simply the development, especially in tournaments, of a kind of magnanimity toward other nobles. None of them were Christian in origin or showed much Christian influence. Generosity was much more like the largesse giving of pagan German kings than like Christian charity and lived on into modern times as a kind of aristocratic contempt for financial responsibility.

---

[7]Sidney Painter, *French Chivalry* (Baltimore, 1940; ppbk., Cornell University Press, 1957). The treatment of chivalry here is based largely on Painter's work.

The teachings of the church were not necessarily opposed to any of these in principle; even the love of glory was acceptable if one sought the glory that was in a good life. In their interpretation and practice of them, however, the feudality were widely at variance with the church and remained so. Prowess as medieval knights understood it inevitably involved them in homicide as a part of their way of life; and practices which the church condemned as rapine were the only ways many knights managed to continue their knightly careers. The tournament, an institution created to facilitate both prowess and rapine in times of peace, was vigorously attacked by the church. The Council of Clermont in 1130 and the Lateran Councils of 1139 and 1179 condemned them and refused burial in consecrated ground to anybody killed in one. Pope Gregory IX incorporated the ban on tournaments into canon law. Yet the church's efforts were largely ineffectual. Tournaments continued until changes in the art of war brought about their decline.

Painter distinguishes two ways in which the church sought to Christianize the feudality of Europe. One was through a general appeal to the nobles to obey the general ethical teachings of the church. The other was to include obligations of a Christian character in the ideal of knightliness itself. Neither of these was very successful. The Peace of God and the Truce of God belong in the former category. Although the eleventh- and twelfth-century peace movements were not without effect and were one of the ways in which Christian influence permeated medieval politics, the results fell so far short of the lofty aims of the church that the movement unmistakably reveals the lacuna between the Christian faith and the actual culture of Europe as late as the twelfth century. One of the brightest chapters in the history of the church is the concern of the bishops who initiated the peace movement for the plight of the poor and defenseless in those areas of Europe where political order had most completely broken down. But the movement so far failed that the church itself, after sweeping compromises with political and military reality, had finally to support the social hierarchy and constituted authorities against the democratic pseudopolitical movements to which its efforts had given rise.[8]

---

[8]Bloch, *Feudal Society*, 412-20.

Even in the matter of getting the nobles to practice monogamy as a life-long relationship, a matter in which the position of the church was strongly supported by other traditions of the medieval nobles, Christian influence on the culture was slow and hard.

> . . . repudiation of wives was still [in the eleventh century] a common practice. Not until the latter part of the twelfth century did the church seriously threaten the noble's right to marry and repudiate at will and then it did little more than gain some control over the practice by insisting that it be accomplished through a formal action in its courts.[9]

In his chapter on "Religious Chivalry" Painter makes clear that the effort of the church to turn chivalry into a Christian vocation was even less influential on the medieval feudality than its other efforts to make their behavior more Christian. The first clear expression of religious chivalry is in John of Salisbury's *Policraticus*. The effort to create a religious chivalry was not merely to get acceptance of the idea that the knight as a Christian should obey the church and protect it and the weak, who were the special care of the church. The point, as Painter presents it, was to make these virtues essential to being a real knight. This last he thinks was never accepted by any considerable number of the nobles; still less did they give up all the ideas that the church opposed. "Certainly," said Painter, "I can find no evidence that any feudal noble felt that homicide committed in tourney or private war and the taking of booty and ransoms were anything but eminently proper in a knight."[10] The ideals of feudal chivalry and religious chivalry remained fundamentally irreconcilable and, despite some literary efforts to blend them, they were known to be irreconcilable by medieval men.[11]

Elements of the medieval conception of religious chivalry did, however, continue in the literary traditions of Europe and become a part of what might be called a literary myth of knighthood. Partly though the influence of this myth, the idea also entered into later

---

[9]Painter, *French Chivalry*, 100.

[10]Ibid., 89-90.

[11]Ibid., 149ff.

conceptions of the Christian gentleman and the Christian soldier, though in neither were the contradictions between humility and pride in one's honor really overcome. Insofar as these later ideals are an adulterated Christian culture, they illustrate how the Christianizing of culture begun in the Middle Ages continued in the subsequent history of Europe.

On the strictly political side progressive Christianization is problematic. The traditions of monarchy were much more compatible with Christianity than were those of the feudality, and the concern of both territorial rulers and the church for an orderly society and peace, at least within the territories of a given prince, strengthened the positive relationship between them. The rise of the monarchies and the decline of feudalism did, therefore, have the effect of making the political life and institutions of Europe more acceptable to the church, more effective in its support and protection, and more compatible with Christian faith generally. Despite the Reformation's breach in the unity of Western Christendom and the continuation in Europe of so much that could not be defended as Christian, the achievement of something like organic Christian societies was probably more nearly realized in specific political communities in the sixteenth century than in the thirteenth. But the question whether monarchy as such was more Christian under Philip Augustus or Francis I or Henry IV is not easy to answer. Were John and Henry III more inclined to treat seriously the religious dimension of politics than were Henry VIII and Elizabeth? The answers to such a question are more likely to reflect general historical interpretations than to produce them. What is typical of an age for one scholar may seem exceptional to another. Frederick II was no doubt exceptional, but were there any thirteenth-century emperors who were more Christian than Charles V?

The literary traditions of courtly love offer a clearer example of how Christian faith gradually permeated European culture and transformed an element of that culture that was clearly non-Christian in origin. This example has the merit of having been carefully studied by C. S. Lewis in his *Allegory of Love*,[12] though Lewis's treatment is largely confined to English literature.

---

[12]C. S. Lewis, *The Allegory of Love, A Study in Medieval Tradition* (London, 1936).

The origins of courtly love are obscure. Neoplatonic influence seems clear, but Neoplatonism came to the Middle Ages by many routes. A. J. Denomy suggests Avicenna and some of the Arabic poets as the most likely source[13]; Theodore Silverstein thinks Apuleius a possibility[14]; even the Albigensians have been mentioned and may have had an influence.[15] Older efforts to find a Christian origin in Saint Bernard or Chartres or the veneration of the Virgin have been generally abandoned.[16]

This essentially anti-Christian ethic of courtly love was hard for modern scholars to accept in what they took for granted was the classic case of a Christian culture. Yet anti-Christian it certainly was as we find it in the twelfth century, and it was understood to be so by the troubadours who celebrated it. Denomy, whose excellent analysis of courtly love emphasizes the contradiction with Christianity, finds it hard to understand how such a thing could happen in the Middle Ages:

> That they [the troubadours] should conceive of pure love as desire for union with the beloved to be fanned by every means short of actual intercourse, by what Catholic and Christian term evil thoughts and desires, impure looks and touches, by proximate occasions to impurity is not normal or natural in the Catholic and Christian age and atmostphere in which they lived. It is quite easy to see how, even under these circumstances, an individual poet or even several, should do so and exalt adultery and fornication: it is not quite so easy to see how a whole succession of poets should adopt such ideas and ideals and have them codified into a system. . . . The poems which express the ideas of Courtly Love were written by men who, for the most part were Catholics and Christians

---

[13]Alexander J. Denomy, *The Heresy of Courtly Love* (New York, 1947); "An Inquiry into the Origins of Courtly Love," *Medieval Studies* 6 (1944): 175-260; and "Fin' Amors: the Pure Love of the Troubadours, its Amorality and Possible Source," ibid.; 7 (1945): 139-207.

[14]Theodore Silverstein, "Andreas, Plato, and the Arabs," *Modern Philology* 47 (1949): 123-24.

[15]Denomy, "Inquiry," 257-58.

[16]Silverstein, "Andreas, Plato, and the Arabs," 117, 120. Guido Errante, who still contended for a Christian origin, is treated respectfully by Silverstein, but effectively refuted.

and who had been reared in that faith and that atmosphere. It is strange, then, that apart from a purely surface coloring and the concept of Christian virtues, there is so little trace of that Christianity and Catholicity in their love lyrics. It is equally strange that the conception of love they developed and expressed be so directly at variance with Christian and Catholic morality. For, from that point of view, their conception of love is wholly immoral. It is impossible to reconcile the tenets of Courtly Love with . . . the teaching of Christ and of His Church. Fron the point of view of the troubadours, however, love illicit and adulterous . . . is the source of all good, of all virtue.[17]

Denomy's problem is produced by his assumption that the age and "atmosphere" was more Catholic and Christian than it was. He is not, to be sure, personally responsible for an assumption that has been a staple of historical interpretation as long as history has been a serious discipline. The idea of the Christian Middle Ages has been occasionally qualified, but almost never challenged as a basic concept. Some of the old Protestants, like C. H. Lea, thought the period more Catholic than Christian; some have pointed out its weaknesses as evidences against the Christian faith; some have argued that secularization started earlier than has been commonly believed; many have seen that it failed to realize the ideals of its Christian thinkers; but the idea of the Christian Middle Ages has shown a remarkable persistence. Challenges to it have been largely works confined to some particular aspect of culture, like Painter on French chivalry, and have refrained from generalizing about the whole period and the whole culture.

It is not, of course, here suggested that the term "Christian Middle Ages" cannot be given a legitimate meaning. The Middle Ages was in some sense Christian, and Christian faith was the most dynamic and, as things turned out, the strongest of those forces which were shaping and integrating the culture of Western Europe. These forces also included, in addition to Christianity, the classical heritage and a common Indo-European warlikeness.[18] But

---

[17]Denomy, "Fin'Amors," 179.

[18]William H. McNeill says that, except for the Japanese, the society of Western Europe has been the most warlike of any civilized people. *The Rise of the West* (Chicago, 1963) 103-104, 539.

the concept of a Christian Middle Ages has included and perpetuated two related myths that continued scholarship has undermined. One of these is that Europeans and European culture were more Christian in the Middle Ages than in any subsequent period; the other is that the history of European culture since the legendary Christian age has grown progressively less religious.

Denomy had run into evidence contradicting the established conception of the Middle Ages. In fact, the class to whom courtly love appealed included the same knights who accepted homicide and rapine as legitimate activities of the knight in opposition to the clear teaching of the church. It was not merely that they failed to live up to the demands of the Christian ethics of the day, but that they incorporated what the church opposed into what was deemed proper for a knight.[19] Courtly love, like the warrior ethic, was an example of non-Christian culture juxtaposed with Christianity in a society still far from being consistently Christian.

Donald Howard, dealing with the same problem as Denomy and like him taking for granted conventional assumptions about the Christian character of the Middle Ages, argues that courtly love did not weaken Christianity except as "one element in a climate of increasing secularity."[20] To speak of increasing secularity in the age of the troubadours pushes the *really* Christian Middle Ages back early indeed! Moreover, one could harldy pick a less likely example of increasing secularity than the tradition of courtly love because C. S. Lewis in his remarkable study of the history of the tradition has shown that, although at first irreconcilable with Christianity, courtly love was increasingly Christianized as poets struggled with the contradiction.[21]

---

[19]See the passage from Painter quoted above.

[20]Donald R. Howard, *The Three Temptations* (Princeton, 1966) 87-88. This is not the solution to the problem Howard thinks is fundamental, but his remark about "increasing secularity" illustrates a more widespread method of accounting for non-Christian elements in medieval culture. His argument that Christian acceptance of anti-Christian tenets of courtly love was a subrational extension of the medieval idea of grades of perfection can hardly be taken to explain the serious moral tension felt by poets in whom the courtly and the Christian ideals are juxtaposed.

[21]C. S. Lewis, *Allegory*. Cf. Richard W. Southern, *The Making of the Middle Ages* (London, 1953) 245-46.

By the time Lewis takes up the history in the late twelfth century, the tradition has matured enough that Chrétien de Troyes can
be seen not as representing an undeveloped stage in its development, but as a poet deviating significantly from what was already
a well-defined tradition.[22] The first clear contemporary analysis and
description of the ideas and ideals of courtly love is found in Andreas Capellanus. According to Lewis we can see in Andreas's con-
demnation of those who seek the favor of ladies by contempt for the
church that already the contradictions between the new love theory
and Christianity were recognized, and it is likely some were inclined to emphasize the contradictions. Andreas, on the other
hand, wanted to reconcile the two as far as possible, but his efforts
produced little more than pointing up the fine moral qualities that
love develops in the lover and cautioning lovers against heresy and
abuse of the church. The fundamental contradictions remain, and
Andreas is quite explicit about them in a number of passages. He
felt the tension so strongly that in his last book he counsels against
the theory of love that he has been at such pains to elaborate and
commend, warning that "No man through any good deeds can
please God so long as he serves in the service of Love."[23]

Poets in the courtly love tradition after Andreas felt the same
tension and sought with varying degrees of success to bring Love
into harmony with faith and accepted standards of Christian conduct. The courtly tradition had a kind of integrity of its own, and
its persistence for a matter of centuries against increasing Christian
pressure is an impressive example of the viability of such a pattern
of ideas, values, and behavior once it is established. Nevertheless,
the efforts at reconciliation showed a progressive development
along two different lines that bore their respective fruits in Dante
and Spenser.

Both developments owed something to the Platonic naturalism
of the School of Chartres, which performed a mediating function
by softening the edges of both the courtly love tradition and Christian ethics and by offering Nature as a kind of *tertium quid* between

---

[22]Lewis, *Allegory*, 24.

[23]Ibid., 40-41.

them.[24] Alanus ab Insulis, writing in the twelfth century, seems to have felt no tension between the courtesy of the troubadours and Christianity. He understood both in terms of a Platonic naturalism and simply assumed their compatibility. For him knighthood did not imply adultery. According to Lewis he juxtaposed and even blended the two traditions, but he did not reconcile them. His work was, however, both popular and influential, and he set a precedent for later compromise. Jean de Meun, who stood in both the development toward Dante and that toward Spenser, was influenced by the Platonism and the naturalism of Chartres and Alanus and sought to avoid the conflict by departing from the conventions of the courtly school into naturalistic love.[25]

In Dante the courtly tradition is brought within a Christian context by the fact that the poet's own love for Beatrice became for him an image of the divine love. The way for this development had been prepared by the effective use in the Bible of parallels between the love of husband and wife and the relationship between God and Israel or God and the church.[26] As Lewis points out, the romantic love tradition was not a mere literary convention, but was an extremely significant change in human sentiment—in Lewis's opinion one with only two or three equals in human history.[27] The love which Dante had for Beatrice was love in the new mode. When this experience became for him an image of the Divine love, the sentiment was that of romantic love stripped of its heresies and immoralities. Not only did this create a literary tradition that is present today in the works of Charles Williams, C. S. Lewis, and, I think, W. H. Auden; it has influenced the development of theology also.[28]

The maturing of various literary traditions not identifiably Christian into the great Christian literary masterpiece of the *Divine*

---

[24]Ibid., 104-105.

[25]Ibid., 148.

[26]The fullest development of this theme is the book of Hosea. See also Isaiah 62:5; Ephesians 5:24-29; Revelation 21:2, 9-11; 22:17.

[27]Lewis, *Allegory*, 4, 11.

[28]Mary McDermott Shideler has published a book on the theology of Charles Williams entitled *The Theology of Romantic Love* (New York, 1962).

Comedy is instructive for the thesis of this chapter. This particular aspect of Christian culture did not mature until the fourteenth century, and it was earlier maturing, not later, than many of the other developments of Christian culture observable in the Middle Ages— perhaps earlier than most. The Harvard undergraduate who described Dante as "standing with one foot in the Middle Ages while with the other he saluted the rising sun of the Renaissance" was involved in more than a mixed metaphor. He ascribed to Dante an awkwardness more properly belonging to ourselves when we try to follow conventional distinctions between Middle Ages and Renaissance. Dante's relationship to his past and his influence on the literature of the future illustrate the continuity of cultural development through periods we have artificially and falsely distinguished.

The other development of the romantic love tradition is even more instructive for our purposes for the very reason that it took longer. The most obvious contradiction between courtly love and Christianity was in the courtly idealization of adulterous love. Conflict was heightened and the issue clarified by the denial on the part of the exponents of courtesy that romantic love was possible in marriage. This was the issue that troubled and embarrassed a long succession of poets. Their struggle with the problem this posed for their Christian consciences produced a gradual modification of the original romantic tradition in a direction more acceptable to Christian monogamy. C. S. Lewis, who was admirably qualified to do so, has traced the process in English literature with great subtlety and erudition. This history will not be repeated here, but its highlights may be noted. In *Troilus and Cryseide* Chaucer brought the literary expression of courtly love to its highest perfection. The adulterous love celebrated in the poem has been so ennobled that it is ready for Christian adoption, but the process is not complete.[29] Lewis points out that "*Troilus* is for Chaucer something to be repented of."[30]

---

[29]Lewis, *Allegory*, 197.

[30]C. S. Lewis, *Studies in Medieval and Renaissance Literature* (Cambridge, 1966) 9.

In the following two centuries poems of secondary quality crossed the boundary up to which Chaucer had brought the tradition and identified romantic love with marriage. King James in the *Kingis Quair* is emancipated from the shackles of the tradition by the fact that he writes of his own experience. The love he describes is not adulterous but a courtship leading to marriage. Lewis calls it "the first modern book of love."[31] Lydgate's *Temple of Glas*, written about the same time, is the story of an adulterous love, but Lewis interprets the conclusion of the story to mean that the lovers can do nothing but wait hopefully for Venus to clear the way for them— presumably by removing the lady's husband.[32] Courtship that looks forward to marriage as its only satisfactory end is again the theme in Hawes's *The Pastime of Pleasure* (early sixteenth century); and William Nevill, also early sixteenth century, goes so far as to recognize that in marriage there will occur a reversal in which the servant of his lady becomes her master.[33]

The long development finds its conclusion in the *Faerie Queen*. In the allegory of the third book Spenser attacks strongly and successfully the illicit love of the courtly tradition, which is symbolized in Malecasta and the House of Busirane, the former representing the attractions and the latter the bitter end of courtly love. As a literary form the conventions of the School of Love did not survive Spenser's onslaught. But the substance of the sentiment of romantic love did survive both in literature and in the Western experience of love. The virtuous love which is victorious in the *Faerie Queen* is not the cold relationship approved by scholastic ethics, but the passionate love of the troubadours now experienced as married love or love which intends marriage. Contradiction was no longer felt, and "the romantic conception of marriage . . . is the basis of all our love literature from Shakespeare to Meredith."[34]

The history Lewis has traced shows an important part of European culture which, whatever its origins, was pagan and self-con-

---

[31]Lewis, *Allegory*, 237.

[32]Ibid., 240.

[33]Ibid., 255-79, 282.

[34]Ibid., 340-41, 360.

sciously unchristian in the twelfth and thirteenth centuries but which was subject to Christian influence for several centuries until at the end of the sixteenth century it was transformed into a tradition consistent with the ethical ideals of the Christian church.

This tradition was not merely literary; it has shaped important norms of Western society related to the place of women in society and the accepted ideals of relations between the sexes in both courtship and marriage. The fact that romantic love was in the process of *becoming* Christian until the time of Spenser and that in both literature and life the tradition from Spenser through the nineteenth century has been more Christian than it was from the time of the troubadours through the sixteenth century argues strongly for a revision of our conventional assumptions about the chronology of the cultural influence of Christian faith.

At least, it may be thought, in the realm of formal scholarship the concept of a Middle Ages Christian from its beginning is a sound principle of historical interpretation. Medieval scholars were overwhelmingly clergymen, and their essential concern was Christian understanding. That some of them had secondary interests like the twelfth-century appreciation of classical literature discovered by Professor Haskins is not a serious qualification of the thesis. Scholasticism, as it has been conventionally understood, was not only typically medieval and thoroughly Christian, but it is of sufficient importance to support the idea of a Christian Middle Ages almost without additional evidence—especially insofar as the development of the intellectual culture of Europe is concerned.

Perhaps so, if we could accept the conventional understanding of scholasticism, but the conventional, textbook account is no longer tenable. Scholasticism was essentially a method rather than a finished body of doctrine. The inadequacies of the method were discovered by the Schoolmen themselves in their rigorous application of it. Scholasticism was a failure and had to be abandoned, but it may well have been the most fruitful, creative failure in the entire history of the human mind. It forced attention to fundamental issues in the Western tradition, and in the very process of self-destruction it laid the foundations of modern science, and raised the questions in philosophy, particularly in epistemology, that have been the central issues of Western philosophy to the present day.

Our new understanding of scholasticism and its achievement is at that awkward stage in which enough basic research has been done to undermine old interpretations and indicate the lines new interpretations must take, but the new synthesis has not yet been given a compelling statement that will make it effective outside the small number of specialists who have laid and are laying the basis for it. Neither space nor the learning of the author allows such a synthesis to be attempted here, but it would be folly to attempt a study of religious sources of modern Western culture against the background of outmoded conceptions of the Middle Ages that are still being repeated in general histories. When all disclaimers of specialized knowledge in the field have been made, it is still necessary to indicate some of the results of recent scholarship in the history of formal thought in the Middle Ages.

Theologians of the ancient church had found the ideas and categories of classical philosophy both inescapable and useful. They were not unmindful of problems and dangers involved in using pagan concepts to elucidate the faith, but use them they did. Stoicism and Platonism were particularly congenial to Christian thinkers. Where conflict with the biblical tradition was recognized, the pagan views were, of course, repudiated, but not all the incompatibilities were recognized. The Christian intellectual tradition inherited by the early Middle Ages, therefore, carried a considerable freight of classical thought, and, due to the influence of Augustine, the Platonic element was particularly strong. Thus from the beginning there was a strong classical component in medieval thought and a more or less diffident, but positive, orientation toward classical philosophy. What kind of Christian intellectual culture might have developed out of this background if it had not been cut short by the Viking and Moslem invasions is a matter of speculation. In Bede and Gregory of Tours there is at least the suggestion that it might have had an orientation toward history and developed that aspect of the biblical tradition more fully than was done before the nineteenth century. This beginning was, however, abortive, and after the Viking invasions intellectual recovery took a new direction.

R. W. Southern begins his *Making of the Middle Ages* with the journey, probably in 972, of the young scholar Gerbert (later Sylves-

ter II) from Rome to Rheims to study logic there. Southern thinks
the personal influence of Gerbert, and especially the logical
method of pedagogy that he developed, may have been responsible
for that uniquely characteristic emphasis on logic during the next
few centuries. Whatever the reasons, and Gerbert was not the only
influence in that direction, medieval Europe became the age of
logic. The influence of his logic gave to Aristotle's philosophy a
prestige—indeed a predominance—in the intellectual life of the
Middle Ages which it had not enjoyed in the ancient world. Scholasticism can be defined as the effort to understand the Christian
faith by means of Aristotelian logic.[35] All human experience, including relationship with God and involvement in creation, was
within the perspective of Christian faith, and, therefore, nothing
was in principle outside the scope of scholastic interest.

Since the *traditio* that came down from the Bible and the fathers
had a Platonic philosophical bias, scholastic method forced attention to the fundamental issues separating the two giants of classical
philosophy. Even more important, the two ancient traditions on
which the culture of Western Europe was so largely founded, the
biblical and the classical, confronted each other in a context that demanded exact definition and logical clarity. Medieval scholars were
involved by their method in an effort to reconcile the two traditions.[36] That is why Gilson could say that the central intellectual
problem of the Middle Ages was the problem of reason and revelation—meaning by reason the logic of Aristotle and the conclusions to which it had led "the Philosopher" and by revelation the
Hebrew-Christian *traditio*.[37] This, of course, was only one aspect of
a much broader and more complex area of contradiction.

In the long run the two traditions proved irreconcilable at fundamental points. In that sense scholasticism failed. Its great
achievement was that it explored the issues rigorously and with
great integrity so that the failure of the method to achieve its original aim was a process by which fundamental elements of the West-

---

[35]Cf. Moody, "Empiricism and Metaphysics," 154.

[36]Cf. Charles Trinkaus, *In Our Image and Likeness* 2 vols. (London, 1970) 1:18.

[37]Etienne Gilson, *Reason and Revelation in the Middle Ages* (New York, c. 1938).

ern consciousness were brought into clear focus as intellectual problems. Of particular importance was the definition of implications of the Christian faith which might never have been seen if the method had been less rigorously logical or if Christian scholars had not been challenged so compellingly by the alternate classical *Weltanschauung* of their pagan mentor.

Aristotle's contribution to the origins of modern science is ambiguous. Eventually his influence had to be broken so that the stultifying rationalism that had ended the creativity of Hellenistic science might be superseded by a freer method.[38] Initially however, his interest in knowledge of the physical world helped to make medieval scholars receptive to the science available from the Arabs. Euclid, Ptolemy, Galen, Hippocrates, and a number of Arabic writers were translated into Latin during the twelfth century, mostly toward the end of the century.[39] It was the impact of this science and of the rest of Aristotle, particularly his *Physics, de Anima*, and *Metaphysics*, that created the intellectual crisis at the end of the twelfth and during the thirteenth century.[40] Commitment to Aristotelian logic as a method made it impossible to avoid the broader philosophical positions associated with his understanding of the physical world and shared to a considerable degree by later Hellenistic scientists.

The thirteenth century was a time of great intellectual tension. It was no game the scholars were playing, and concern was deeper than any merely professional interests could have provoked. The things men felt most compelled to believe, things they *could* not doubt, were in contradiction, and the contradictions touched the very meaning and reality of their lives—what they would have called their salvation.

---

[38]A. R. Hall, *The Scientific Revolution, 1500-1800* (London, 1954) xvi; see also Karl Jaspers, *Nietzsche and Christianity*, trans. E. B. Ashton (Chicago, 1961) 67-81; and below, ch. 4.

[39]Southern, *The Making of the Middle Ages*, 64-67.

[40]Ibid. David Knowles, *The Evolution of Medieval Thought* (Baltimore, 1962) 221-30.

Greek philosophy had developed in the context of a cosmological world view.[41] For Aristotle the world was eternal, and at the
most fundamental level reality was unchanging. When one pene-
trated beyond ephemeral appearances to the underlying, unchanging truth, his knowledge was absolute. God could exist in this view
only as the principle of order or rationality. Since a vacuum would
contradict the order of the world according to Aristotle, it followed
that even God could not create a vacuum. But this was a problem
for Christians who were committed to the biblical conception of
creation as it had been defined and explored in Christian thought.
The biblical God transcended the world and was in no way ontologically continuous with it. In the language of twentieth-century
theologians he was "utterly other" than the world, which had no
ground of existence except God's will operating in absolute freedom. The world thus remained even in the tiniest details dependent upon God's will.[42] The freedom of God and the contingency
of the world were two sides of the same coin—whatever order exists
in the world exists by his continuing will. Since God remained completely free, it made no sense to say that he *could* not create a vacuum. Whether he *had* done so or not was a matter for investigation.
Even if it should be discovered that he had not, this fact in no way
bound God in the future to refrain from doing so. The Christian
doctrine of creation implied both the contingency and the dynamism of the world. The order of the world was not eternally inherent in it but was imposed on it from outside by the transcendent
God. Particular creatures of God were neither universal nor necessary; this led to the development of a nominalistic solution to the
problem of universals. Human knowledge of the world had, therefore, to be knowledge of particular creatures in a contingent and dynamic world, could not be deduced from universal cosmic truths,
and could never arrive at absolute certainty.

---

[41]Mircea Eliade, *Cosmos and History*, trans. Willard R. Trask (New York, c. 1959)
34-35, and *The Sacred and the Profane*, trans. Willard R. Trask (New York, c. 1959;
Harper Torchbook edition, 1961) 107-10.

[42]Augustine, *The City of God*, trans. Marcus Dods (Modern Library edition)
(New York, c. 1950) 158 (Book V, 11); Matthew 10:29-30.

All of these implications were not worked out before the fourteenth century. Thomas Aquinas was not the apex of medieval thought, but merely a very important figure in its history. His solution to the problem of relating the biblical and classical was not generally accepted by his contemporaries or by the generations immediately following him.[43] Nor were the fourteenth-century theologians and philosophers degenerate scholastics. They were, or the best of them were, pursuing the matter to its end; and the end was not a post-medieval emancipation from Christianity, but a Christian emancipation from Aristotle. That is what was significant for the later history of Western thought.[44]

The late scholastics concentrated on the problem of our knowledge of the world and in so doing they defined and refined that cast of mind which allowed the West, and only the West, to break through the closed systems of cosmological thought to the development of modern science. They also gave to Western philosophy that dominant interest in epistemology that has characterized it ever since.

Emphasis of late scholasticism on our knowledge of the physical world has had a curious result in twentieth-century historiography: it is not the theologians but historians of science who have taken the lead in discovering the importance of the fourteenth century in our intellectual history. Pierre Duhem at the beginning of this century, and after him a number of others including A. C. Crombie, M. B. Foster, Lynn Thorndike, George Sarton, and Anneliese Maier made it impossible to treat the age of Ockham, Bradwardine, Buridan, Albert of Saxony, Nicholas d'Oresme, and others as a decadent age in science or philosophy. The origins of modern science will be treated in a later chapter; here we merely note the fact that historians of science have been in the forefront of late medieval studies. It is our purpose to show that the intellectual history of the Middle Ages was a process by which European culture was being Chris-

---

[43]Paul O. Kristeller points out that Thomism was more influential in the sixteenth century than at anytime in the Middle Ages, *Renaissance Thought* (New York, 1961) 38, and "Philosophical Movements of the Renaissance," *Studies in Renaissance Thought and Letters* (Rome, 1956) 21.

[44]Cf. Moody, "Empiricism and Metaphysics," 146, 153-61.

tianized through the achieving of a better definition and understanding of the intellectual implications of Christian faith. It was
not, as it has been so frequently depicted, a process in which a
more purely Christian worldview of the early Middle Ages was
eroded by the increase of learning.

Nominalism, empiricism, and skepticism concerning any absolute certainty in human knowledge were salient characteristics of
fourteenth-century thought; and despite some deviations in the
age of the Renaissance and since, they have become fundamental
parts of the structure of the modern Western mind. All these characteristics were derivations from the Christian doctrine of creation.
One of the ironies produced by our conventional periodization of
European history is that the very fact that these aspects of the Western worldview are modern has led us to suppose them to be incongruous with the Middle Ages and hence with Christianity. Far from
habitually recognizing their Christian origin, historians have most
frequently mentioned them as instances of the breaking down of
the supposedly more Christian intellectual culture of the thirteenth
century.[45] What was breaking down was scholasticism as a fruitful
method of investigation. Paradoxically, the breakdown itself was
most fruitful. The glory of scholasticism was not the Thomist synthesis as a synthesis, but the rigorous pursuit by Thomas and others of the efforts to reconcile Aristotle and the Christian intellectual
tradition. Scholasticism broke down as a method because the two
proved irreconcilable. As an Aristotelian tradition, however, it continued alive, especially at Padua; but post-Reformation scholasticism—both Protestant and Catholic—was a kind of intellectualistic
obscurantism that transformed it from a rigorous method of inquiry into a dead weight of abstruse dogma. This end was radically
different from the dynamic intellectual life from Anselm (1033-1109)
through the fourteenth-century Franciscans.

Bruno Nardi has pointed out that the Franciscan thinkers of the
fourteenth century had not abandoned reason or the philosophic
enterprise; they were simply insisting that the Christian revelation
had certain philosophical implications and that philosophy which

---

[45]Moody, "Empiricism and Metaphysics."

ignored them was bound to err fundamentally.[46] Modern identifi-
cation of "Christian philosophy" with a closed and dogmatic syn-
thesis of knowledge stems from the false assumption that
Thomas's *Summa* was the end product of Christian thought in the
Middle Ages and that it served his age as such a closed synthesis.
This is, of course, quite far from the dynamic truth.

The influence of Aristotle had turned attention to our knowledge of the natural world, and medieval scholars on the whole insisted that in considering nature and our knowledge of it we not
neglect the Creation and all that was implied in the Christian teaching concerning it. The freedom of God and the contingency of the
world and each creature in it as absolutely dependent upon him
must not be contradicted. The success of nominalism in the Middle
Ages is due to the fact that the implications of the doctrine of creation are strongly nominalistic. Particular creatures are not necessary but contingent upon God's will; therefore they cannot be
known by reference to any eternal and universal cosmic order. Nor
is God related to individuals through some ontological continuum
or by the mediation of demigods. He knows each creature immediately, directly, and wholly. Not a sparrow falls that he does not
know it. Every hair on one's head is known in its uniqueness.[47] William of Ockham did not know whether universals are in the mind
of God or not,[48] but there was no doubt of the reality of the particular thing or of God's knowlege of it.

The term nominalism was used in the late Middle Ages less precisely than modern philosophy finds necessary. Many whom moderns would call conceptualists were designated nominalists by

---

[46]Bruno Nardi, *Studi di filosofia medievale* (Rome, 1960) 201-202. Professor Langdon Gilkey in his *Maker of Heaven and Earth* (New York, 1959) likewise recognizes
that the doctrine of creation has philosophical implications (42, 124, 134-38), although he does not seem aware of the depth of medieval thought on the subject
(116). Much of recent theology has been blighted by the fear that recognizing the
philosophical implications of the Christian tradition would lead to a closed synthesis. This is a serious misunderstanding because the implications seen by the
fourteenth-century Franciscans and Gilkey are precisely what would make such a
closed system impossible.

[47]Matthew 10:29-30.

[48]Ernest A. Moody, *The Logic of William of Ockham* (New York, 1935) 86-94.

their medieval contemporaries.[49] One reason for this looseness of terminology may be that medieval scholars were less vitally interested in the question, What is a universal? than in insisting on the reality of particular creatures.[50] These particular creatures constitute a universe not because they are rooted in some eternal cosmic reality, but because they are related to each other in the purpose of God. It is true, to be sure, that God's purpose involves the establishment by him of an order in the world, but this order is in no way binding upon him.[51] Since the purposes of God are largely inscrutable, and since, even when he has made his purpose known, he pursues it in the absolute freedom of omnipotence, a trustworthy knowledge of the natural world cannot be achieved by deduction. There is no eternal cosmic order in terms of which man can have absolute, certain, necessary knowledge of nature. Man's natural knowlege is always partial and never achieves certainty; the world itself, in the phrase of Ernest Moody, is only "conditionally pre-

---

[49]Richard I. Aaron, *The Theory of Universals* (Oxford, 1967) 20.

[50]Nardi, *Studi di filosofia medievale*, 204.

[51]I am indebted to Professor Harold Ditmanson for calling to my attention that nominalism is consistent with the unity of the world when it is assumed that the world is ordered by a single Divine will or purpose. This idea, which was too generally agreed to in the fourteenth century to require much discussion, was appealed to later by Descartes and Locke and in a different way by Berkeley to explain the relation of the human mind to the world it knows. For them, even for Descartes, it was an assumption that was not likely to be questioned. The possibilities of the idea of a transcendent purpose as the source of unity in the world have not been fully developed. One reason is the bias created by the nonteleological methods of physics. In the last three centuries it has also been opposed by a very strong anti-Christian prejudice in Western thought. An adequate development of the concept would lead to an essentially historical understanding of reality; this might make it possible to bring the very strong Western sense of historical existence into a satisfactory relationship to science and the philosophical concepts associated most closely with science.

Concern to avoid a return to a teleology inherent in things has inhibited any discussion of what in recent times has pointed toward a teleology in evolution and in history. The purposefulness of a transcendent God offers an explanation that is not in conflict with modern science and is, indeed, what freed science from immanent teleologies in the first place. This alternative has not, however, been investigated outside a very small and isolated theological elite, and their speculations have not been significantly related to science or philosophy. See below, ch. 7.

dictable." Christian scholars were thus drawn to that position of relative skepticism which admits some kind of validity to human knowledge but which denies to it the kind of certainty that stands in the way of criticism and advance in scientific knowledge. This relative skepticism, although it has not held the field unchallenged, has since characterized the Western mind in both science and philosophy.

The empirical emphasis of the fourteenth century, which has been equally significant in subsequent intellectual history, was a part of the same complex set of ideas.[52] Since one could not know the facts of nature by deduction from an absolute world order, attention was turned to empirical data in order to learn what order had in fact been established. Though Christian scholars continued to believe in the general regularity of nature, established by what they called the *potentia ordinata* of God, the empirical method by which that order was known required a piecemeal approach to science. Not only was the hypothetical nature of all scientific knowledge recognized, but widespread discontinuity in our knowledge of the world had to be accepted. The way was opened for those specific and limited investigations which have been the hallmark of modern science. Empiricism has been so closely related in our history with a skepticism regarding the capacity of the human mind to achieve certainty in the knowledge of the world or to penetrate to the ultimate and essential nature of things that the two terms are in some contexts practically synonymous. That skepticism regarding systems and ultimate essences arose in the context of the doctrine of creation and in intimate association with the vindication of our direct knowledge of particular things[53] has been of the utmost importance for the development of Western thought, both scientific and philosophical.

The mainstream of Greek philosophy was rationalistic, cosmological, speculative, and centered in metaphysics; the mainstream of modern philosophy has been empirical, analytical, critical, and centered in epistemology. What has too often gone unnoticed is

---

[52]Moody, "Empiricism and Metaphysics," 156-58.

[53]Nardi, *Studi di filosofia medievale*, 204.

that the radical change in the nature and interests of philosophical inquiry was, in the words of Ernest A. Moody, "due primarily to the influence of the Christian religion, and to the work of the theologians of the Middle Ages." "The transformation of the *form* of philosophical inquiry, from the speculative to the analytic," he says, ". . . gave a new character and direction to all later philosophy of which we have not yet seen the end."[54] Etienne Gilson recognizes the same deep and long-lasting influence of the late scholastics and generously praises them for the fruitfulness of their work in science and even in mathematics; but as a Thomist he deplores the effect on philosophy as "a complete abdication of philosophy as a rational discipline" and asks, "But was it impossible to pave the way to science without destroying philosophy?" Gilson's criticism, as much as Moody's praise, is a recognition of the seminal role the late scholastics had in forming the structure of the modern mind.[55]

The history of nominalism, skepticism, and empiricism illustrates the long-term influence of medieval Christianity on our culture. At the same time it furnishes a most important example of the gradual development of peculiarly and characteristically biblical-Christian insights in the course of medieval history. The Middle Ages was not a culture Christian from its inception, but a culture in process of a Christianization which never reached completion. In the struggle between classical and biblical traditions that was the fundamental problem of scholasticism, it was the biblical that prevailed. In its emancipation from Aristotle the Christian philosophy of the fourteenth-century Franciscans is the source of a major part of the structure of the Western mind.[56]

The long-range effectiveness of developments in the schools was possible because they were giving articulate expression to modes of being aware of the world and attitudes toward historical existence that permeated the society as a whole. The Christianiza-

---

[54]Moody, "Empiricism and Metaphysics," 146, 161.

[55]Etienne Gilson, *The Unity of Philosóphical Experience* (New York, c. 1937) 117-18. The importance of Ockham for modern philosophy has probably been recognized more widely among Thomist opponents of Ockham than in any other group of scholars.

[56]Moody, "Empiricism and Metaphysics."

tion of Europe was proceeding along a broad front. The progress of the church's educational, Christianizing mission finds an ironic measure in the history of medieval heresy. By the twelfth century there was enough lay interest in theology and the Christian life for heresy to take the form of popular movements. The heresies of Pierre de Bruys, Henry of Lausanne, Arnold of Brescia, and Peter Waldo—all in the twelfth century—differed from the previous heresies of isolated intellectuals in that they all became popular movements. The Albigensians of southern France date from the previous century, to be sure, but they are a special case. Although the medieval church treated them as heretics, the term is misleading. Actually they were not a variety of Christian belief but Manichaean dualists and ought to be thought of as a non-Christian religion. The fact that such a religion could get so strong a foothold in a large section of the medieval West and flourish as it did until rooted out by military power in the thirteenth century is evidence against the conventional concept of the Christian Middle Ages. It is doubtful if such a thing could have occurred in Europe from the fourteenth century through the seventeenth.

The Albigensians indicate how serious the task of the church was, but the other heresies, which were basically Christian, indicate the success of the church even more than its limitations. In the thirteenth century the Franciscans might easily have been forced into heresy as the strongest such movement up to that time if the church had handled them less wisely. As it was, they became more effective than the traditional monastic orders as an agency for the spread of a truer faith among the common people. The Dominicans, organized specifically to combat heresy among the laity, were similarly effective.

By the fourteenth century lay piety had developed to an unprecedented degree. Large numbers of people who had no thought of entering a monastery or convent were concerned about the religious quality of their personal lives. The "books of hours" used by the monks in their prayers were translated into the vernacular for the sake of pious laymen. Again the appeal of popular heresy offers a perverse measure of the growing interest in the faith. Movements like those of Wyclif and Hus could hardly have existed on such a scale in any previous century. Although these movements were put

down as overt movements, their influence continued in the growing religious interest of the laity in Euope, an interest which did
not, of course, include everybody, but which did involve people in
all classes of medieval society.[57]

Measured by the standards of the kingdom of God, Europe was
still a long way from being Christian and interests were still pursued in a manner that can be called "secular" in the sense of not
being Christian in intent or conscious relationship; but to describe
the century of Wyclif, Hus, Dante, and the Franciscan theologians
as characterized by a *growing* secularity is quite wide of the mark.
Petrarch and Chaucer, who are often cited as indications of the secular direction of European culture, were in fact devout Christians.
Petrarch, who had taken minor orders, passionately defended the
faith against Averroists,[58] and Chaucer repented the non-Christian
elements in his *Troilus*. The formation of the Brethren of the Common Life near the end of the fourteenth century was symbolic of
what was going on. Despite the much commented-on moral and
spiritual decadence in the church, especially in its upper echelons,
religious interest and commitment continued to grow in Europe
through the period of the Conciliar Movement and beyond until it
reached a crescendo in the Reformation.

---

[57]Heiko A. Oberman, "Some Notes on the Theology of Nominalism with Attention to its Relation to the Renaissance," *Harvard Theological Review* 53 (1960): 74.

[58]Ernst Cassirer, Paul Oskar Kristeller, John Herman Randall, Jr., *The Renaissance Philosophy of Man* (Chicago, 1948) 140-41, 143.

III THE RENAISSANCE VIEW OF MAN

In a brilliant essay republished in a collection of his shorter works in 1960, Bruno Nardi pointed out that the criticism of the four-teenth-century nominalists had undermined Aristotle as the basis of philosophy and that they envisioned the creation of a new Christian philosophy based upon the implications of the Christian revelation for a true understanding of God, the world, and man.[1] Certainly they had made a significant beginning toward such a construction because their criticism of Aristotle had been based on implications of the doctrine of creation regarding the absolute freedom of God, the contingency of the world, and the hypothetical nature of all human knowledge of the world. As pointed out in the previous chapter, the nominalism by which they are commonly designated as a group was itself a derivative out of their understanding of the relation of the Creator to his creatures.

The power of this line of thought is evidenced in the fact that it deflected the mainstream of philosophy from Greek rationalism to

---

[1] *Studi di filosofia medievale* (Rome, 1960) 193-207.

the critical, and in a modified sense of the word, skeptical philosophy of the modern West.[2] Yet the program of a Christian philosophy developed rigorously from the foundation laid by the fourteenth-century Franciscans was not carried out. Why it was not is a historical problem of enormous scope and beyond what is envisioned in this study. Even the continuity of seventeenth-century empiricism with the empiricism of the Ockhamites is not easily traced.[3] Most modern empirical, analytical philosophers would be surprised to learn how much they owe historically to Christian theology; and even those among them who may be confessing Christians would hardly understand themselves as involved in an enterprise to produce a Christian philosophy! Indeed, the idea of a Christian philosophy would be as much anathema to Protestant theologians of the present day as it would be to philosophers. Theologians identify such an idea with a closed synthesis like Thomism. What the medieval Franciscans had in mind was, of course, something very different. Their epistemology was hardly conducive to a closed system of thought.

The Franciscans simply recognized what on a common-sense basis must be obvious: that if the biblical understanding of creation is taken seriously, it involves belief in a transcendent God and has implications for the nature of man and the reality he confronts.[4] There did not, however, develop a comprehensive, coherent, Christian philosophy such as Nardi thinks the nominalists had in mind.

---

[2]Ernest A. Moody, "Empiricism and Metaphysics in Medieval Philosophy," *The Philosophical Review* 67 (1958): 145-163.

[3]Michael Oakeshott, "Introduction," to the *Leviathan* (Oxford, 1957) xvii, xxvii.

[4]Richard R. Niebuhr uses the term "Christian metaphysics" and recognizes that such is implied in the doctine of creation *ex nihilo*, and in a brief but brilliant book makes a good beginning toward laying the foundation for a Christian philosophy that would relate our experience of history with our understanding of nature. Richard R. Niebuhr, *Resurrection and Historical Reason* (New York, c. 1957) 168, passim. Langdon Gilkey and Wolfhart Pannenberg from different points of view have also recognized the possibility of a Christian philosophy. Niebuhr's work offers the most promising possibilities, but at this writing it has not been further developed. The idea of a Christian philosophy is not popular in present-day Protestant theological circles. It is more common for theologians to seek a foundation for theology in some supposedly autonomous philosophy. Giving up her role as "Queen of the Sciences," theology has chosen to be a kind of camp follower.

Their criticism of Aristotle involved a Christian analysis of fundamental aspects of the cosmological world Greek philosophy had explored and exhibited. The consequences of this analysis shaped the
mind of the modern West, but the consequences were worked out
in a variety of traditions that sometimes seemed widely divergent
from each other: modern science, the empirical tradition in philosophy, Reformation theology, the historical consciousness of modern
man, existentialism.

For the nominalists the contingency of the world had meant that
the world had no purpose of its own; the purpose that operated in
it was overwhelmingly God's purpose and secondarily man's. Thus
was born the "dead" world that modern science explores un-
impeded by any consideration of inherent purposes in things. In
this the nominalists did a thorough job. The revival of Platonism in
the fifteenth century obscured the new mode of knowing the world
for many intelligent and creative people, but was probably never a
serious threat to the cast of mind that had made modern science
possible. The nominalists had worked out with regard to the world
and our knowledge of it what was implied by faith in the Transcendent God of the biblical tradition who acts in absolute freedom and
with absolute power. But what this God and the contingent world
implied about the existence of man had not received their full attention. That implication of the biblical tradition was to be the concern of Renaissance humanists, whose approach to it was very
different from the rigorously logical methods of scholasticism.

What continuity there might have been between the nominalists and the humanists is not easy to say. Humanism had developed
out of the rhetorical traditions of the Middle Ages, particularly in
Italy, and there was a certain hostility between them and the scholastic thinkers that was in large part the kind of rivalry between academic traditions that obtains in American universities today
between historians and sociologists.[5] The humanists had a sincere
distaste for and distrust of the dialectical method of the Schoolmen;
yet in many basic matters they were in substantial agreement with
the nominalists. Charles Trinkaus points out that although Pe-

---

[5]Paul Oskar Kristeller, *Renaissance Thought* (New York, 1961) 113; Charles Trinkaus, *In Our Image and Likeness*, 2 vols. (London, 1970) 1:23.

trarch and Salutati were antagonistic towards the Ockhamites, "there was a remarkable coincidence in their religious views and those of Gregory of Rimini." In another passage Trinkaus specifically mentions both Bradwardine and Gregory as examples of theologians whose Augustinian inspiration had led to their revival of a Trinitarian view of man that had affinities with humanist anthropology.[6] The humanists had little interest in the problem of universals as it had been defined by the philosophers, but their own sense of reality, a widely pervading Platonic influence notwithstanding, was strongly nominalistic.[7] The voluntarism of the nominalists had involved an understanding of man as radically free, transcending any causal necessity in his relation to the created world. This view was parallel to the humanist emphasis on man as ordained ruler of the world. And with the humanists as with the nominalists it contained a serious threat of Pelagianism. In many of the humanists there was also a skepticism regarding natural philosophy that gave them some affinities with the more rigorously thought-out qualifications the nominalists had put on our knowledge of the world. In both cases there was a resulting tendency to fideism.

Whether the humanists were in any direct way indebted to the nominalists for these components of their thought it is very difficult to say; and it is probably not of very great importance. Both were operating within the immensely rich and profound biblical-Christian tradition, and both were oriented in that tradition by similar elements from Augustine. All medieval scholars were in a profound way Augustinians, but the nominalists even more than most so that the specific tradition to which they contribute is sometimes distinguished from the rest of medieval scholarship as "Augustinian." As for the humanists, Augustine far more than any other ancient writer shaped and directed their thought. It would, perhaps, make for a more plausible interpretation of the general sweep of Western intellectual history if we assume that there was little direct

---

[6]Trinkaus, In Our Image, 1:60-62, 199.

[7]Heiko A. Oberman, "Some Notes on the Theology of Nominalism with Attention to its Relation to the Renaissance," Harvard Theological Review 53 (1960): 47-76. Trinkaus agrees in general, though he points out that the humanists were not nominalists in a technical sense, and he objects to Oberman using the term nominalist to describe the ideas of Ficino. Trinkaus, In Our Image, 1:60, 2:467.

continuity between nominalism and humanism, but only the indirect continuity that resulted from the nominalist contribution to the general Christian culture and life orientation of their own and subsequent times.

Two things it is important to note. One is that the Renaissance view of man has important affinities with the nominalistic philosophical position. The second thing to remember is that the development of the various implications of the tradition that the nominalists explored was along independent lines and no clear integration of them into a single tradition has been achieved, although the common origin of these developments suggests the possibility of such an integration.

The magnitude of the humanist achievement would be hard to overestimate. In developing the basically Christian doctrine of man more fully than had been done before, the humanists gave to modern Western man an understanding of the characteristic mode of consciousness out of which he develops his science, his philosophies, his culture in general. Paradoxical it may be, but modern atheistic man shares in this way of being aware of himself quite as fully as his Christian contemporaries. Moderns were justified in seeing the Renaissance as the source of their own understanding of man; and since in their age this view had no necessary connection with Christian commitment, it is understandable that they should assume that the Renaissance marked the widespread repudiation of Christian faith, imputing to the fifteenth century what did not occur until the end of the seventeenth. The irony is that in their dissociation of Renaissance humanism from Christianity those who most admired and praised the humanists obscured the originality of the Renaissance view of man by presenting it as merely a revival of classical paganism and even treating it as an obvious, common sense conception of man that needed only to be freed from the distortions and gloom of medieval theology. Actually it was a highly sophisticated development of one of the unique characteristics of the biblical tradition and is peculiar to the civilization of Western Europe.[8]

---

[8]Western civilization has, of course, in recent times come to dominate the whole world, so that this peculiarly Western conception and mode of existence like many other Western characteristics is now present virtually everywhere.

It will be convenient here to describe how the biblical view of man differs from that of classical antiquity.

The uniqueness of the Hebrew people was that they became aware of themselves as existing under a transcendent God.[9] Transcendence here means that God was not in the world as a member of the cosmos, nor was he an aspect of the world, as, for example, Cicero's God was the Rational Principle of the cosmos. God was beyond the world—as some recent theologians have put it, God was "utterly other" than the world—and he was in absolute control of history and of nature. The history of the Hebrew people was the working out of implications of their knowledge of the transcendent God. The story is complex and the detailed analysis of it is the concern of Old Testament scholars. We are here concerned only with the major elements that developed. The Hebrews first became aware of God in the midst of their history, probably in connection with the exodus from Egypt. They knew that God had acted and that they must respond. Then God would respond to their response, and so forth. History was the central reality, a dialectical relationship between them and God. If God controlled their history, he had to be in control of the Egyptians, the Assyrians, and other peoples with whom they dealt. Also God had to be in control of nature. The idea of creation developed as one of the most sophisticated products of the maturing faith. Emerging as it did in the context of a reality understood as historical, the creation was conceived as an historical act, a free act of God.[10] The created world did not stand over against God in some cosmic dualism; it was absolutely dependent upon him for its very existence. This is the essential meaning of the later Christian formula of creation *ex nihilo*.

The purposes of God operated in the world, but the world itself was without purpose. This was the contingent world of Augustine and the medieval theologians—the world whose order and structure the nominalists had pointed out could not be deduced by any laws of necessity because it was the product of a God acting in ab-

---

[9]Eric Voegelin, *Order and History*, Vol. I: *Israel and Revelation* (Baton Rouge, c. 1956) 123-33, 420-27, passim.

[10]Ibid., 135.

solute freedom. It was the "dead" world of modern science, known to man only empirically.

So much the Schoolmen had seen with great clarity; but they had not developed so well the understanding of man's very peculiar relationship both to God and to the rest of creation. Like all creatures man was sustained in his existence by God's will and creative power; but man had in addition a very special relationship with God. He was related to God in the interacting responses of history; he was intended for fellowship with God, for the mutual relationship of a community of love and understanding. This was the meaning of the idea of the image of God in man. In the highest capacities of mind and spirit man transcended the orders of creation by virtue of his relationship to the transcendent God. This transcendence made man radically free. His was not the absolute freedom of God because he was involved in the relationships of the ordered world; but man transcended the orders of the world and was capable of free and creative action in regard to the world. He was a subcreator under God. Man was a *historical* creature, creating culture and changing even the physical world; he had a certain freedom even in relation to God. There was the clear suggestion in the Bible that the purpose of God in the whole creation was his relationship to man in the community of the kingdom of God, or to use the less common biblical phrase which Augustine preferred, the City of God.[11]

This was a very exalted conception of man as one who transcended the very cosmos itself and upon whose future development no limits could be set. Man's relation to the world was in fact to be its ruler. In the Genesis story of creation God said to the first man and woman: "Be fruitful and increase, fill the earth and subdue it, rule over the fish in the sea, the birds of heaven, and every living thing that moves upon the earth."

The classical view of man was quite different. The Greeks had praised man highly. They had noticed his inventiveness and were well aware of his superiority to the other animals. But the final real-

---

[11]Genesis 1:26-30; Psalms 8; Matthew 25:34; Ephesians 1:9-10, 19-23; 3:8-11; John Bright, *The Kingdom of God* (Nashville, New York, c. 1953). Cf. Trinkaus, *In Our Image*, 1:316.

ity for the Greeks was not a transcendent God, but the world itself. The cosmos was not contingent; it was eternal, and basically it was unchanging. Mircea Eliade points out that even Plato's philosophy was a highly sophisticated understanding of a cosmological world view that had been almost universal up until his time.[12] All the Greeks did not think alike, but the context of their thinking was the eternal and unchanging cosmos. In this world man had a place; it was for most Greeks a place of great dignity, but it was not the highest place. If a person arrogantly sought a higher place, if he tried to usurp the place of a god, he was guilty of hybris, and the result was his destruction.

This sense of a fixed place in an unchanging cosmos was missing in the Renaissance philosophy of man. The radical freedom of man finds what is, perhaps, its most famous early expression in Giovanni Pico della Mirandola, and since his time it has been the modern mode of human consciousness. Since the Renaissance man has understood himself to be free with regard to the world, responsible for his own historical future, and responsible only to God—or in recent atheism only to himself or to posterity. Modern man has no understanding of hybris; what Eliade calls "the terror of history" he does know, but that is a very different thing.

Renaissance humanism developed out of the traditions of medieval rhetoric.[13] This tradition led the humanists easily into an acquaintance with and an appreciation of classical literature. The ethics, the politics, and the aesthetics of the pagans were of particular interest to them. It was Augustine, however, who had been the strongest single influence on medieval thought, and his influence continued unabated through the Renaissance. The fact that Augustine himself had been educated in rhetoric rather than in philosophy strengthened the affinities the humanists felt with him.

Out of this varied background the humanists evolved their philosophy of man, and despite the rich garnishing from classical sources the essential ingredients were biblical and Christian. The

---

[12]Mircea Eliade, *Cosmos and History*, trans. Willard R. Trask (New York, c. 1959) 34-35; and *The Sacred and the Profane*, trans. Willard R. Trask (New York, c. 1959; Harper Torchbook edition, 1961) 107-10.

[13]Kristeller, *Renaissance Thought*, 11-13.

most thorough study of this aspect of the Renaissance to date is a two-volume work of Charles Trinkaus to which he gave the shocking title *In Our Image and Likeness*, a direct quotation from the Genesis story of creation. Trinkaus's work is the culmination of a century of scholarship in which recognition of the Christian influence on Renaissance thought has been steadily growing, but growing against what for long seemed the almost overwhelming opposition of a conventional interpretation that saw the Renaissance as essentially pagan and secular and rationalistic. The first significant work in this development was Henry Thode's argument that the naturalism of Renaissance art was derived from Franciscan sources. He linked the attention to particular, concrete fact in Renaissance painting and sculpture to the nominalistic philosophy of fourteenth-century Franciscan scholars.[14] Wallace K. Ferguson points out that Thode's work had little influence among historians until Paul Sabatier's biography of Francis supported his general interpretation of the Franciscans.[15] The lecture in which Ferguson pointed this out was given in 1956. Since that time the interpretations of some important aspects of the Renaissance have been virtually reversed. The Renaissance philosophy of man is, perhaps, the most significant example. In his Foreword Trinkaus announces: "It will be our thesis that the new vision of man in this period found its inspiration in a revival of the patristic exegesis of the Genesis passage: 'And He said: Let us make man in our image, after our likeness.' "[16] According to Trinkaus the Renaissance philosophy of man was rooted in ideas of the Church Fathers, particularly Augustine and Lactantius, which had been the prevailing view of man through the early Middle Ages, but that the scholastic philosophers had shown less interest in.

It was a combination of their rhetorical revolt against scholastic theology and philosophy, and of their revival of patristic theological

---

[14]Henry Thode, *Franz von Assisi und die Anfänge der Kunst der Renaissance in Italien* (Berlin, 1885).

[15]Wallace K. Ferguson, "The Reinterpretation of the Renaissance," *Facets of the Renaissance: the Arensberg Lectures* (Los Angeles, 1959).

[16]Trinkaus, *In Our Image*, 1:xiv. See also 2:507, passim.

anthropology that gave the humanists' vision of man a centrally Christian and religious character. The classical visions of man did not always fit these humanists' insights, and they were cautiously and arbitrarily used only where they could fit.[17]

The doctrine of creation in the image of God and its complement of man's divine commission to subdue the world and rule it was the central theme, but other biblical and theological doctrines were frequently appealed to. The Incarnation was of special importance. It was because man was made in the image of God that the Incarnation could occur. In Ficino's Platonic theology there was the further idea that the universality of man as the only creature who was "capable of all relations with all things" made man the appropriate creature for God's incarnation.[18] Traditional comment on the Incarnation had been inclined to emphasize the lowliness of man in order to magnify the love of God and the sacrifice of Christ. This theme is not absent among the humanists, but they preferred to draw a very different conclusion: God's act in becoming man was not only a dramatic affirmation of the image of God in man; it conferred still greater honor and glory upon him. Manetti even argued that if man had not sinned the Incarnation would still have occurred so that God "might marvellously and unbelievably honour and glorify man."[19] The Incarnation had opened the way for an ascent of man beyond the angels. There was patristic evidence for this; but the scholastics, under the influence of Aristotle and a hierarchical world view had tended, with some exceptions, to ascribe a higher dignity to the angels.[20]

The question whether the dignity of man is higher or lower than that of angels may seem a matter of little interest today, but the po-

---

[17]Ibid., 1:xxiii.

[18]Paul O. Kristeller, *The Philosophy of Marsilio Ficino* (New York, 1943) 405. For a discussion of Ficino's concept of the universality of man see ibid., chapter 7. For the varying view of Pico della Mirandola see ibid., Appendix II.

[19]Trinkaus, *In Our Image*, 1:37-38, 191, 252-53, 2:739-41, passim.

[20]Ibid., 1:188-91; 2:511-12, 519; Giovanni Pico della Mirandola, *Heptaplus*, trans. Douglas Carmichael, in Giovanni Pico della Mirandola, *On the Dignity of Man* (Indianapolis, 1965) 115-16.

sition taken on that question by the humanists was the result of a basic and highly significant contribution which they have made to modern man's understanding of himself. They were moving away from efforts to understand man in terms of his place in some cosmic hierarchy and were recovering and developing a tradition of man as one who transcends nature itself and is capable of acting upon the world creatively. The understanding of man implied in the Christian faith had so permeated the thought and consciousness of Europe by the fifteenth century that it even subverted the hierarchical concept in Ficino's Platonism, giving to man in the center of the hierarcy an importance greater than that of any other creature. And if there had been any doubt about this, the Incarnation would have removed it.[21] Man's relationship to God in the Christian faith is simply not consistent with any intermediaries and implies a radical freedom on the part of man. Pomponazzi, the Aristotelian who denied with such force Ficino's claim that the immortality of the soul was capable of rational proof, yet agreed with Ficino about man's general place in the cosmos.

Pico della Mirandola, second only to Ficino among the Italian Platonists, went even further in his emphasis on the radical freedom of man that transcends nature itself. Pico accepted the Neoplatonic idea of a hierarchy of being. But man, he thought, had no place in the hierarchy. He is free to move up and down it and take for himself whatever attributes he wills. Kristeller comments: "Thus the hierarchy is no longer all-conclusive, while man, because of his . . . freedom, seems to be set entirely apart from the order of objective reality." Man was not out of touch with nature and his creaturehood was not denied; but though involved in the natural world, he did transcend its order.[22] Pico's *Oration*, although it contains his most original contribution to the Renaissance philosophy

---

[21]Paul O. Kristeller, "Ficino and Pomponazzi on the Place of Man in the Universe," *Studies in Renaissance Thought and Letters* (Rome, 1956) 284-85. Ficino is not, however, completely consistent in this. His Platonism gives the angels an upper hand in some contexts. See Kristeller, *Philosophy of Ficino*, 83.

[22]This is the theme of the first part of Pico's *Oration on the Dignity of Man*. See also Kristeller, "Ficino and Pomponazzi," 286; Trinkaus, *In Our Image*, 2:506-26; Paul J. W. Miller, Introduction to a volume of Pico's works (Indianapolis, 1965) xv-xvi.

of man, does not present the whole range and depth of his Christian anthropology. Taken by itself it has a strongly Pelagian ring; on the face of it he seems to be saying that sin is a folly the wise can avoid and that man by his own will can achieve beatitude:

> The seeds that each man cultivates will grow and bear their fruit in him. If he cultivates vegetable seeds, he will become a plant. If the seeds of sensation, he will grow into brute. If rational, he will come out a heavenly animal. If intellectual, he will be an angel, and a son of God. And if he is not contented with the lot of any creature but takes himself up into the center of his own unity, then, made one spirit with God and settled in the solitary darkness of the Father, who is above all things, he will stand ahead of all things. Who does not wonder at this chameleon which we are?[23]

Taken out of its context in an account of creation, this sounds hardly Christian at all. It is hard to make it consistent with what he wrote later in *Heptaplus* even when some allowance is made for rhetorical flourish. In the *Heptaplus* Pico makes clear that sin has seriously distorted, if not destroyed, the image of God in us and, indeed, injured the whole creation; that there could be no salvation apart from Christ; that the ascent to God was possible only by God's drawing us (which is Pico's definition of grace); that to attempt to ascend by one's own power was a deadly sin.[24]

The radical anthropology of Pico, especially his doctrine of the transcendence of man, rests not on philosophical but on theological grounds. Pico's philosophy would have indicated a place for man in the great chain of being, but the Incarnation was a breaking into the cosmos by the transcendent God. The humanity of Christ revealed and guaranteed the unique relationship of man and the God who had become man for man's sake. The metaphysics of the cosmos was transcended in the act of God and in man's relationship to God.[25] Trinkaus points out that also in Lorenzo Valla it is easy to

---

[23]Pico della Mirandola, *On the Dignity of Man*. Trans. Charles Genn Wallis and included in a volume of Pico's works with an Introduction by Paul J. W. Miller (Indianapolis, 1965) 5.

[24]Pico, *Heptaplus*, 125-26, 136-37, 145-46, 152.

[25]Trinkaus, *In Our Image*, 2:512.

see that the transcendence of man beyond nature is due to his relation to the transcendent God. Valla repudiates the idea of any hierarchy of gradual steps from the inanimate to the divine. He stresses how much like the other animals man is in all natural ways so that he can emphasize the transcendent character of his glory. "By nature man is an animal, by supernatural divine action he is a god."[26]

Aristotelian and Platonist could agree in their vision of man's exalted nature because it was deeper in their consciousness than their philosophical conclusions were. The tradition was far older than humanism itself and had been a major theme among the humanists since Petrarch. Pico's statement of the radical freedom of man was striking because of Pico's rhetorical skill and because of its context in an otherwise hierarchical philosophy; but Trinkaus thinks the originality of the idea itself has been exaggerated. He points to anticipations of the ideas of the "multipotentiality" and freedom of man, not only in Ficino and Manetti, but also in Gregory of Nyssa and, above all, in Augustine. Augustine has been the chief interpreter to Western Europe of the whole biblical-Christian tradition. All the varied, turbulent thought of the ancient church, and a good bit of pagan thought as well, was funneled through him, and out of him it spread into virtually every aspect of European life. Augustine did not exactly *invent* personality. Personality is the obverse of community. The concept is inherent in the Christian idea of the redemption of individuals into the community of the City of God. But if he did not invent personality, it was in him that it got its first adequate definition and expression. The chapter in Cochrane's *Christianity and Classical Culture* which bears the subtitle "The Discovery of Personality" deals primarily with Augustine.[27] In all previous antiquity there was no book like Augustine's *Confessions*.

Augustine's analysis of his own self, or person, put the will in the fundamental and central position. His development of this un-

---

[26]Ibid., 1:155-56.

[27]C. N. Cochrane, *Christianity and Classical Culture* (London, New York, Toronto, 1944).

derstanding of human psychology became the source of subsequent voluntaristic philosophies in the West.[28] With it went the
understanding of the whole of human culture as the artificial creation of man. When Burckhardt entitled a chapter of his famous
interpretation of the Renaissance "The State as a Work of Art," he
was, whether he knew it or not, expressing a basically Augustinian
idea. Michael Oakeshott rightly identifies the political tradition in
which "will" and "artifice" are key works as "Augustinian."[29] Like
the late medieval nominalists, who were Augustinians too, the humanists subordinated the intellect to the will; but while the interest
of the scholastics was primarily epistemological, the thrust of the
humanists was an anthropology of freedom and action. Hume
might have been surprised to learn that his dictum, "Reason is, and
ought only to be the slave of the passions," had been anticipated by
Petrarch and Salutati and Lorenzo Valla.[30] Their emphasis on the
will turned them toward action in the world. Valla said that no definition of man should leave out "action without which man does
not exist."[31]

The voluntarism of the humanists was closely related to their
emphasis on man's God-given role as the ruler of the created
world. Man could rule over nature because he transcended nature.
Natural necessity, said Salutati, determines the intellect, but the
will can turn the intellect to this object or that.[32] Man operating
freely in the world was a sub-creator under God, and his creations
were the world of history and culture. This was not merely a theory
for the classroom or study; it was a mode of consciousness, and it

---

[28]Kristeller, *Philosophy of Ficino*, 256-57. Kristeller points out that the concept of
will was almost wholly absent from classical Greek thought. See also a review by
Kristeller in *Speculum* 42 (1967): 374.

[29]Oakeshott, Introduction to the *Leviathan*, lii-liv; Willis B. Glover, "Human Nature and the State in Hobbes," *Journal of the History of Philosophy* 4 (1966): 293-311.

[30]Trinkaus, *In Our Image*, 2:769, passim.

[31]Ibid., 1:153.

[32]Ibid., 1:64-65. Trinkaus points out the similarity of this position to that of
Duns Scotus. In his discussion of Pomponazzi, Trinkaus treats him as an excep-
tion because for him: "Man is in nature, not above nature as the Renaissance
Christian exegesis of *Genesis* i had made him." Ibid., 2:547

released a burst of personal energy which characterized the period. Trinkaus credits Valla with having the best grasp of this aspect of humanism and of giving it the most vigorous expression. Valla's position, though with "significant specific disagreements," was "a version of Christianity solidly based on a rephrasing and transformation of Augustine's own voluntarism, eudaemonism and theology of grace." What was most significantly new in Valla was the vigorous activism. There is no denial of God's providence in history, but the emphasis is on man's historical creativity.[33]

The Renaissance recovery of interest in history has long been celebrated and the sense the humanists had of the distance in time that separated them from the ancient classical world contrasted with the lack of such a sense in the Middle Ages. Their historical consciousness, however, was not merely their appreciation of the works of classical historians, their own interest in writing history, and their sense of chronological perspective. They also had a sense of existing historically; their activism was an integral part of their historical mindedness. Yet it is doubtful that the Renaissance historians themselves identified activism and orientation toward the future as aspects of a historical consciousness. Their interest in and respect for the historians of antiquity seems to have obscured for them, as it has for modern scholars, how far beyond the Greek and Roman historians they had moved. In the histories they wrote the humanists tended to follow classical models, and like the ancients they saw the chief value of the study of history to be the discovery of unchanging truths, especially moral truths. The first great age of history as a scholarly discipline exploring a reality in which no event is ever repeated, a reality the charm and the terror of which is the unending presentation of novelty, was to wait until the nineteenth century. But the Renaissance sense of historical existence was more profound than the ideas they had about the histories they wrote and read.

Transcendent man, free, creative, with no fixed limits as to his achievement, is precisely the historical being that modern man knows himself to be. In the concluding paragraph of his chapter on Lorenzo Valla, Trinkaus says of the humanists generally:

---

[33]Ibid., 1:168-70; 2:765.

the humanists first grasped and were stunned by the mightiness of
. . . human forces. . . . They best saw . . . that in the name of God,
the Creator, the world had better be embraced than fled. Human
energy was mightier than metaphysics; the force of human history,
shaped by an inscrutable divine providence, too dynamic to be
contained within static theologies. The human world, which is the
historical world, was overcoming nature and claiming divinity for
itself. Man alone with his gift of word and his Gift of the Word
could overcome and direct, by rhetorical appeal and political device, the minds and hearts of the men who were the carriers of this
surging collective energy. The key to understanding it lay in history, sacred and profane, since it composed a reality of actions, divine and human, rather than a structure of forms and substances.[34]

Such exaltation of historical man was preeminently present in
Valla. It was a vigorous concern with secular affairs; yet it was not
secular in the sense of a turning away from religion; rather it was
the incorporation of the secular into a Christian understanding of
man. However such confidence in man may have encouraged others in a much later age to declare their independence of God himself, this was far from the case with Valla or with the humanists in
general. According to Trinkaus, "The religious philosophy of Lorenzo Valla represents in every sense the triumph of man"; but he
also declares it to be "one of the most powerful assertions of the
reality of human experience within a Christian framework in his
own age or in any age" and that it was "fully consistent with at least
the Augustinian tradition."[35] Trinkaus interprets Valla's treatment
of Epicureanism as an attempt to discredit it by an ironic defense
and at the same time discredit Stoicism by insisting that it was less
moral then Epicureanism. Valla was, in fact, against all rationalistic
morality; for him the only true morality was within the Christian
faith.

The humanists' sense of personal historical existence inevitably
had some effect on their understanding of the past. They were
aware of the cultural achievements of antiquity as historical events

---

[34]Ibid., 1:169-70. Cf. the discussion of Manetti, ibid., 177.

[35]Ibid., 1:168-69.

bringing novelty into the world, and they felt an obligation to emulate them in their own time. No doubt Valla's understanding of man and his interest in ordinary affairs carried over into his grasp of history and even into his critical studies of historical documents—the Donation of Constantine, the Apostle's Creed, the New Testament text.[36] But classical views of history lacked the dynamism and the orientation toward the future that was the unique contribution of the Hebrews; and this classical approach to history within the context of a closed, unchanging cosmos had its effect on the humanists, preventing their grasping fully what their new vision of man meant for the discipline of history. Maria Colish quotes the Spanish humanist, Ludovicus Vives, as saying:

> . . . there are those who persuade themselves that a knowledge of the past is useless, since the ways of life have changed everywhere. . . . It is undeniable that everything has changed, and changes daily, for, to be sure, these changes spring from our will and industry. But such alterations do not take place in those things encompassed by Nature. . . . It is more important by far to know this fact than to know how men of old dressed or constructed buildings. For what greater prudence is there than to know how and what the human passions are; how they are aroused, how quelled? . . . History acts as an example of what we should follow, and what we should avoid.[37]

This is a very interesting passage. History is not here subsumed into nature; a clear distinction between the two is assumed. Whether the relation of historical change to "will" and "industry" is anything more than common sense may be questioned, but it is a sense common to a society that expected purposeful action to produce novelties. Yet the rest of the passage, instead of justifying history as a way of explaining a situation in terms of its development in time, reverts to a classical approach that saw history as valuable only because it pointed beyond itself to an essentially

---

[36]Ibid., 1:148.

[37]Marcia L. Colish, "The Mime of God: Vives on the Nature of Man," *Journal of the History of Ideas* 23 (1962):15.

unhistorical reality where unchanging truth was to be found. Marcus Aurelius had said:

> For everywhere, above and below, you will find nothing but the selfsame things; they fill the pages of all history, ancient, modern, and contemporary; and they fill our cities and homes today. There is no such thing as novelty; all is as trite as it is transitory.[38]

The place of history in a world so conceived would be a minor one. Renaissance men did not conceive the world that way, but the classical influence retarded the full development of the historical sense implied in their much more dynamic world view.

The Renaissance ambiguity regarding history persisted through the Enlightenment, when the classical component in it was reenforced by the implications for a fundamentally static reality contained in a mechanistic world view. But even Hume, who was not a mechanist and who was a historian, thought the reason for studying history was "to discover the constant and universal principles of human nature."[39]

It is ironic that historians for so long made Petrarch's climb up Mount Ventoux a symbol of the secular Renaissance. It has been thought that Petrarch discovered "the world of Nature and of Man" and the modern world began. The irony is that the climax of Petrarch's experience on this celebrated occasion was his renewed awareness that man is more marvelous than all the wonders of nature; and the reminder came to him, not out of Cicero, but out of Augustine's *Confessions*, which he opened at random when he had arrived at the top of the mountain. The concept of a secular Renaissance has been slow in dying, but it is now about laid to rest. Something like general agreement among scholars that the civilization of Europe in the fifteenth and sixteenth centuries was an essentially Christian culture—at least as Christian as the thirteenth—has come only in the past few years. What the full effects may be of this revolution in interpretation are not yet clear; it will, no doubt,

---

[38]Marcus Aurelius, *Meditations*, tr. with Introduction by Maxwell Staniforth. (Penguin ed. Baltimore, 1964) Book 7, 105.

[39]David Hume, *An Inquiry Concerning Human Understanding* (New York, c. 1955) 93.

be a long time before an adequate adjustment is made. Something peculiarly modern was going on in the Renaissance, something as important to atheistic humanists[40] as to present-day Christians; and yet it was the product of an essentially Christian movement. Some far-reaching changes will obviously be needed in our general inter-pretation and periodization of European history.

Already the humanists can be seen in a different context and the power of their influence seen as less mysterious. The humanists were not an elite group of intellectuals staging an intellectual re-bellion against the theology and philosophy of their culture. Their movement was much more positive than that and had much more depth. In the past there has been a persistent insistence that Re-naissance thought was important coupled with a sometimes reluc-tant recognition that it is not very important in the history of philosophy. Now it appears that the Renaissance view of man was important precisely because it was not a merely intellectual move-ment. Far from being a group of intellectual rebels, the humanists were full participants in the Christian culture of their day. There is no longer any reason to think their piety was less sincere or less profound than that of Hussites or Protestants. In that culture the humanists were the leaders in developing one important facet of a very rich tradition. With Augustine as their mentor, it was the hu-manists who grasped and expressed the new mode of conscious-ness of transcendent, historical man that had developed in Europe after centuries of commitment in some significant way to the Chris-tian faith. The Renaissance philosophy of man was not just a the-ory, but a way of being aware of the world and of man and especially of one's own personal experience. The power of Renais-sance thought is not in philosophical defenses or demonstrations but in the fact that, uninhibited by formal metaphysical consider-ations, it was the expression of a new kind of self-consciousness de-veloped over centuries out of a very profound religious and intellectual tradition, a mode of consciousness that by the time of the Renaissance had permeated the whole society.

---

[40]The word "humanist" is here used in a very different sense from the proper use of the term in discussing Renaissance humanism.

The Renaissance vision of man has remained a most essential element in the structure of the modern mind. In the Enlightenment it became divorced from the Christian faith and later from any belief in God at all; but it remains in European culture a common ground between Christian and atheist and one of the principal integrating forces in Western civilization. The relative weakness of formal philosophy in the Renaissance has been often commented on; but no philosopher since the Renaissance and no school of philosophy has had so much influence on modern culture as has the Renaissance view of man.

The story of formal philosophy in the fifteenth and sixteenth centuries can now be set in a different context. It is a curious thing that the nominalistic, empirical philosophy of the fourteenth century did not continue to develop. The future ultimately was with it, and the history of philosophy from the seventeenth century to the present has shown the possibilities that were open to it; but there is a strange lacuna of some two hundred years. The nominalists in their criticism of Aristotle (and paradigmatically through him of classical philosophy in general) had discovered philosophical positions and approaches more congenial to the developing Christian society. And yet, though elements of Ockhamism lived on in theology and science and a diffused suspicion of rationalistic philosophy, the continuity with seventeenth-century philosophy is hard to trace.

One might almost say it was by default that formal philosophy was left to a continuing Aristotelianism and a growing Platonism.[41] At Padua, which was the center of Aristotelianism from the fourteenth century on, Aristotle was associated with science rather than with theology and was hence subjected to less critical pressure than had been the case earlier at Paris.[42] Aristotelianism con-

---

[41]The decline of the universities of Oxford and Paris, accompanied and perhaps caused by religious controversy and external interference, may have been a factor in the failure of nominalism to continue to develop as a formal philosophy. On the other hand, that failure may have caused the decline of the universities. Perhaps, the challenge of Aristotelianism having been in their eyes dealt with, the attention of the nominalists was simply drawn to science or to theological problems.

[42]Paul Oskar Kristeller, "Philosophical Movements of the Renaissance," *Studies in Renaissance Thought and Letters* (Rome, 1956) 22.

tinued into the seventeenth century and was an influence supporting the largely barren scholasticism of post-Reformation theology, both Catholic and Protestant. In the late seventeenth century in his long and able polemic against Hobbes, Bishop Bramhall made continuous use of scholastic terms and concepts despite the contempt and ridicule to which Hobbes treated them. In the history of philosophy, however, neither the Aristotelianism nor the Platonism of the Renaissance is of any great significance. Trinkaus sums it up.

> The anti-nominalistic implications of Ficino's philosophy did battle with the future of western philosophy as much as its past, whereas so-called "Averroism" [the most prominent form of Aristotelianism], as both Randall and Vasoli have suggested, represented a vestigial survival in the Renaissance of a non-dynamic heiratic freezing of the cosmos and was essentially conservative with regard to the imperative intellectual problems of the Renaissance.[43]

The future of Western philosophy was to be in the directions of empiricism and existentialism, plus the development beginning in the eighteenth century of philosophies that developed ideas of process and the dialectical movement of a dynamic reality that had affinities with the history-centered biblical tradition.

It was as widely diffused influences on theology, literature, and education that the formal philosophy of the Renaissance has been most significant. Two areas of such influence are particularly pertinent to the present study. One is the influence of Platonism on Christian thought. Plato, like Aristotle, had written in the general context of cosmological religion; his philosophy, therefore, contradicts the biblical tradition at a number of points; but no criticism of Plato from a Christian point of view developed at a depth and a clarity corresponding to the scholastic criticism of Aristotle. The Schoolmen had been driven to their criticism by the logic of Aristotle himself. No such imperative moved the Platonists. Furthermore, there had been for so long a Platonic influence in Christian thought that suspicions were allayed. This is not to say that the Platonists were not aware that their pagan mentors needed correction

---

[43]Trinkaus, *In Our Image*, 2:467.

at some points;[44] but the corrections hardly struck at the basis of the conflict between irreconcilable worldviews.

The points of conflict were several. Most basic was that Neoplatonism assigned God a place in the cosmos. Even though God's was the highest place and even though all other beings emanated out of him, he was ontologically continuous with all other beings. This denied the transcendence of God in the biblical sense and obscured the relationship of the Christian faith to those important aspects of Western culture that had derived from the understanding of God as transcendent. It is interesting that so devout and learned a Christian as Milton should have been drawn into heresy at this point. Not finding the formula *ex nihilo* in the Bible, Milton concluded that God had formed the world out of a primeval material exuded out of himself.[45] Ficino was aware of a problem here. He affirms creation *ex nihilo* and modified Plotinus to retain the biblical doctrine that God is directly related to each creature, but he did not arrive at a consistent position. He was concerned to be true to the teachings of the church, but he seems not to have realized the significance of the doctrine of creation.[46] The Greek conception of perfection as inconsistent with change or action is so strong in Ficino that his treatment of God is essentially ontological and does not include consideration of God as one who acts in historical relationship with man. The concept of history is not lost, but it is very much subordinated to the idea that the final perfection of all being will be a state of rest because all movement is imperfect.[47]

Ficino avoids the error of making God subject to a moral order as the later Cambridge Platonists were to do, but he did not grasp the Augustinian and medieval understanding that God acts in absolute freedom. For him God's action in creation is a necessary con-

---

[44]See for example Kristeller, *Philosophy of Ficino*, 168-69, 188-89.

[45]John Milton, *Complete Prose Works*, Vol. VI: *Christian Doctrine*, trans. John Carey, ed. Maurice Kelley (New Haven, London, 1973) 308; George Newton Conklin, *Biblical Criticism and Heresy in Milton* (New York, 1949) 67-70; C. S. Lewis, *A Preface to Paradise Lost* (London, 1942) 88.

[46]Kristeller, *Philosophy of Ficino*, 60, 83, 121, 167-69, 232.

[47]Ibid., 188-89, 198, 244.

sequence of his own essence. The Augustinian emphasis on the will is absent.[48] In his psychology also, in distinction from Augustine, Ficino subordinates the will to the intellect.[49]

Salvation itself was a fulfillment of the intellect in contemplation rather than the perfected community of the City of God. Ficino valued friendship and community very highly, but what one loved in a friend was really God. The ultimate salvation according to Ficino was the contemplation of God in a nonhistorical state of rest. All evil was simply a deficiency of good. Sin in man was a deficiency in the intellect; when man knows the good, he naturally desires it. Salvation is not a matter of repentance, faith, and forgiveness; it is achieved by the true knowledge that comes through contemplation.[50] In this aspect of his theology Ficino's Platonism has completely prevailed over his Christian faith.

Neoplatonism is not an absolute dualism, but it involved a relative dualism because of man's central place between matter and spirit. For man the attraction downward toward matter is bad; the attraction upward toward spirit and God is good. There is an obvious tendency here toward a metaphysical-moral dualism. Ficino, like the ancient Neoplatonists, is drawn very far in this direction.[51] Such a dualism would have hopelessly compromised the basis for his exaltation of man, which was the universality of man's contact with all of being, material and spiritual. From this Ficino is saved by the Christian doctrine of the resurrection of the body. The soul needs to free itself from the body in order to ascend to the contemplation of God; but the soul has an abiding love for the body, which ultimately will be satisfied by the resurrection.

> Since at the end of all days its desire for God is satisfied forever through eternal beatitude and its tendency toward the body through resurrection, the Soul will evidently be the bond and middle between the corporeal sphere and the intelligible sphere even

---

[48]Ibid., 60-61.

[49]Ibid., 256-58. So does Pico. See *Heptaplus*, 109.

[50]Kristeller, *Philosophy of Ficino*, 64-66, 211, 256-58, 356-57.

[51]Ibid., 214-17, 224.

in the final order of things after the movement of the world comes to rest.[52]

In the later Christian Platonists the dualistic tendency sometimes led to a substitution of the immortality of the soul for the resurrection of the body.

Ficino affirms the need man has for God's grace if he is to ascend the ladder of contemplation; but God's grace and his love for men is interpreted as the attraction God exerts on the human soul. This attraction is a very different thing from the active, outgoing love of God which is the New Testament meaning of agape. Though Ficino does not mean to give up the Christian concept, he in fact transforms it on God's side into a passive and impersonal attraction to which the appropriate human response is a Platonic eros. Pico had essentially the same view.[53]

To the Renaissance Platonists Platonism seemed to have such amazing affinities with the Christian faith that they conceived two lines by which God prepared the way for Christ: one through the history of the Hebrews and the teachings of the Old Testament; the other through a theological tradition including historical and legendary characters from Mercurius Trismegistus (or in Ficino's later writings, Zoroaster) to Plato.[54] This compromised the uniqueness of the Christian revelation and led to considering Christianity as one member, albeit the superior member, of the genus religion. Pico went further than Ficino in religious eclecticism. A major theme of his *Oration on the Dignity of Man* is that there is truth to be found in all religions.[55] A tendency implicit in this pluralism was to make human reason the final arbiter between competing religious

---

[52]Ibid., 399. See also pages 195-97, 390.

[53]Nygren's attack on Ficino at this point is fundamentally correct, but it is so unqualified as to give the false impression that Ficino had moved completely away from the biblical-Christian tradition. Anders Nygren, *Agape and Eros* (Philadelphia, 1953) 668-80. Both Kristeller (*Philosophy of Ficino*, 278n) and Trinkaus (*In Our Image*, 2:751-52) defend Ficino from Nygren's attack. For Pico see *Heptaplus*, 151-52).

[54]Kristeller, *Philosophy of Ficino*, 25-26.

[55]Ibid., 319. For Pico see Trinkaus, *In Our Image*, 2:506, 753-60; Kristeller, "Philosophical Movements of the Renaissance," 27.

ideas and thus to subordinate revelation to the critical reason. This was not explicit in Pico, who, in fact, declares emphatically that salvation can be found in no other religion than the Christian faith.[56] His eclecticism was, nevertheless, a first step toward deism.

Ficino and Pico were able and pious men who sincerely sought to live Christian lives and understand the Christian faith. The Platonic influence was so strong in them, however, as to blur some of the fundamental doctrines of the theology that had developed in the biblical-Christian tradition. Whatever evaluation one may put on the quality of their philosophy in its own right, neither of them can be said to have made any significant contribution to Christian theology, except for their part in the development of the Renaissance vision of man. Their Platonism was effective in that largely by providing a contrasting context that threw into sharp relief the nonhierarchical, transcendent man of the biblical tradition. Platonism also resulted in an attenuation in both of them of the historical, activist emphasis one finds in the humanists.[57]

Their place in the history of philosophy may be a minor one, but the Renaissance Platonists are very important in the intellectual history of Europe. Ficino's translations of Plato and the prestige of his Academy greatly stimulated a Platonic influence already widely diffused through European culture.

Religious Platonism has been appealing to a considerable variety of thinkers: some as close to traditional Christianity as Milton and C. S. Lewis; others as unorthodox as Emerson and the transcendentalists. In some, like the Cambridge Platonists, it is a strong self-conscious tradition; in others it is a vague and unidentified influence. The Cambridge Platonists, C. S. Lewis, and Charles Williams found in it a weapon against mechanism. It has certainly enriched the experience and thought of many people, but on the whole, its influence has inhibited the development of the biblical-Christian tradition.

---

[56]Pico, *Heptaplus*, 145-46.

[57]Ficino saw the contemplative life as the superior form of human life, the voluptuous life as second, and the active life as lowest. Kristeller, *Philosophy of Ficino*, 358. For Pico see Trinkaus, *In Our Image*, 2:519-21.

This religious Platonism has been harmful in that it has obscured and blurred the radical and irreconcilable differences between the biblical-Christian understanding of God, man, and the
world and that of the classical tradition. One result of this was that
Christians for three hundred years had no idea of the contribution
Christian theology had made to the origins of modern science;
hence their efforts to relate the Christian tradition to science were
largely superficial and misleading. The Cambridge Platonists were
poor champions against mechanistic philosophy; what was needed
was an epistemological criticism of it along the lines of Ockham or
Hume. By the time of Hume, however, the relation of the doctrine
of creation to the empirical tradition in philosophy had been so
completely lost to sight that the apologetic value of Hume's skepticism, though it produced a revival of fideism in a few theologians
of the nineteenth century,[58] had practically no impact on the question of how science relates to Christian faith before the twentieth
century; and even then its influence has not been great. The most
celebrated conflicts between "science and religion" have been spurious, pathetic, and a source of additional confusion. It was not until historians of science in the twentieth century began to discover
how science was emancipated from Aristotle in the thirteenth and
fourteenth centuries that the ground for a sounder understanding
came to be laid.

Another harmful influence of religious Platonism has been to
distort the relationship between philosophy and Christian theology. Ernest Moody makes a convincing case that it was the influence of the Christian faith that has made the mainstream of
modern philosophy so different from the mainstream of classical
philosophy: the one being, in his terms, critical and empirical; the
other rationalistic and speculative.[59] But one would scarcely guess
this from most of the theology of the past three hundred years. Platonism cannot be assigned the whole blame. It had its part, however, in identifying the Christian faith in the minds of many with a

---

[58]David Hume, "Editor's Introduction," *Dialogues concerning Natural Religion*,
ed. Richard H. Popkin (Indianapolis, Cambridge, c. 1980) xv.

[59]Ernest A. Moody, "Empiricism and Metaphysics."

rationalism that had little standing in philosophy and divorcing it from the skeptical and empirical positions with which it had, when rightly understood, much stronger affinities.

Heresies regarding creation, sin, and redemption that may be charged to Platonism are significant from a traditional Christian perspective; but they are less important than the general confusion and misunderstanding bred by religious Platonism in regard to crucially important traditions that have shaped the mind and consciousness of the West. This latter must be deplored by Christian and atheist alike.

The humanists, as distinct from the Platonic philosophers, also contributed to a blurring of the distinctions between biblical and classical traditions. Their interest in philosophy was largely confined to aesthetics and ethics.[60] Their aesthetics is not highly relevant to the present study. It is, nevertheless, interesting to observe that Renaissance art theory, when it was not dealing with techniques, was generally Platonic; yet the sense of reality that informed the naturalistic painting and sculpture of the period was nominalistic.[61] It is a striking example of the divergence that can occur between the rational expression of a society and its deeper consciousness. Michelangelo frequently talked like a Platonist, but his painting and sculpture show his sense of the reality of particular concrete things.

The humanist interest in ethics was destined to be much more influential than their aesthetics. Finding much of classical ethics attractive, they incorporated it into their religious thought, generally without any awareness that the Greek approach to ethics was fundamentally different from the ethics of the Bible. The Greeks derived ethical principles out of human nature. Right conduct was conduct appropriate to the nature of man; that was good which fulfilled one's true nature as a human being. Plato, Aristotle, the Stoics, the Epicureans—all proceeded in this manner. In the Bible,

---

[60]Trinkaus, *In Our Image*, 1:24; Kristeller, *Renaissance Thought*, 101-102.

[61]Frank P. Chambers, *The History of Taste* (New York, 1932) 64-65. Nesca Adeline Robb, *Neoplatonism of the Italian Renaissance* (London, 1935) 213-15; Harry B. Gutman, "The Rebirth of the Fine Arts and Franciscan Thought," *Franciscan Studies* n.s., 5 (1945): 218, 223-24.

on the other hand, practically nothing is said about self-fulfillment. Ethics is other oriented—it is oriented outward toward God and one's neighbor. There is a basic obligation to be concerned for widows, orphans, and strangers. Greeks and Romans had some noble things to say about the obligation of one friend to another, but Christ said, "Love your enemies." It was not a case of hyperbole— it was a radically different ethical principle derived out of a unique understanding of who man is in relation to God and his fellows.

Rhetoric did not probe or reveal this kind of distinction. Petrarch felt no tension between Cicero and his Augustinian Christian faith. Lorenzo Valla's penetrating critique of pagan ethics is exceptional. What was true in Stoicism and Epicureanism was, in Valla's interpretation, transformed in the process of being subsumed under a Christian understanding of the love of God. Trinkaus remarks on the originality of Valla's contribution to theology.[62] What has been historically effective, however, in Renaissance ethics has not been Valla but rather the superficial blending of contradicting ethical traditions into a kind of learned practical wisdom. From the Renaissance through the nineteenth century this blend of classical and Christian ethics was the staple of European education; and in the blend the classical predominated, and practical ethics was divorced from serious philosophy. A Christian is tempted to assert a Gresham's law of morals! It was, perhaps, for all its lack of intellectual clarity, a serviceable guide in practical action. At any rate, now that it is no longer a staple, we do not seem to be better off, though here and there one sees some evidence of an increase in other-directed ethics in the general culture.

The humanists were professionals in their own areas of teaching, philology, rhetoric, and even history, but many, if not most of them, were amateurs in philosophy and theology.[63] The continuing increase in popular piety in the period of the Renaissance not only made possible the Reformation as a widely based popular movement, but it produced throughout Europe large numbers of sincere

---

[62]Trinkaus, *In Our Image*, 1:137, 167-68. Trinkaus's chapter on Lorenzo Valla, pages 103-170, is one of the most interesting parts of his study.

[63]Kristeller, *Renaissance Thought*, 7, 17, 99-101.

laymen who were disposed to think about their faith and express their convictions publicly. The humanists were by no means the only such laymen, but they were among the best educated, and their influence was correspondingly great. The result of this lay activity, humanistic and otherwise, was a great mish-mash of religious speculation not subject to any accepted methodology nor to the criticism of any community of scholarship capable of speaking for the society as a whole.[64] Among the more extravagant of such speculations are those of Bruno, Paracelsus, and other Renaissance naturalists late in the period.[65] Amateurish religious speculation and eclecticism continued through the seventeenth century and opened the way for that widespread repudiation of the Chrisitian faith that marked the beginning of the Enlightenment.

On its positive side the Enlightenment was a triumphant affirmation of man that had its roots in the Christian anthropology of the Renaissance. In this too the exuberance of theological amateurs carried them to extravagant overstatements that, in the absence of careful definition and qualification, could be given meanings quite different from those intended by their pious authors. Theology that took a rhetorical form was prone to exaggeration in dealing with issues like the glory and dignity of man.[66] In numerous passages the humanists, including Ficino and Pico, speak of man as a god or as destined to be a son of God, a companion of God, a brother to God, or even of his "becoming God."[67] Sometimes it is obvious that the meaning is simply that in the world to come people will realize the image of God in themselves and become godlike, creatures even higher than the angels. The term *gods* was sometimes used to refer to angels. Pico says that is the meaning in the biblical phrase "God of gods" (Deuteronomy 10:17; Psalms 136:2; Daniel 2:47), and he

---

[64]Cf. Trinkaus, *In Our Image*, 1:26-27, 41-50; 2:768, 773-74.

[65]Kristeller, *Renaissance Thought*, 44, 61-62.

[66]Trinkaus uses the term *theologia rhetorica* to describe the religious thought of the humanists; though he says he had not actually seen the term in their writings. *In Our Image*, 1:127; 2:770 and elsewhere. The term *theologia poetica* was used by the humanists. Pico promised to write a book so entitled, but never did. Ibid., 2:520.

[67]Trinkaus gives numerous quotations. See *In Our Image*, 1:156, 301, 312, 316; 2:476, 485, 488-95, 528, 637, 739-41, 754.

goes on to say "but when we say 'God' in an absolute sense we do not understand one of them but the indivisible Trinity presiding over them."[68] This, of course, was also the case when men are called gods.

Ficino identified immortality with divinity. Both angels and men in this sense were divine. He was hardly saying more than this in the passage Nygren incorrectly translated as a claim that man is in an unqualified way a *rival of God*.[69] What the passage actually says is: "He is undoubtedly out of his mind who denies that the soul, which in art and government is the rival of God, is divine." Trinkaus quotes a passage from Lorenzo Valla which ends: "just as He transforms that bread [in the Eucharist], so he transforms us in the day of judgement into God." But Valla continues, "For we will be his members as he is the head of the whole body."[70] The shocking and seemingly heretical statement about man being transformed into God becomes a simple play on a familiar biblical figure of speech.

Other passages, especially in Ficino, about man becoming God are the result of attempting to put Christian ideas in Neoplatonic terms which were not well adapted for the purpose. When Plotinus spoke of the return of the soul to the one, he was thinking of the loss of particularity in an ontological union.[71] But Ficino was thinking of the beatitude of individual personal immortality. When this is remembered, it is clear that some of his statements deifying man cannot be taken in the literal sense they have for modern men. Ficino could use such terminology because in the Platonic tradition the intellect in knowing takes on the form of the thing known.[72]

The truth is that although they were not very careful or consistent theologians on the whole and made the kind of errors one

---

[68]*Heptaplus*, 97.

[69]Nygren, *Agape and Eros*, 675.

[70]Trinkaus gives the latter sentence as a paraphrase after the quotation and the longer Latin passage containing both sentences in a footnote. *In Our Image*, II:637, 840.

[71]Miller, introduction to Pico, *Heptaplus*, xvi, xxv.

[72]Trinkaus, *In Our Image*, 2:489-90.

might expect of amateurs, their extravagant statements about man hardly go beyond some of the language of the Bible.[73]

When all allowances have been made, however, the humanists and Platonists were frequently carried away by their own rhetoric into extravagant language and positions not consistent with Christian theology. In their thinking the dignity of man had as its complement the misery of the present human condition; but these two themes were often separated in their writings.[74] Later generations by the natural selective process of their own interests and tastes were able to mistake the Christian anthropology of the Renaissance for a secular affirmation of man's promethean prowess. It is one of the supreme ironies of Western history that this Christian anthropology should have had so little impact on a subsequent Christian theology and yet be claimed enthusiastically by the secular humanism of more modern times.

Partly because they were literary men and because they were not inhibited by too rigorous a methodology, the humanists had the imagination to pursue the hints they found in the Bible of a glorious future that awaits mankind in the intention of God. They also had sufficient learning to build upon the tradition already begun by the ancient Fathers of the church; they grounded their imaginative flights solidly in the doctrines of creation and Incarnation.

By the end of the Renaissance Christian Europe had achieved a distinctive mode of consciousness, a way of being aware of the world and of one's own existence that was distinctively biblical and Christian and that was unique in human history. Christian theology had played a major part in this development, but the phenomenon was not merely intellectual. In fact, the new biblical consciousness in large part determined which ideas in philosophy and theology were convincing and would prevail. Better than others the nominalists at the end of the Middle Ages had expressed the implications of the transcendence of God, his absolute power and freedom, for the nature of the world and of our knowledge of it.

---

[73]Romans 8:14-21; 1 Corinthians 3:21-23; 6:3; 15:42-50; Galations 4:4-7; Ephesians 3:18-19; 2 Timothy 2:12; 2 Peter 1:4; 1 John 3:2.

[74]Trinkaus, *In Our Image*, 1:174.

God's relation to his creatures supported nominalism. It was a meaningful world, but it was absolutely subordinated to the free, creative action of God; it was God's purposes that gave it meaning, for the world had no purpose of its own. It was an ordered world because God had ordered it, but the order could not be deduced from any general principles because no such principles were binding on God. The world's order could be known only by observing to see how God had chosen to order it. Man's knowledge was valid but never absolute; never certain in the way Aristotle had understood true knowledge to be. The way was prepared for modern science.

The place of man in relation to God and the world had been more discussed in ancient and early medieval times than had the nature of the physical world. It was the challenge of Aristotle that had provoked the latter. In the earlier theology man's sinful relation to God and his need for the redemption God provided had got the emphasis rather than the more positive, hopeful aspects of being this uniquely great and valuable one of God's creatures. The adequate expression of the glory and dignity of man was the contribution of the humanists. Man transcended the rest of creation in his personal relationship to the transcendent God. The orders of the world applied to him, yet in his transcendence of them he could act with freedom. The creation had been given to him to control and to use. He was a sub-creator under God; in his freedom he brought novelty into the world. He was historical man, the creator of culture and history.

By the time of the high Renaissance, the distinctive cast of mind that was to characterize the West to our own time was already formed. In the next century it was to launch that scientific movement that is, perhaps, the most obvious distinctive feature of the culture that has come to dominate the world. Modern science was so impressive in its achievements that its influence on the developing Western consciousness was to be of decisive importance.

Europe was headed for the greatest cultural, religious crisis so far in its history, and science was to have a major part in producing it.

IV SCIENCE
AND
THEOLOGY

Unless it be the technology that has been so intimately related to it, there is nothing more obviously characteristic of the modern West than its unique development of natural science. The religious implications of this development, especially its relationship to the Christian faith, have been a matter of interest and deep concern throughout the whole history of modern science. Misunderstanding of this relationship, frequently taking the form in the last two centuries of largely spurious "conflicts between science and religion," has led to a general confusion regarding the religious bases of Western civilization and to many superficial and erroneous judgments about both science and Christianity.

Historical scholarship in the present century has revealed new dimensions of the problem of science and religion and has afforded a fresh perspective from which to attempt a better understanding. The material to be surveyed from this new perspective is immense, and its resolution into some kind of ordered consensus involves such philosophical, religious, and historical subtleties that it will no doubt occupy the next several generations of scholars in those

areas. The question is, nevertheless, so fundamental to any assessment of the religious dimensions of modern culture that even this
brief essay must undertake to describe in at least general terms
what this aspect of our history looks like from the vantage point of
recent scholarship.

It is the historians of the origins of modern science aided by students of the general intellectual history of the relevant periods who
have done most to provide us with a new approach. The most surprising result of their research has been to discover the essential
and positive role of Christian theology in the early history of our
science. The seminal work was done by Pierre Duhem in his *Études*
sur Leonard de Vinci, published in Paris, 1906-1913, and in his mon-
umental *Le Système du monde, Histoire des doctrines cosmologiques de*
Platon à Copernic, Paris, 1913-1917. Duhem called attention to the importance of original work in physics done at Paris and Oxford in the
fourteenth century and to the grounds for this work in Christian
theology. He gave particular emphasis to the decisions of a church
council called in 1277 by Étienne Tempier, Bishop of Paris, at the in-
stigation of the Pope. Several of the propositions condemned as heretical by the council were propositions in physics that set limits on
what God could do. The most famous of them involved the idea
that even God could not create a vacuum. The break with Aristotle
was clear-cut; in order to understand how important this was, it is
necessary to review the effects of Aristotle's conception of scientific
knowlege on Hellenistic and later on Islamic science.

The thought of Aristotle, like that of Plato and other classical
philosophers, developed in the context of a cosmological worldview. The world itself was eternal, its fundamental order unchanging; the changing phenomena of nature and history were not only
ephemeral but superficial. The order and intelligibility of the world
were due to the eternal forms that existed in its objects and made
them definable. Knowledge was the perception of these forms by
the mind. Hellenistic science was empirical in that it sought knowledge by observing the objects in which the eternal forms were em-
bodied; but once the forms (intelligible essences) were grasped by
the mind, knowledge of them was final and not subject to challenge

by experience.[1] Greek science was, therefore, in a real sense empirical; but the principle of empirical verification was not a part of its method. Any so-called knowledge that was not clear apprehension of the eternal forms was not real knowledge but merely opinion (*doxa*) and had no place in science.

In the two centuries following Aristotle, Hellenistic science made notable progress. Eratosthenes computed the size of the earth with remarkable accuracy. Archimedes discovered the famous principle of floating bodies named after him, worked out the mathematical principles of the lever, the pulley, and the screw, and made numerous other contributions to both mathematics and physics. Hipparchus computed the length of the solar year to within six minutes and fourteen seconds of the now-accepted figure and the length of the lunar month with an error of only one second! These are only a few of many Hellenistic contributions to the knowledge of physics and astronomy. But the very success of Hellenistic physics was its nemesis; for as the body of knowledge grew and was systematized around the erroneous Aristotelian laws of motion, this system, absolutized and beyond criticism as it was, became an obstacle to further discovery. Although science was still a matter of live interest in the Greek world when the Moslems invaded it in the seventh century A.D., few new discoveries had been made since the second century B.C.

The Moslems appropriated Greek science and added to it what they learned from Persians and others. Their interest in it was not less than that of the Greeks themselves, and the cross-fertilization of cultures enabled them to make original contributions; but in physics these contributions were limited, and physics stagnated in Islam as it had in the ancient world. One reason, and very probably the chief reason, is that they had, along with Greek science, also appropriated Aristotle's understanding of the nature of scientific knowledge.[2]

---

[1]Michael B. Foster, "Christian Theology and Modern Science of Nature," *Mind* 44 (1935): 460.

[2]Moslems, of course, were heirs of the biblical tradition; and the idea that the transcendence of God implies the contingency of the world was not unknown in Islam. See William J. Courtenay, "The Critique on Natural Causality in the Mutakallimun and Nominalism," *Harvard Theological Review* 66 (1973): 77-94. It is,

There have been, of course, other peoples, notably the Chinese, who have acquired considerable knowledge of the physical world; but no civilization except the Christian West has gone on to the creation of a scientific method capable of taking it indefinitely beyond the science of the Greeks and Arabs. The civilizations of these latter flourished long after science had stagnated in them; and yet it was the no-longer-advancing science of the Greeks and Arabs that brought the medieval West up to the threshold of modern science. It is an obviously significant question, Why did the West, and the West alone, achieve a breakthrough into a still-developing modern science? The answer suggested by Pierre Duhem at the beginning of this century has won increasing acceptance by students of late medieval science. The breakthrough was not accomplished by merely condemning some propositions of Aristotle; the significance of the condemnations of the Council of Paris in 1277 is that the ground for the action was the doctrine of creation. Although the action of this council was cited many times in subsequent generations, the council is important only as a convenient expression of principles that would have been effective without it. The matter was fundamental to medieval thought. Commenting on the new orientation toward science in the period from the fourteenth century through the sixteenth, A. R. Hall notes that "the universe could be seen through Aristotle's eyes no more"; and he recognizes that the change was due in part to the Christian faith:

No Christian could ultimately escape the implications of the fact

---

therefore, a question of considerable interest why the Moslems did not, then, produce a cumulatively progressive science comparable to that of Western Europe. Ernest A. Moody's study of William of Ockham suggests that the Aristotelianism of Averroes and the Neoplatonism of Avicenna were too strong to be overcome (Ernest A. Moody, *The Logic of William Of Ockham* [New York, 1935] 10-18, and especially the footnote on p. 86). Relevant to this suggestion is the fact that Islam had no Augustine.

With the limited knowledge of Islamic culture at my disposal I can only conjecture; but it seems possible that Moslem scholars who took seriously the skeptical implications of the contingency of the world gave up science for reasons like those of Nicholas of Autrecourt and that only those who retained Aristotle's understanding of scientific knowledge continued an interest in the subject. Cf. Francis Oakley, "Christian Theology and the Newtonian Science; The Rise of the Concept of the Laws of Nature," *Church History* 30 (1961): 453, footnote 35.

that Aristotle's cosmos knew no Jehovah. Christianity taught him to see it as a divine artifact rather than as a self-contained organism. The universe was subject to God's laws; its regularities and harmonies were . . . a result of providential design. The ultimate mystery resided in God rather than in Nature. . . . The only sort of explanation science could give must be in terms of descriptions of processes, mechanisms, interconnections of parts. Greek animism was dead. . . . The universe of classical physics, in which the only realities were matter and motion, could begin to take shape.[3]

The effort to appropriate Aristotle had forced medieval theology to a thorough examination of the biblical doctrine of creation. What resulted was a renewed affirmation of a Creator God who completely transcended the world, which he had brought into being by an absolutely free act of his will. This doctrine of God implied a doctrine of the created world as contingent, entirely dependent on the will of God for its existence. God in this biblical understanding remained absolutely free in his relation to the world. No order of the world is binding upon God; whatever order exists is there because God continues to will it. G. K. Chesterton put the principle succinctly when he told of the man who would get up in the morning, look at the sunrise, and exclaim: "Well, He did it again!"

The voluntarism of the late medieval nominalists, of whom William of Ockham is the best-known representative, expressed this aspect of the doctrine of creation. The will of God directs his thought, and not the other way round. Not even a rational intelligence in the mind of God took primacy over the absolute freedom of God's will. Thus the nominalists avoided the Averroistic heresy of thinking God acted in accordance with some necessity of his own nature. Because creation was a completely free act of God, its very existence was not necessary. And because God was completely free to establish any order of creation he pleased, the order that he did in fact establish cannot be known by deduction from any principles whatsoever but only by observation or revelation. So far as the physical world was concerned, knowledge of its objects and

---

[3]A. R. Hall, *The Scientific Revolution, 1500-1800*, 2nd ed. (Boston, 1966) xvi-xvii; see also p. 172. Cf. Karl Jaspers, *Nietzsche and Christianity*, trans. E. B. Ashton (Chicago, 1961) 67-75.

of the relationships that existed between them could be known only empirically. The purpose which informed creation was inscrutable (except insofar as God had revealed it); it was God's purpose and was not inherent in created objects. Final causation was thus banished from physics; the aim of physics was to discover the efficient causation that operated in the order that God had established for physical objects in the world. This was the crucial step from ancient physics to the physics of the modern world, and it cannot be credited to any one man. In the words of Ernest Moody it was a response to a problem that

> was common to all [fourteenth-century philosophy], entailed by the fact that the eternal, necessary and predictable natural world of Aristotle had been replaced by the created, contingent, and only conditionally predictable natural order compatible with the Christian Faith.[4]

The contingency of the world on the absolute freedom of God had skeptical implications. God could do anything he pleased free of any rational order which might guide the human mind in its predictions; nothing, therefore, was predictable in any absolute sense. If one insisted with Aristotle that only what could be known with certainty was valid knowledge, then all physical science was a vain undertaking. Nicholas of Autrecourt drew this conclusion. If everyone had taken such an attitude, there would have been no further science. The nominalists and voluntarists, however, did not generally so conclude.[5]

The biblical tradition that had led them to question the possibility of absolute knowledge of the world also impressed upon them the reality and worth of the material creation. Furthermore, nominalists and voluntarists already were aware of regularity and order in the world. They accepted the significance of what conditional knowledge of the world was possible to them. The historical fact is that scientific interest was stimulated in them, and they were

---

[4]Ernest A. Moody, "Ockham, Buridan, and Nicholas of Autrecourt," *Franciscan Studies* n.s. 7 (1947): 142.

[5]Ibid., 113-46. See also J. R. O'Donnell, "The Philosophy of Nicholas of Autrecourt," *Medieval Studies* 4 (1942): 98-99.

free to make the limited, piecemeal studies of the physical world which have been the hallmark of modern science and the way to its great accomplishments.[6]

The tension existing between the theological conviction of the absolute freedom of God and awareness of regularity and order observable in the world took the form of a distinction between the *potentia absoluta* of God and his *potentia ordinata*. (This was a very useful analysis; but the absolutizing of the *potentia ordinata* in a later age led to fundamental contradictions in Western thought.) God had freely chosen to establish an order in the world and in general he governed the world through this order. He could, however, have established any other order. To know what order had in fact been established one could not proceed by deduction from any fundamental principles but had simply to look and see. This was the *potentia ordinata*. God, of course, was not bound by the order so freely established; his *potentia absoluta* remained in full force.

The thesis of Duhem was revolutionary and it did not go unchallenged. Since the appearance of his *Études sur Leonard de Vinci* (1906-1913), two generations of scholars have examined his claims for medieval science. The works of Anneliese Maier have been especially thorough. In the enthusiasm of discovery Duhem overstated his case; but when the necessary corrections, qualifications, and clarifications have been made, the interpretation of Duhem remains in its essentials intact; and it calls for a new structuring of the history of early modern science.[7] That restructuring is not yet complete. Two problems raised by the discussion are of particular interest to the present study.

The first is the question of the continuity of medieval science with the scientific revolution initiated especially by Galileo. At first there seemed to be a hiatus of about two centuries when science made little or no progress. Continued study has, however, gone far to fill in the gap. Interest in science virtually disappeared at Paris

---

[6]Moody, "Ockham, Buridan, and Nicholas," 113-16.

[7]A brief discussion of the main outlines of this chapter in the historiography of science by an American scholar who has made major contributions to it is found in the Introduction to Marshall Clagett, *The Science of Mechanics in the Middle Ages* (Madison WI, 1959) xx-xxiii.

and Oxford after the fourteenth century; but in the fifteenth and sixteenth centuries there was a very lively interest in it in Italy, especially at Padua. The major manuscripts of the Parisians and the Mertonians (Thomas Bradwardine and his followers at Merton College, Oxford) were available in the library at Padua during these centuries and were frequently cited. The question whether Galileo was indebted to these manuscripts may never be definitely settled. The evidence that he was so indebted is circumstantial. When he was at Pisa his mechanics was based on the theory of motion of Avempace, which he sought to explain by a mathematical method adapted from Archimedes.[8] The results were vitiated by the false assumptions of Avempace; but Galileo did not abandon his Pisan mechanics until after he had moved to the University of Padua in 1592. There he shifted to the more fruitful approach which was to make him the initiator of a scientific revolution. Was the change simply a result of the empirical invalidation of his earlier mechanics? Or did Galileo learn at Padua of the repudiation of Avempace by the fourteenth-century Mertonians and Parisians, who had gone far in both kinetics and dynamics to anticipate his own work? Whether or not there was a direct influence of fourteenth-century mechanics on Galileo, increased knowledge of the wide diffusion of those ideas in the fifteenth and sixteenth centuries make the fact of continuity between late medieval and seventeenth-century physics unmistakable. Galileo was not working in isolation.[9]

Although there is no longer any question that a continuity of scientific thought did exist in Europe from the Middle Ages on, it is still a problem why the period between the early fourteenth century and Galileo did not exhibit the same cumulative progressiveness that is so obvious in science after Galileo. I do not think any

---

[8]Ernest A. Moody, "Galileo and Avempace," *Journal of the History of Ideas* 12 (1951): 413-14.

[9]A very large literature has accumulated on the subject—far more than I am acquainted with. Among the works which have been particularly helpful to me on this point are: Moody, "Galileo and Avempace"; Clagett, *The Science of Mechanics in the Middle Ages,* especially the introductory sections and the conclusion; Stillman Drake and I. E. Drabkin, eds., *Mechanics in Sixteenth-Century Italy* (Madison WI, 1969); John Herman Randall, *The School of Padua and the Emergence of Modern Science* (Padova, 1961).

simple solution to this problem is likely. A number of factors seem relevant. For one thing, some progress *was* made, particularly in mathematics, and that provided the mathematical tools used so effectively in the seventeenth century. There is also the fact that the medieval emancipation from Aristotle was not so sudden or so complete as Duhem assumed.[10]

During this whole period new ideas were likely to be presented as interpretations of Aristotle or Averroes. A striking example is Bradwardine's exponential interpretation of Aristotle's law of motion.[11] This tendency to refer to Aristotle or other philosophically oriented authorities had the effect of keeping science too closely tied to philosophy and tempted scholars to opt for a particular position regarding motion because it was compatible with some particular form of Platonism or of Aristotelianism. Moody's article just cited makes this abundantly clear.

The philosophical contexts within which science was pursued hindered the development of any genuine community of scientists. Stillman Drake identifies two distinct Italian schools of mechanics in the sixteenth century, one in northern Italy and one in central Italy, and comments that "the two groups appear to have been scarcely aware of one another's existence, though all the men concerned were working actively and publishing in a new and exciting field of study."[12] Mathematics seems to have achieved autonomy as a discipline before physics did. It was not until the time of Galileo himself that an international community of science emerged.

A second problem in the history of the origins of modern science is the question of the source of the mathematical method of

---

[10]See, for example, Moody, "Galileo and Avempace"; and Paul O. Kristeller, *Renaissance Thought II* (New York, 1965) 112.

[11]Moody, "Galileo and Avempace," 191; Clagett, *Science of Mechanics*, 421-503. Both authors discuss the widespread influence of Bradwardine's fourteenth-century formulation and cite Anneliese Maier as stressing the significance and novelty of Bradwardine's formula and denying that it was what Aristotle meant in her *Die Vorläufer Galileis im 14. Jahrhundert* (Rome, 1949). Both the works cited also give many other illustrations, as would, indeed, any recent history of science in this period.

[12]*Mechanics in Sixteenth-Century Italy*, 13.

seventeenth-century physics. Galileo certainly emphasized the importance of geometrizing as essential to the new physics. The use of mathematics was in fact so crucial to early modern physics that it is understandable that some historians have seen (erroneously, I think) the use of mathematics as what has distinguished modern physics from the physics of the ancient world and the Middle Ages. If one then sought an explanation for what was supposed to be a new interest in the use of mathematics, it was plausible to look for it in the Platonism that was so prominent a part of Renaissance thought. Platonism had always emphasized the importance of mathematical ideas as fundamental structures of the world, and Platonists and Pythagoreans had stood in awe of the mysteries of mathematics. Edwin A. Burtt in his widely influential *Metaphysical Foundations of Modern Physical Science* (New York, 1925) makes the revival of Neoplatonism and Pythagoreanism the clue to the break with medieval Aristotelianism and the origin of a new mathematical method in science.

In 1936 Edward W. Strong published a closely reasoned and fully documented refutation of this generally held view.[13] Strong showed that the appreciation of mathematics by the early scientists and their use of it was practical and instrumental, very different from the mystical, transcendental interest in mathematics of the Pythagoreans and Neoplatonists. From the history of mathematics itself he showed that the mathematicians of the sixteenth century cannot be identified with any traditional philosophical position for the simple reason that mathematics had achieved an automony that allowed its pursuit without regard for philosophy.[14] But Strong was a young scholar and not at the time well known. For a long time his study did not have the effects that might have been expected. Better known people in the field, especially Alexandre Koyré, challenged his thesis or ignored it. Koyré denied any continuity between medieval and modern physics; and though he admitted that Galileo referred often to observation, he minimized the empirical element in Galileo's method. It was in the Platonic influence

---

[13]Edward W. Strong, *Procedures and Metaphysics* (Berkeley, 1936).

[14]Ibid., 47-90, especially 48, 55, 60, 68, 69, and 85.

on Galileo that he saw the origins of the new mathematical physics.[15] On the surface a plausible case can be made for Koyré's position; but it has not survived serious criticism.

Nicholas of Cusa is the only one of the outstanding Renaissance
Platonists who has a place in the history of mathematics, and his is
a minor one. Kepler more than other important figures in science
at the beginning of the seventeenth century was influenced by Neoplatonic and Pythagorean traditions. His motivation to scientific
work was sometimes due to such influence; and sometimes this influence was something to be overcome. It is hardly going too far to
say that the Platonic element in his thought was accidental to his
contribution to astronomy. His famous laws of planetary motion
were the result of an instrumental application of mathematics to
the exact observations of Tycho Brahe. If Kepler had taken less seriously the importance of exactness of observation, his discovery of
these laws would not have occurred.[16] His three laws are, in fact,
classic examples of the empirical basis, the instrumental use of
mathematics, and the concept of the laws of nature that were characteristic of early modern science.

As for Galileo, his identification with Platonists as against Ar-
istotelians had no significance for the development of mathematical
physics. Serious mathematics had been independent of philosophy
since the Middle Ages,[17] and in the sixteenth century it was developing among artisans and engineers as well as in the universities.
Kristeller and Randall go so far as to affirm that Aristotelianism (despite his opposition to it) was a greater factor than Platonism in
producing Galileo:

> Indeed, that mathematical and mechanical development which by
> the end of the sixteenth century produced Galileo owes very little

---

[15]Alexandre Koyré, "Galileo and Plato," *Journal of the History of Ideas* 4 (1943):
400-28.

[16]A. R. Hall, *Scientific Revolution*, 118-24. Cf. Ernst Cassirer "On the Originality
of the Renaissance," *Journal of the History of Ideas* 4 (1943): 53.

[17]Paul O. Kristeller, "From Platonism to Neoplatonism," *Journal of the History of
Ideas* 19 (1958): 131.

to the Platonic revival but received powerful stimulus from the critical Aristotelianism of the Italian Universities.[18]

Galileo's mentor was Archimedes and not Plato; but, of course, he went beyond Archimedes in his systematic application of mathematics to physics. A clear exposition of Galileo's use of mathematics is found in the contribution of Edward W. Strong to a book entitled *Homage to Galileo*.[19] Galileo learned to quantify physical problems by abstracting properties of bodies through accurate measurement. In this way Galileo introduced into physics the demonstrative character of mathematics. He considered his results to be exact science; but he did not lose sight of the empirical origin of his data or of the validity of empirical checks on his conclusions. He was thus using mathematics as his instrument in what was a basically empirical science. If this method was not directly implied in the nominalism and voluntarism of the fourteenth century, it was thoroughly consistent with it.

Renaissance Platonism was associated with just that animism that had to be rejected before the methods of modern science could be developed. Those who, like Paracelsus and Bruno, retained belief in a world soul and an immanentist theology might exhibit imaginative brilliance in cosmological speculation; but they were outside the main current of intellectual development and made little contribution to science.[20] In the next century the Cambridge Platonists had real difficulties with the spirit of the new science, and

---

[18]*The Renaissance Philosophy of Man*, ed. Ernst Cassirer, Paul Oskar Kristeller, and John Herman Randall, Jr. (Chicago, 1948), "General Introduction" by Kristeller and Randall, 12. Cf. Koyré, "Galileo and Plato," 421. Koyré betrays little understanding of the significance of the empirical element in Galileo's method and, in fact, is led by his enthusiasm for Platonism to oppose mathematics to empiricism when the distinguishing genius of the new physics was to unite them.

[19]Edward W. Strong, "Galileo on Measurement," one of six papers published in *Homage to Galileo*, ed. Morton F. Kaplon (Cambridge, 1965).

[20]Paul O. Kristeller, *Studies in Renaissance Thought and Letters* (Rome, 1956) 28; *Renaissance Thought* (New York, 1961) 44, 61-62; Robert Lenoble, *Mersenne ou la naissance du mécanisme* (Paris, 1943) 5-12. A particularly clear statement on this subject is made by E. J. Dijksterhuis in a review of Dorothea Singer's *Giordano Bruno* in *Centaur* 4 (1955-1956): 87.

it was not their Christianity but their Platonism that produced the incompatibility.

The concept of the laws of nature as it was understood in seventeenth-century science had not been known in the ancient world. Natural law in ancient classical thought had been law immanent in nature and in particular natural objects; natural law as it was conceived by seventeenth-century *virtuosi*, on the other hand, was a law imposed on nature by a law-giver who was beyond and outside of nature. It is not here contended that this was an inevitable consequence of the biblical doctrine of creation. At least insofar as voluntarism is concerned, it would seem that God in his freedom might have established just such a universe governed by immanent law as Greek philosophers envisioned. Voluntarism did, however, certainly open the way to the fundamental change in the concept of nature that characterized early modern science; and it is significant that such a view of natural law did not develop in any nonbiblical culture.

The nominalism of many of the voluntarists was a major factor influencing them toward the new view of laws of nature. Not everyone who has believed in the biblical view of creation as opposed to any cosmological view has been a nominalist. Augustine was not, for example, nor was Thomas. In fact, the concept seems to have stemmed originally from a remark of the Neoplatonist Porphyry and been introduced to the West by Boethius. But once the question was broached, there were strong affinities between a religious faith which emphasized the reality and worth of every particular creature and some version of nominalism. Not a sparrow falls that God does not know it. His power sustains and operates directly on each created being. In a nominalistic world it is easy to refer all purpose and meaning to the Transcendent God. This view was reinforced by biblical emphasis on God's immediate sovereignty over nature as well as history. The God who had given a moral law in Ten Commandments had also given "to the sea his law that the waters should not pass his commandment."[21]

---

[21]Francis Oakley brings out very clearly the importance of the biblical understanding of God as One who orders and commands to the origin of the idea of the laws of nature in his "Christian Theology and the Newtonian Science." This scripture, which he quotes on page 436, is from Proverbs 8:29.

As has been pointed out previously the voluntarism of the Ock-hamites could have led to a skepticism that would have precluded the development of science; but, with the interesting exception of Nicholas of Autrecourt, voluntarism chose a different course which accepted what knowledge of the world is possible to man. The reg-ularities of nature were explained in terms of an order established by God and through which he *normally* acted in the world; this ac-tion of God was his *potentia ordinata* and it never circumscribed or limited the *potentia absoluta* which expressed his absolute freedom even in respect to the natural order he had established.[22] The mod-ern conception of the laws of nature developed in this context. Oak-ley says its "overt starting point" was in the condemnations of the Council of Paris in 1277.[23] Oberman credits Anneliese Maier with having established its application to physics by the school of John Buridan in the fourteenth century.[24] Although recognizing its me-dieval origins, Oakley sees the concept as having been given a much more explicit role in physics in the seventeenth century.[25] Oakley's study convincingly demonstrates the continuity of the theological basis of the modern idea of natural law from the late Middle Ages through the time of Newton. In the sixteenth and sev-enteenth centuries it was common to Protestant and Catholic tra-ditions, and it was frequently mentioned by leading scientists of the seventeenth century in the context of a voluntarist theology.

If from the sixteenth century on it was possible for scientists to think in terms of "imposed laws of nature" without reference to theology, this automony of science was itself due in large measure to the voluntarist tradition of a *potentia ordinata*. The use by Oakley and others of terms like "imposed" laws of nature can be mislead-ing. It might be held on theological grounds that God had imposed

---

[22]A brief, clear description of these concepts is found in Oakley, "Christian Theology," 442-45. A much more detailed discussion of them as they relate to eth-ics and theology is found in Heiko A. Oberman, *The Harvest of Medieval Theology* (Cambridge, 1963) 30-56.

[23]"Christian Theology," 438.

[24]See Heiko A. Oberman's review of Maier's *Zwischen Philsophie und Mechanik* in *Speculum* 35 (1960): 137-38.

[25]"Christian Theology," 443.

an order on nature; but what was knowable through empirical observation was not the act of such imposition but the relationships which had been so imposed upon natural objects. The new empirical science could, therefore, be pursued without regard to any historical origins in theology of its basic concepts. Science had been freed from consideration of final causes by the transfer of purpose from the world itself to God; but since the purposes of God remained inscrutable and certainly not known by empirical observation of the world, science continued with its proximate attention to efficient causation and was not, as science, concerned with theological contexts and explanations.

This capacity of the order of nature ordained by God to be treated in independence of theology ironically led to its being absolutized into a new world order in which the mechanistic methods of science were converted into a mechanistic metaphysics. That conversion was a very complicated development, the history of which has not yet been unraveled. The fact of the conversion of mechanism from method to metaphysics is, nevertheless, clear; and some elements in its development are not hard to discern.

Mechanism, as Robert Lenoble uses the term in his life of Mersenne, was the method of the new science. The method was basically empirical, and it proceeded by the explanation of phenomena in terms of efficient causation and mathematical demonstration. It was skeptical regarding metaphysical knowledge; and in theology it was fideistic, tending to accept the propositional teachings of the church as revealed truth. It distinguished empirical knowledge, which was always subject to error, from logically demonstrated conclusions, which it regarded as certain. In this distinction it anticipated modern logical positivism. Because all knowledge of the world was empirically based, such knowledge was recognized as hypothetical. The metaphysical skepticism of this method and its recognition of the hypothetical character of its conclusions kept it open-ended toward the future of science and capable of investigations of limited scope directed toward the solution of specific problems in physics without undue regard for the philosophical implications of its conclusions.[26] This method, with variations de-

---

[26]Robert Lenoble, *Mersenne*, 314, 325-28, 391, passim.

veloping in the history of science itself and various subtleties of interpretation introduced by recent philosophy, has remained basic in Western science to the present day. It is, therefore, one of the supreme ironies of modern culture that this mechanistic method should have given rise early in its history to a mechanistic metaphysics that negated its basically nonmetaphysical nature.

The development of a mechanistic worldview may have owed something to the concept of laws of nature. When Buridan and Oresme constructed heliocentric systems that "saved the appearances" in the manner of ancient astronomy, they were not concerned to establish them as literal descriptions of reality. Oresme, however, did take the possibility seriously enough to offer arguments against it based on terrestrial observations. What made the later construction of Copernicus so much more important was that he did think his theory described reality and that some other people, notably Kepler and Galileo, were convinced. The idea that scientific knowledge was hypothetical was not lost. Mersenne certainly believed it; and even Hobbes, despite the dogmatism of his mechanistic materialism in other contexts is equally emphatic that all knowledge of the world is uncertain. Explanation by causes, argued Hobbes, is always hypothetical because a different set of causes, some of which we are not aware of, may actually have produced the effect.[27] It is, nevertheless, probable that in scientific investigation the hypothetical nature of science was less in the forefront of the scientist's consciousness than his inspiring belief that he was getting at reality itself.[28]

The confidence scientists had in the validity of their discoveries as literally and objectively what was "there" in nature was enhanced by the mathematical nature of the method developed by Galileo. Galileo never ceased to adhere to empirical verification as a final test of the truth of scientific propositions, but his emphasis was on the demonstrability of the new mathematical physics in

---

[27]Thomas Hobbes, *The English Works*, ed. Sir William Molesworth, 7 vols. (London, 1865; 2nd reprint, Darmstadt, Germany, 1966) 7: "Seven Philosophical Problems," 3-4; "Six Lessons to the Professors of the Mathematics," 183-84.

[28]Edward Grant, "Late Medieval Thought, Copernicus, and the Scientific Revolution," *Journal of the History of Ideas* 23 (1962): 197-220.

which by a process of abstraction he quantified the elements of physical problems and proceeded to mathematical solutions. If the mathematical conclusions were not contradicted by empirical observation, Galileo assumed that he had by rigorous methods discovered a truth that was somehow out there in nature. With Galileo the process of developing a mechanistic metaphysics did not go further because his interest was not in philosophy but in physics per se. "Mechanism" remained with him an open-ended method.[29] Some minds, however, are not content with such open-endedness; they want the loose ends tied up. Such an intellect was Descartes's. Lenoble sees in Descartes a defection from mechanism. "It is possible," he says, "to write the history of the birth of mechanism without speaking of Descartes"; in that history Descartes was "a metaphysical accident."[30] Since Descartes is generally known as the chief founder of mechanistic philosophy, this judgment has to be understood in terms of Lenoble's identification of mechanism with the method described above and not with the metaphysics derived from it. Descartes's contributions to science and mathematics cannot be gainsaid; but his passion for speculative system building took him in some respects outside the mainstream of scientific development.[31] His emphasis on "clear and distinct ideas," while not itself Aristotelian, is reminiscent of the absolute quality which Aristotle attributed to all genuine knowledge. Descartes's general influence, as well as the specific system of mechanistic philosophy which he elaborated, supported the development of a mechanistic metaphysics on the basis of the impressive successes of seventeenth-century physics.

Another element making for the development of a mechanistic philosophy was atomistic materialism. In the nominalistic atmosphere of seventeenth-century science with its conception of laws of nature imposed from outside governing the relationship between objects, the atmosphere of a physics of matter and motion,

---

[29]Strong, *Procedures*, 135-61; cf. Lenoble, *Mersenne*, 314.

[30]Lenoble, *Mersenne*, 348, 437-49, 610-15. The quotations are from pages 606 and 614.

[31]A good example would be his theory of vortices.

the atomistic philosophy of Democritus and Lucretius proved congenial to the thinking of many of the *virtuosi*. Atomistic materialism was attractive and yet suspect because of its atheistic associations in classical thought. There were not many atheists in seventeenth-century Europe, but the widespread attraction of atomism generated a strong fear of it.[32] The fear of atheism was not wholly unfounded because atomism contributed to the metaphysical world of the deists, from which God was effectively excluded.

Above all the very success of the new science and the autonomy it had achieved in regard to theology and philosophy produced in many the conviction that its discoveries were our surest grasp on reality. Especially after Newton had brought practically all that was known in physics and astronomy into one self-consistent and empirically verifiable system, it was easy to believe that the created world was a closed causal plexus. Newton himself believed that God had not only created the world but that he continues its existence by his will and actively governs all aspects of it. Newton's comment that flaws in the solar system would require correction by direct action of God can be used to make him appear naive. Leibnitz said Newton made God an inept watchmaker. This judgment ignores the profound grasp Newton had of God's dominion over the created world, which was far closer to the traditional doctrine of creation than Leibnitz's notion of a perfect watchmaker God.[33] Newton's contemporaries virtually apotheosized him, but his theology could not withstand the mechanistic implications people saw in the new physics.

It was not that theological expressions of the freedom and sovereignty of God or of the contingency of the world were lacking. Even in a short article Oakley is able to give an impressive list of both theologians and scientists who were saying these things right

---

[32]Richard S. Westfall, *Science and Religion in Seventeenth-Century England* (New Haven, 1958) 20, 106-10. Hobbes's materialism was, no doubt, one of the reasons for the accusation that he was an atheist, though Hobbes was not an atomist but believed in a wide variety of basic material substances. See Willis B. Glover, "God and Thomas Hobbes," *Hobbes Studies* (Oxford, 1965) 143-44.

[33]This understanding of Newton's religion follows Frank E. Manuel, *The Religion of Isaac Newton* (Oxford, 1974) rather than the interpretation of Westfall, *Science and Religion*, 201-20.

through the end of the seventeenth century. Most of the scientists by this time were, of course, laymen, and many of them had an inadequate understanding of their own beliefs. That was to be expected and would, perhaps, be of little importance except that the lay scientists were more and more the molders of the European mind. Those with a better theological understanding like Pascal had a less general influence. Paul Hazard has pointed out that an important thing to note about Pascal is that "he had no disciples."[34] Why there should have been a fading at this time of just those aspects of the Christian intellectual tradition that were most relevant to the new science—and not only relevant to it but congenial to it— is an intricate historical problem to which no adequate answer can be given here. The fact itself is beyond question and of the greatest importance in the intellectual history of Western culture.

Theological rationalism was a serious retrogression and it put Christian theology in a very poor position to deal with the developing situation. Theology was losing its grasp on just those aspects of its great intellectual heritage that would have enabled it to understand the new science and even to have kept it more closely related to the philosophical contexts out of which it had arisen and to which it was destined eventually to return. The future of philosophy insofar as it had a direct and meaningful relation to science was to be critical and empirical. At the end of the seventeenth century, however, empirical science seemed wedded to a rationalistic and dogmatic mechanism from which it took the critical power of Hume to divorce it. The rationalistic theology that was dominant at the time led into the shallow apologetics of the eighteenth century which tried futilely to secure itself on the alien ground of mechanistic metaphysics.

A fundamental change was occurring in the European consciousness.[35] It was the beginning of the Enlightenment, and the new non-Christian humanistic faith of Europe was associated in its long formative stage with the mechanistic worldview that seemed

---

[34]Paul Hazard, *The European Mind, 1680-1715*, trans. J. Lewis May (Cleveland, New York, 1963) 144.

[35]Hazard, *The European Mind*.

implied in Newtonian science. Mechanism was more than just a theory; it was a new mode of consciousness. The idea of the world as a closed system of mechanical order came to dominate the imagination of Europe, to be for Western man a new way of being aware of reality. Mechanism as a metaphysical absolute has never had very strong philosophical support, and recently such support as it once had in the projection of physical models to the whole of reality has been undermined by developments in physics itself; yet so firm a hold did the mechanistic mode of being aware of the world get over the Western imagination that it even now requires some intellectual sophistication to emancipate oneself from it, and it is doubtful if very many even of the sophisticated are ever really free of it in their prerational awareness of things.

Mechanism was not consistent with the absolute freedom of God even though some people—Hobbes, for example, and many lesser thinkers of the eighteenth century—might assert them both. The problem this posed for Christian faith will be discussed in the next chapter. Nor was mechanism consistent with the transcendent freedom of man as a historical being responsible for his own future. This has been a source of contradiction and confusion over wide areas of modern culture from various areas of philosophy to psychology and criminal law. Though individuals may lean one way or the other, in general modern man has not been able to deny either his awareness of himself as transcendently free or his conception of the world, which includes him, as a closed system of order.

The transcendent God of the biblical-Christian tradition offers a way of reconciliation by qualifying the freedom of man and deabsolutizing the world order; yet Christian theology has never dealt effectively with mechanism. This in spite of the fact that the earliest effective answers to mechanism come right out of the empirical philosophical tradition that had its own source in medieval theology. Bishop Berkeley's answer was too much an affront to common sense (at least to the sense that was common in Europe) to have much general influence; but David Hume's criticism was devastating. Hume did not say the last word in philosophy. Some subsequent philosophers have taken a radically different approach. Furthermore, mechanism has continued a major element in the Western imagination; but mechanism as a serious metaphysical position can hardly be called tenable since Hume's criticism. The curious thing is that Christian theology had by the middle of the eighteenth century so far lost its hold on its own intellectual heritage that it failed to recognize the apologetic value of Hume's skepticism and treated him as an enemy. Hume is generally admitted to have been unorthodox and just what his personal religious opinions were has been the subject of considerable discussion; but be that as it may, he himself pointed out that his skeptical philosophy, just because it declared some questions beyond rational solution, opened the way to a religion based on revelation. In his *Dialogues concerning Natural Religion*, he has one of the characters, Philo, say:

> A person, seasoned with a just sense of the imperfections of natural reason, will fly to revealed truth with the greatest avidity: While the haughty dogmatist, persuaded that he can erect a complete system of theology by the mere help of philosophy, disdains any further aid and rejects this adventitious instructor. To be a philosophical skeptic is, in a man of letters, the first and most essential step towards being a sound, believing Chrisitian.[36]

The skepticism of Hume offers an obvious possibility for undermining mechanistic metaphysics; but the possibility was not realized in nineteenth-century theology. It was Kant's reponse to Hume to which Protestant theologians looked for a way out of the problem posed by mechanism. Kant's philosophy was critical, and he made a basic epistemological distinction between our knowledge of phenomena and our understanding of noumenal realities which include God, freedom, and duty. The noumenal world is the creation of God. The phenomenal world is a world of appearances; it is a creation of man. Things-in-themselves of the noumenal world are in some unexplained sense the source of the sense data out of which the human mind constructs phenomena. Noumenal objects cannot be known directly as phenomena or dealt with by "pure reason." Attempts to understand noumena with the pure reason or as

---

[36]David Hume, *Dialogues concerning Natural Religion*, ed. with an introduction by Richard H. Popkin (Indianapolis, Cambridge, 1980), 89. It has been much debated which one of the participants in the *Dialogues* speaks for Hume. The end of the *Dialogues* explicitly cites Cleanthes as the choice of the author; but there are reasons to think Hume's real affinities were with Philo.

though they were phenomena can result only in nonsense. Cause and effect and necessity are categories supplied by the human mind in the construction of phenomena out of sense data; they have no legitimate application to noumena, not even to those noumena that are the source of sensory data. If free action in the noumenal world resulted in phenomenal knowledge, that knowledge would conform to the causal necessity provided by the categories with which the mind constructs phenomena. The causal relationships important to science were preserved for the phenomenal world with which alone science is concerned; but they no longer contradicted the experiences of freedom and moral responsibility.

Kant's philosophy is not a true ontological dualism. There is a kind of epistemological dualism between the way we know phenomena and the more direct way we are aware of some noumenal realities. In some of Kant's followers, however, the epistemological distinction he had made was transformed into an ontological dualism. In other words, whereas Kant had said we are aware of one reality in more than one way, some Kantians came to conceive of a phenomenal reality as distinct from a noumenal, or spiritual, reality. It is this perversion of Kant that became the dominant basis of Protestant theology. Overwhelmed by the authority of science and identifying science with a mechanistic metaphysics that had long been associated with it, the thrust of neo-Kantian apologetics has been an attempt to reconcile Christian faith with mechanism rather than to explore the irreconcilable contradictions between them. By its acceptance of Kant's phenomenal world as metaphysically real, theology came to preserve the mechanistic world view when it was outmoded in serious philosophy and even, to some extent, in science.[37]

The ontologizing of Kant produced a kind of two-storied world in which a mechanistic determinism operated in history and nature in so far as they were observable; above this mechanistic world was the spiritual world in which the *meaning* of observed events was known. The obvious problem with this is the lack of any ade-

---

[37]Richard R. Niebuhr, *Resurrection and Historical Reason* (New York, c. 1957) 81, passim. Willis B. Glover, "The Irrelevance of Theology," *The Christian Century* 76 (30 December 1959): 1520-22.

quate explanation of how the two stories relate. Did the meaning Paul saw in the crucifixion affect the movement of his body in the observable world? If so, is this not a breach in the closed system of order postulated for that world? Earlier mechanists were much more aware of this problem than recent Protestant theologians. This neo-Kantian apologetic strategy seems, nevertheless, to have relieved the minds of many sophisticated Christians and allowed them to affirm whatever conclusions are reached by what they think is science. The price paid for this relief is that the mechanistic method has led repeatedly to the compromising of the historical events of the Christian revelation. Bultmann's treatment of the Resurrection is a classic case.[38] The plight of Christian thought since 1700 will be discussed more fully in a subsequent chapter. Here it will suffice to remark that recent concern to explore more fully the implications of the historical nature of the Christian revelation offers prospect of a sounder methodology.

Mechanism presented a real problem, but the methods of neo-Kantian theology bypassed it. The problems with science that exercised the minds of large numbers of Christians have been superficial or even spurious. Galileo's trouble with the church has been accorded a significance far beyond its true impact. Whatever may be the merits of that still-debated case, it did not trigger among either Protestants or Catholics any sustained effort to interfere with the developing new science. Churchmen and pious laymen participated in the movement freely and for the most part undisturbed by any sense of tension between their faith and their scientific pursuits. Bruno, who is sometimes cited as a martyr to science, may have been a martyr to intellectual and religious freedom; but he was hardly a representative of what we can see now was the effective scientific revolution.

Deism will be dealt with in the next chapter. The deist conflict was really not about science, despite the fact that the deists were inspired in part by the spirit of the new physics.

It was geology and biological evolution in the nineteenth century that occasioned the widespread and to Christians disturbing

---

[38]Hans Werner Bartsch, ed., *Kerygma and Myth*, trans. Reginald H. Fuller (London, 1954) 1-44.

conflicts between science and religion. There were some real problems for Christian thought raised by these sciences. Even the new
chronology of geology called for rethinking the historical setting of
the biblical revelation. Also some biblical narratives previously
taken as literal history had now to be given a different interpretation. Biological evolution presented other problems that were closer
to the heart of the faith. In what way was man distinct from other
animals? How did this distinction originate in the gradual evolution
of species? In the absence of any historical state of innocence, what
should be our understanding of the Fall? Can man be expected to
evolve into radically different species in the future? Although a few
theologians have addressed themselves to one or more of these
problems, they can hardly be said to have been dealt with adequately. In any case these were not the issues that caused most concern among Christians. What generated so much heat was the
contradiction between biological evolution and the traditional, literal interpretation of the creation story in Genesis. "The conflict
between science and religion" that ensued was a spurious one because the study of the Bible itself had made the traditional interpretation untenable.

Actually the acceptance of the new geology and the new biology
was easier and quicker than general accounts sometimes indicate.
A few colorful debates in which very conservative Christians like
Gladstone, Bishop Wilberforce, or William Jennings Bryan went
down to defeat before a Thomas Huxley or a Clarence Darrow have,
especially in the English-speaking world, obscured the fact that
many educated leaders in all the major churches accepted the new
theories almost as quickly as the scientific community did.

The critical study of the Bible in the nineteenth century was essentially a product of the deepened sense of history that characterized the era and was only incidentally related to science. The
trauma it produced in religious circles was greater than that of geology or biology; but in the long run it greatly relieved the tension
occasioned by the scientific developments because it undercut the
indefensible claim of biblical inerrancy and offered a much sounder
biblical scholarship. Once Christian faith was dissociated from the
claim that the literal text of the Bible was inerrant, it was possible

to argue that science and religion cannot conflict because they operate in different areas.

This view is not identical with neo-Kantian dualism, but it is probably not in the long run a viable position. There is a parallel between theology and science: both deal in hypothetical explanations of something given—theology on the givenness of the Christian revelation and science on the givenness of empirical data. Both are subject to error and subsequent correction. It is, therefore, possible that hypotheses accepted in the community of scientists may not be acceptable in the community of Christian theology. I am not aware of anything at present uncontroverted among scientists which is not capable of assimilation in Christian thought; but if such should occur in the future, the proper response would not be a disavowal of either science or the Christian faith but some suspension of judgment in recognition of the fact that neither science nor theology arrives at absolute certainty in its formulations and that verification is a different process in the two spheres. A convenient illustration of a sophisticated attitude toward such an impasse is found in a recent pronouncement by a Nobel prize-winning physicist concerning a matter not directly involving the Christian faith at all.

Dirac, writing in *Scientific American* in 1963, points out that at the present time quantum physics has indeterminist implications; but Dirac himself has a strong inclination toward a kind of determinism. He suggests that those with similar inclinations continue to believe in determinism in the hope that a future stage of scientific development may support such a belief.[39] Fortunately, no such impasse seems to exist at present between undeniable conclusions of science and Christian faith; but it would be wise not to be too dogmatic in arguing that it could never occur.

More important than any possible conflict between specific conclusions of scientists and Christianity are the strong affinities that exist between the Christian theological tradition and the more sophisticated understandings of science in the twentieth century. Philosophy of science now varies from positivism to Polanyi; and efforts at clarifying concepts like "law" or "causation" have led to

---

[39]P. A. M. Dirac, "The Physicist's Picture of Nature," *Scientific American* 208 (1963): 47-48.

analyses of ever-increasing complexity.[40] In it all, however, there is general agreement on the hypothetical nature of the interpretive structures by which data is understood.

The prevailing philosophy of science at the present time has developed in and out of the empirical tradition and has regained a sophistication lost in the classical age of science; it thus has more affinities with fourteenth-century thought than with the mechanism associated with classical physics. Yet theology has not taken cognizance of this and continues a neo-Kantian apologetic that is largely irrelevant to the intellectual life of our time.[41] Not only theology but philosophy of science and even science itself might profit from an understanding of the biblical-Christian source of much that is basic to the Western mind and relevant to science.

When Hume eventually drew the skeptical conclusions implicit in the empirical tradition with systematic thoroughness, he did so without dependence on any theological considerations. As a result his epistemology had no ontological base; that is essentially what is meant by calling it critical philosophy. Philosophies of science that have developed since in the empirical tradition have also been essentially epistemologies that have lacked any ontological ground. Without such ground they have solipsist implications which are rarely admitted. Berkeley showed the possibility of treating sensations without reference to any source of them in an external world. Berkeley, of course, posited a God who was the direct source of sensations. Leave God out and the solipsist implications of an empirical epistemology unrelated to any ontological basis become evident. Neither scientists nor philosophers, of course, have come to solipsist conclusions but have continued to make ontological assumptions of a common sense sort which are philosophically naive. Belief that the world the scientist investigates is really there and worth his efforts is a basic characteristic of Western culture, but its historical origin in the biblical tradition is rarely understood outside religious circles.

---

[40]See, e.g., William A. Wallace, *Causality and Scientific Explanation*, 2 vols. (Ann Arbor, 1974) 2:163-326.

[41]Niebuhr, *Resurrection*; Glover, "Irrelevance."

Except for Bergson and Whitehead, influential philosophers of science who have broken with the empirical tradition have offered alternate epistemologies but not an explicitly developed ontology. This is true of Kant and more recently of Polanyi. Neo-Kantians who have converted Kant's epistemology into a speculative ontology have not only capitulated to an outmoded mechanism but have entangled themselves beyond extrication in a naive dualism. Alfred North Whitehead's deliberate effort to provide an adequate non-mechanical ontology for science resulted in one of the most interesting intellectual constructions of modern times. It is subtle, sophisticated, highly original—a fitting monument to the imaginative genius of the great mathematician who produced it. Speculative philosophies have not, however, proved viable in a West whose mind was so largely formed by the critical thought of the fourteenth-century theologians. Even Hegelianism has not in the long run succeeded in being more than a minority influence on Western thought. Whitehead was quite clear as to the hypothetical nature of his construction; [42] but a hypothesis of such complexity that offers no possiblity of empirical verification has not been convincing to the scientific community. Process philosophy is a minority movement in philosophy and is one of the straws at which diffident theologians can grasp when they no longer understand or believe in the strength of their own intellectual heritage; but scientists have shown little interest in Whitehead's exciting subtleties.

Scientific investigation continues and its achievements show no sign of diminution, but it continues in a state of confusion concerning the ground of the object of its investigation.[43] Whether interest in science and success in its pursuit can continue indefinitely in this situation has been questioned; but there is at present no basis for a definitive answer.

Another question about which there has been much greater concern has to do with the difficulty of integrating science into the general culture. The autonomy of science has stimulated its growth by the removal of inhibitions to its pursuit. The price we pay for this

---

[42]Alfred North Whitehead, *Process and Reality* (New York, 1929) 11-12, 20-21.

[43]Cf. Dirac, "The Physicist's Picture."

autonomous science may, however, prove excessively high. Since
World War II there have been both within and without the scientific
community serious misgivings about the difficulty of relating science to our ethical concerns, our capacity for generating awesome
political powers, and our overwhelming sense of historical responsibility. Existentialist insights into the nature of our personal lives,
insights that inform so much of our literature, do not seem a part
of the same world in which scientists are motivated to extend their
researches. Yet existentialism, our sense of history, much of our political theory and basic political orientations derive from the same
religious heritage as our science. Historically a relationship between these aspects of our culture can be found. A fundamental
question for our time is whether mere historical understanding is
powerful enough in the absence of a common faith to furnish the
cohesive force needed to achieve cultural integration. The odds
would seem to be against it; and that is most disquieting because
genuine religious faith cannot be produced as a means to cultural
salvation.

V THE ENLIGHTENMENT: THE BEGINNING OF THE MODERN WORLD

The style of the Enlightenment gives an impression of simple, rational clarity that can be quite misleading to any serious effort at historical understanding. The clarity that characterized the self-consciousness of the period was superficial. The Enlightened could believe that truth is simple and the world rational only at the expense of not recognizing the contradictions that abounded in their own intellectual culture. As the various aspects of the period's grasp of reality were probed more deeply, the Enlightenment with its clarity disappeared amid the babble of contradictory voices that have since contended in the post-Enlightenment West.

Superficial as much of its thought may have been, the Enlightenment was, nevertheless, a crucial period in the formation of the modern mind. It was a spiritual movement of great depth and power; and if it left European culture fragmented and insecure, it also provided much of the dynamism that has characterized the modern West. There is a persistent sense that the modern world differs in some fundamental way from an earlier Europe. The crucial time that marks the beginning of the modern period is not, however, as was once thought, the Renaissance, but the age of Locke and Newton. Paul Hazard says that the new direction was taken in the single generation between 1680 and 1715. It was in that generation that for the first time in the history of Europe any significant number of the leaders of culture openly repudiated the Christian faith.[1] This was not a merely negative movement.

The emancipation from Christianity occurred within a culture already formed in some of its most fundamental aspects by the biblical tradition. The biblical contribution had not been restricted to a few great seminal ideas but had brought a new mode of human consciousness. Biblical awareness of existence under a transcendent God had radically altered man's self-consciousness and also his way of being aware of the world. As mentioned in previous chapters, the world, in biblical understanding, was a world in which God's purpose operated; but it had no inherent purpose or meaning of its own. It was the dead world which science explored and on which man through his science operated. Man in this view, by virtue of his supernatural relation to the transcendent God, also transcended the world and was free to operate upon it in accordance with his human purposes. These propositions, it must be emphasized, were not merely ideas; they designate a new level of human consciousness. What happened in the Enlightenment was that man achieved an emancipation in his own consciousness from the transcendent God, but he retained an essentially biblical understanding of himself and the world—essentially biblical, but not without a fundamental modification. Without the limitations imposed by awareness of the transcendent God man lost his sense of sin and found his freedom inflated to the point of self-deification. There was thus born a new religion radically to be distinguished from Judaism, Christianity, or Islam and yet taking its place beside them as a fourth biblical religion. The new religion may be referred to as humanism. "Humanism" is admittedly a very ambiguous

---

[1]Paul Hazard, *La crise de la conscience européenne (1680-1715)*, (Paris, c. 1935): trans. into English by J. Lewis May under the title *The European Mind, 1680-1715* (London, 1953).

term. Renaissance humanism was the pursuit of certain intellectual disciplines.[2] A more general usage simply refers to an approach to learning and to society that emphasizes the humane qualities characteristic of Western culture at its best. Douglas Bush uses it in this sense when he speaks of the Christian humanism of sixteenth- and seventeenth-century England.[3] Despite this ambiguity, it seems the appropriate term to designate the effort of modern man to find the meaning of his life in his own purposes or in his communities and historical causes. This is the meaning most often intended in this study.

Transition to the new faith was both obscured and facilitated by the phenomenon of deism. Deism was not a genuine religious faith but a set of ideas congenial to the mind of the eighteenth century under the shelter of which the new humanistic faith developed.[4] The sources of deism were diverse and can be mentioned here only in the briefest and most cursory manner. The intellectual discipline which had guided and restrained religious speculation in the Middle Ages had lost much of its effectiveness when educated laymen of serious religious concern began to speculate about religious truth. The Reformation did something to encourage lay ventures into theology, but such ventures had begun before the Reformation and would no doubt have continued without it. At any rate, it was not the great theologians of the Reformation but the amateurs of the Renaissance and early modern times who, for the most part unwittingly, prepared the way for the apostasy of the Enlightenment. Wilder speculations like those of Paracelsus and Bruno probably had less influence than the innocent Neoplatonic eclecticism of people like Pico.[5] The idea that revelations less complete than that in Christ had informed other religions was not uncommon by the

---

[2]Paul Oskar Kristeller, *Renaissance Thought* (New York, 1961) 9-10.

[3]Douglas Bush, *The Renaissance and English Humanism* (Toronto, 1939).

[4]Cf. Leslie Stephen, *History of English Thought in the Eighteenth Century* 3rd ed. reprinted (New York, 1902); 1:169. (The original edition of this work was published in 1876).

[5]Giovanni Pico della Mirandola. See Charles Trinkaus, *In Our Image and Likeness*, 2 vols. (Chicago, 1970) 2:724-25 and 753-60.

late sixteenth century, especially in France; and Lord Herbert of Cherbury is frequently mentioned as an early seventeenth-century forerunner of English deism. Eclecticism in religious thought made reason the arbiter of religious truth. It was an easy step to subject Christianity to this same arbitration; and as "reason" became more and more the discursive reason used in the new science, the Platonic element in the older proto-deism faded from the picture. In this context the eighteenth-century concept of natural religion and the phenomenon of deism are easily understandable.

"Natural religion" was the religious knowledge thought to be available to man through reason alone. In the deistic controversy most of the Christian apologists accepted the concept of natural religion but contended that further knowledge was needed and that it had been furnished by revelation. The deists held that no religious truth beyond natural religion was accessible to man. Deism was a common-sense, popular residue of Christianity from which had been lopped off—as though they had stuck out from some Procrustean bed—those distinctive elements that were not congenial to the mind of the age. There was, of course, no definition of deist orthodoxy and deists varied somewhat in the terms they used and in the degree of traditional Christian influence they retained. Leslie Stephen has pointed out that the line between deists and the more rationalistic of professing Christians is almost impossible to draw.[6] There were, however, three tenets that were characteristic of deists: belief in (1) a watchmaker God who had created the world as a perfect machine in the workings of which he no longer needed to intervene; (2) a moral law, which was a part of the law of nature; and (3) an afterlife of rewards and punishments.

The first of the tenets listed above effectively removed God from the scene; but the deists reserved for man a transcendent freedom to interfere purposefully with the world machine which they denied to God, although the latter idea was quite as inconsistent with their conception of the world as a closed system of mechanical order.

---

[6]John J. Tayler, *A Retrospect of the Religious Life of England*, 2nd ed. (London, 1853) 280; Stephen, *English Thought*, 1:91-92.

In the English deistic controversy of the early eighteenth century the primary issues were revelation and the providential activity of God. These issues were serious enough, but the handling of them by Christians was so obtuse and superficial as to render the whole controversy largely spurious and irrelevant to the profound cultural crisis of the age. Its polemics continued to have some popular appeal in the nineteenth century, but it had little direct import for the future intellectual history of Europe. Ignoring the deeper meanings of historical revelation and Incarnation, the Christian defenders interpreted revelation to mean simply the propositions recorded in the Bible. They were thus betrayed into defending doctrines of inerrancy that proved embarrassing when exposed to the literary and historical study of the Bible that developed among Christians themselves after 1800.[7] The defense of providence fared no better. Insofar as there survived traditional conceptions of the sovereignty of God over nature, they found little acceptance in the age of Enlightenment. More popular efforts to reconcile providence with the closed mechanical world were, of course, doomed to failure. Caleb Fleming, an English Unitarian who was an active polemicist against the deists, cited as a prime example of providence the "Protestant wind" that had blown King William's ships to England in 1688 while bottling James's fleet in the Thames estuary. God, he explained, had in creation excepted the wind from the closed system of natural order. As the scriptures say, "the wind bloweth where it listeth" (John 3:8), and this gave God a continuing entrée into his world.[8] Not all the arguments were this naive; but the apologists were generally themselves too much a part of the prevailing climate of opinion to take advantage of the devastating attacks Bishop Berkeley and later Hume made at the very foundations of mechanism.

Leslie Stephen, a fair-minded "freethinker" of the nineteenth century, has recognized that the weight of ability in England was on the side of the opponents of deism; but he points out that the

---

[7]Willis B. Glover, *Evangelical Nonconformists and Higher Criticism in the Nineteenth Century* (London, 1954) 21-22, 72-90, 103, passim.

[8]Caleb Fleming, *Remarks on Mr. Thomas Chubb's Vindication of His True Gospel* (London, 1739) 62.

decay of deism was not a clear logical triumph of the Christian apologists. The Christians had met the deists more than half way and
thus compromised their position. Deism had declined primarily
from internal weakness. It was, as Stephen says, a vapid, optimistic
creed that "was never really alive." Its failure was that it had no
power to deal with the real human situation.[9] As a kind of residual
Christianity ideas like those of the deists are still quite common; but
by the end of the eighteenth century deism was not a position many
sophisticated people wanted to defend. It disappeared without
causing any traumas because it was not really anybody's living
faith, and the new humanism no longer needed it as a crutch.

In France the question of sin was more prominent in public de-
bate. The doctrine of original sin was anathema to the philosophes,
but too many Christians had also abandoned it for the issue to be
fairly joined very often between Christian tradition and the new
way of thinking. In England neither Hobbes nor Locke had denied
original sin. Hobbes's description of man as seeking power after
power over others in what, without the restraining force of civil society, was the war of all against all is a good statement of what is at
least one aspect of sin as it is understood in the Pauline-Augustinian tradition; but Hobbes did not identify any of this with sin, and
instead defined sin in simple commonsense terms as the willful
breaking of a known law.[10] Common sense was, indeed, the key-
note of the new era and it opened the way for a popular kind of Pelagianism even though Hobbes did not take the step of denying
original sin. Locke likewise did not himself deny original sin; yet he
contributed to its denial by many in the age he so greatly influenced
by his commonsense approach to natural law morality and his sen-
sational psychology. By the early eighteenth century general opinion in England was strongly Pelagian. Man was considered able to
do either good or bad and the moral status of an individual was a
summing up of the pluses and minuses. There were exceptions, of

---

[9]Stephen, *English Thought* 1:86-90, 169-70. For more recent comments on the
failure of deism see Roland N. Stromberg, *Religious Liberalism in Eighteenth-Century
England* (London, 1954) 53-54; and Glover, *Evangelical Nonconformists*, 72-77.

[10]Willis B. Glover, "Human Nature and the State in Hobbes," *Journal of the History of Philosophy* 4 (1966): 295-300.

course. The hymns of Isaac Watts and Philip Doddridge represent the continuance of an older tradition even in the period before Wesley.

In France the situation was similar. There the Jansenists gave a vigorous defense of the doctrine of original sin; but the Jesuits, who represented orthodoxy, had departed so far from it that there was not much difference between their position and that of Voltaire. The philosophes seemed to have understood the significance of the question of sin better than the theologians. To find a suitable antagonist Voltaire went back to Pascal, who had died in 1662. In choosing the champion he would oppose Voltaire showed how seriously he considered the issue. Few if any in the whole long history of the Christian intellectual tradition had thought more deeply on the subject of sin than Pascal; Voltaire had not sought an easy antagonist.

The Christian conception of sin is not a simple, pragmatic judgment regarding the prevalence of immorality; it is a highly sophisticated doctrine of the relationship of God and man. Sin is man's willful independence of God. Its result is alienation from God and the centering of each human life falsely in the man himself. This false centering has the further result of disrupting relationships between persons. It is not a doctrine understandable in the categories of the Enlightenment. This aspect of Augustinian Christianity did not, of course, die out. There was even a revival of it on a popular level in the Wesleyan movement, and in the American colonies Jonathan Edwards was one of its abler exponents. The simpler, commonsense ideas of the Enlightenment were not, however, compatible with it.

In the Age of Reason Pascal did not get much of a hearing, and Voltaire's task seemed easier than it was. As Paul Hazard has pointed out, the weakness of Pascal was that he had no disciples.[11] Common sense is not, however, always the best understanding of reality, and truth is not always simple. The Pauline-Augustinian doctrine holds in balance two ideas that together give a more accurate description of human reality than the optimistic views of the

---

[11]Hazard, *The European Mind*, 144. For the popularity of anti-Pascal polemics see Ira O. Wade, *The Intellectual Development of Voltaire* (Princeton, 1969) 577-78.

Enlightened. One of these ideas is an insistence on the essential goodness of man as a creature of God whose end is to live in harmonious community with God and his fellow men. The other idea is that man, alienated from God and falsely centered in himself, is continually disrupting and destroying the community that is essential to his own fulfillment. Man's desperate need for community accounts for the good he does even as a sinner; his tragic incapacity to achieve community in his alienation from God accounts for his wickedness. In the Christian understanding even the good deeds of men are sinful when they are done in willful independence of God. The great Augustine has long been quoted as saying, "The greatest virtues of the pagans are but splendid sins." That sentence is probably not Augustine's, but the idea is clearly presented in *The City of God*.[12] As John Herman Randall, Jr., pointed out in a reappraisal of Saint Augustine, this understanding of the human condition has much to recommend it even to those who deny the supernatural teachings of the Christian faith;[13] but it was hardly a doctrine to be countenanced by the new humanists in the first exhilaration of their emancipation from God.

Like the Renaissance humanists before him Pascal had emphasized the grandeur of man as well as his misery; Voltaire and others of the Enlightened wanted to affirm the former but to treat the wickedness and misery of man as a relatively superficial, accidental matter that could be remedied by human will and reason without the aid of any supernatural grace. It is doubtful that Voltaire ever understood the subtleties of Pascal's argument; the context in which he approached the problem hardly allowed for it, for Voltaire was an early and outstanding exponent of the new humanistic faith.[14] His faith in man was based more than he realized on Augustinian Christianity; but the radical sinfulness of man was one aspect of the older doctrine that had to be abandoned if human capacity to achieve man's proper destiny was to be affirmed.

---

[12]Saint Augustine, *The City of God*, trans. Marcus Dods (New York, 1950) 707 (book XIX, section 25).

[13]John Herman Randall, Jr., "The Manifold Experience of Augustine," *The American Scholar* 30 (Winter 1968-69): 127-28.

[14]Wade, *Voltaire*, 586-88.

There were Christian precedents for Voltaire's position. After all, Pelagius himself had been a bishop. There is a perennial Pelagian tendency in Christianity due in part to the very sophistication of the orthodox teaching, which is frequently misunderstood by less subtle Christians. Also the desire for personal, spiritual independence that Augustine or Pascal would have identified as sin is generally present as a motivation. The Spanish Jesuit Luis de Molina had in the late sixteenth century made a scholarly effort to reconcile the free will of man with the grace and foreknowledge of God. Molina was careful to avoid Pelagianism, but his theory included the concept of a natural state of man into which man had lapsed when by his sin he lost the supernatural gifts with which he had been endowed in his state of innocence. This natural state was in itself a part of the original creation and in it man was free to do good or evil. To less subtle and more commonsense thinkers than Molina this doctrine opened the way to a Pelagian conception of moral freedom, and such was widespread among the Jesuits of Voltaire's time.[15]

Self-interest as the common motive for good action was not necessarily incompatible with Christian orthodoxy. Even Mandeville's argument in *The Fable of the Bees* that all the good in society is produced by selfishness or that public virtue stems from private vices might have been used as an explanation of the good possible to even unregenerate sinners. But the proponents of an egoistic morality (of which, of course, Mandeville was hardly typical) did not usually identify selfishness with sin. The self-interest that Rousseau accepted as proper motivation in naturally good men would have been understood as sin by Pascal.

Voltaire, in this as in so much else the spokesman for his time, pitted common sense against the subtle and sophisticated probing of the moral ambiguities of man that had been the concern of the Christian intellectual tradition. An evaluation of the arguments of Voltaire against those of Pascal is hardly worthwhile. They represented different basic, prerational commitments, both of which

---

[15]R. R. Palmer, *Catholics and Unbelievers in Eighteenth Century France* (New York, 1961; c 1939) 30-43.

have continued strong to the present time. It is Voltaire's position, however, which has been most characteristic of the modern world.

Some historians have sought to explain the Enlightenment as a return to classical paganism. The first volume of Peter Gay's two-volume interpretation of the Enlightenment bears the title: *The Rise of Modern Paganism*.[16] Professor Gay sees the early Enlightenment as a return to ancient paganism in a heroic effort to be emancipated from Christianity. In this interpretation Gay's own anti-Christian zeal carries him to seriously misleading positions. There was a repudiation of Christianity by an influential minority that was destined to be far more powerful in the future; but the anti-Christian movement was part of a more complex whole; Christian and non-Christian shared most of the characteristic ideas of the Enlightenment.[17] Overemphasis on what Harold Parker calls "the cult of antiquity"[18] also obscures the essential spirit of the new humanistic faith, which was radically different from that of the ancient Greeks and Romans. The philosophes, like the earlier Renaissance humanists, were particularly attracted to the ethical and aesthetic writings of the ancients, which they used as a quarry of quotations and arguments to adorn their own works. Not only did the Enlightened tend to ignore Augustine, who had been the most popular ancient writer with the Renaissance scholars, but they had little interest in Aristotle or Plato, and their grasp on the real nature of classical antiquity was no greater than that of their forebears.[19] Serious probing into the spirit of the ancient world awaited the nineteenth and twentieth centuries, when such studies were the domain of specialists whose intellectual context was the more highly developed historical sense of their own age. Rousseau and others might extol

---

[16]Peter Gay, *The Enlightenment: An Interpretation*, vol. 1: *The Rise of Modern Paganism* (New York, 1967).

[17]Palmer points out that the Jesuits did not recognize the anti-Christian intent of the *Encyclopédie* until articles appeared attacking the authority of the church. *Catholics and Unbelievers*, 18-20.

[18]Harold Parker, *The Cult of Antiquity and the French Revolutionaries* (Chicago, 1937).

[19]Gay, *The Enlightenment*, 1:82-86.

the virtues of Sparta or the Roman Republic, but the political thought of the Enlightened is not to be derived from such sources.

Hybris as an idea was not unknown to the philosophes, and it could be used to reinforce the commonsense dictum that pride can lead to a fall. Yet no oppressive fear of fate or of any gods characterized their general attitude. The concept of the great chain of being was a commonplace, and the idea of man as having some fixed place in the scheme of things was not uncommon;[20] but this was a minor theme, contradicting and qualifying but not dominating the spirit of the time. The prevailing view was that all other creatures exist for man's sake. Lovejoy quotes Fénelon as saying: "In nature not only the plants but the animals are made for our use."[21] Man's relation to the world was as its lord to know it and control it for his purposes through his reason and his science. Hybris as the Greeks had understood it was as foreign to the spirit of the Enlightenment as the Christian idea of original sin. With qualifications that were mostly recognition of practical problems or of the corruptions existing in society, the spirit of the age remained a triumphant affirmation of the goodness and rational competence of man.

From the early Middle Ages to the early twentieth century the appeal of classical antiquity was a constant in the thought of Western Europe. Only in our own time have classical studies been restricted to a small group of specialists. No interpretation of the Enlightenment should ignore the fact that the appeal of the Enlightenment has not been seriously diminished by the recent eclipse of classical culture as a common ingredient of intellectual life. Those in this day who still find in the Enlightenment their spiritual home and birthplace do not do so because they are returning to ancient classicism but because they recognize in it that faith in man to which they are committed. That it is increasingly difficult to sustain that faith with the optimism of the eighteenth century just adds to the nostalgia.

---

[20]Arthur O. Lovejoy, *The Great Chain of Being* (Cambridge MA, 1936) 187-207.

[21]Ibid., 186-87.

A biblical humanism without God produced a world without purpose and a humanity without sin. In the traditional faith the purpose of God had dominated both nature and history. The loss of any purposefulness external to man was not keenly felt in the eighteenth century because it was assumed that standards and direction were given in the Laws of Nature. In this protective context the weight of man's responsibility for his destiny was less fully experienced than the exhilaration of his emancipation and control. The secularization of world history was accompanied by a faith in the perfectibility of man and his societies. The concept of perfectibility did not postulate a defined final state of human perfection which man had it in his power to reach by the proper exercise of reason. It was rather belief in an unlimited possibility of human improvement.[22] The idea that man could by his own efforts and without the need of any supernatural grace indefinitely perfect himself was a denial of the radical nature of human evil that Christians explained as sin. But on the other hand, progress and the possibility of *perfectibilité* presupposed, at least as the eighteenth century understood them, a non-recurring historical reality such as is found in the biblical tradition.[23] Furthermore, they involved an understanding of man as transcending the order of nature and using it to his own ends. In their development of this biblical understanding of man Renaissance humanists had given man a somewhat more positive role as an actor in history.[24] This was not, however, a radical departure from earlier concepts of history. The Bible, Augustine, and various medieval writers had seen history as a drama of fall and salvation, a continuum of non-recurring actions that were headed toward a consummation in which the purposes of God for man would be accomplished. History was a dialectical relationship between God and man; but man's role as a shaper of history was secondary and even largely negative. It was God through his judgment and his grace who was really in command. This the-

---

[22]Palmer, *Catholics and Unbelievers*, 114-15, 133.

[23]Ibid., 167.

[24]That the Renaissance glorification of man was consciously derived from Christian theology is the thesis of Charles Trinkaus's *In Our Image and Likeness*. Trinkaus's study is the principal basis of chapter 3 of the present essay.

ology of history certainly involved in its main outline a kind of progress; but the assurance that it led to a better future rested in the power and good intentions of God. The new thing in modern times was that man was taking charge, and the assurance of a better future was in man's intentions and power. Since man's actions were within observable history, this moved meaningful history down to the secular sphere. There were, of course, other secularizing forces at work.

The beginnings of the modern sense of progress can be conveniently dated from Francis Bacon and Descartes, and by the early Enlightenment it had become a dominant motif. As men encouraged by the successes of the new science became more confident of their capacity to create a better future, their sense of dependence upon God was lessened, and one of the foundations of atheistic humanism was secured. Penfield Roberts has remarked that what the Divines of Queen Caroline really wanted was to be emancipated from God himself. What was true of latitudinarian clergy was even more true of the more radical philosophes. According to Carl Becker, "What we have to realize is that in these years God was on trial." Of the Newtonian philosophers he says, "having denatured God, they deified nature." The rhetoric of the Enlightenment did seem to deify nature; but in the long run it became clear that it was man who knows and controls nature who was to be deified. The Enlightenment was not a return to cosmological religion.[25] The emancipation and accompanying exaltation of man was the spirit of the age, and it had been preparing for a long time. For Descartes man's mastery of nature was to be based on the new mathematical physics, and he was concerned that it be through an art or method that was founded upon certain knowledge. His concern for certainty put him at odds with the medieval Christian insistence on the contingency of the world. In the medieval view all human knowledge of the world is less than certain because of the continuing dependence of any order or regularity that exists on an omnipotent God who acts in absolute freedom and can so change that

---

[25]Penfield Roberts, *The Quest for Security, 1715-1740* (New York, 1947) 153. Carl L. Becker, *The Heavenly City of the Eighteenth-Century Philosophers* (New Haven, 1932), 63, 73.

order. Descartes's discovery that he could not doubt his own existence established a point of absolute certainty and in so doing provided a limit to the divine omnipotence. From this he derived what
he considered a certain knowledge of the veracity of God and hence
the dependability of human reason. On this "Archimedean point"
man rested his mastery of the world and even a certain knowledge
of the existence of God.[26] The God so known is not the God of the
Bible, but is closer to the Supreme Being of later deists. Man, now
capable by art of certainty in his knowledge of the world, can by-
pass God. Descartes had an important role in the origin of that
modern gnosticism that became the popular humanism of the
Enlightenment.[27]

The relation of nature and history in a science (in the broadest
sense of that word) that was a human artifact and at the same time
a certain knowledge of nature posed the fundamental dilemma of
modern culture. As Kennington puts it, "by the promise of the
progress of science toward infinite benefits he [Descartes] and Bacon established the 'idea of progress,' or the belief that the good is
the future whose benevolence owes nothing to tradition, to nature,
or to God."[28] The contradiction inherent in the Enlightenment is
here clearly revealed: a progress based on science could hardly
"owe nothing" to the nature which is the object of scientific study.
Progress is to be an achievement of the free human will, of art,
while the certain knowledge of nature which is the foundation and
guarantee of that progress requires the immutability of nature. The

---

[26]Richard Kennington, "René Descartes," *History of Political Philosophy*, ed. Leo
Strauss and Joseph Cropsey (Chicago, 1963) 388. For a recent criticism of Descartes's argument see Hiram Caton, *The Origin of Subjectivity* (New Haven, 1973)
115-30.

[27]Eric Voegelin, *Science, Politics, and Gnosticism* (Chicago, 1968). See also Voegelin's *The New Science of Politics* (Chicago [1952]). Voegelin's interpretation of modern humanistic faiths as forms of a modern gnosticism is a creative insight that
sheds great light on the nature of modern history. With God eliminated, modern
man has found himself a transcendent spirit over against the material world. This
dualism is reminiscent of ancient gnosticism. Voegelin's effort to establish a historical continuity between modern humanism and ancient gnosticism is, however,
not successful, and it obscures the real origins of Enlightenment and post-Enlightenment humanisms and confuses the important issue of their relationship to the
biblical tradition. This matter is discussed in more detail in chapter 8.

[28]Kennington, "Descartes," 394.

consciousness of the men of the Enlightenment was that of a transcendent freedom and yet they felt compelled to understand man as a part of the closed system. The problem was inherent in the new context of a godless world. Fourteenth-century scholar-scientists had no such dilemma because their anchor-point was not the certainty of their knowledge of the world but their relationship to the transcendent God. In this relationship they knew their own freedom, and they were also able to accept the contingency of the world without denying all validity to their knowledge of it. The omnipotence of God implied an uncertain world because nothing limited what he might do next—even to changing the order of nature. Emancipation from such uncertainty was achieved in Cartesianism by inferring from the trustworthiness of God a certainty in man's knowledge of the world; this certainty in turn implied a world no longer contingent upon the immediate will of God. Descartes was thus an important source of deism, in which the dependence of the world on God refers only to a past act of creation and has no other relevance to the present situation. The deists saw clearly that the fixed order of the world precluded any free action of God in the world; but they refused to draw the correlative conclusion that it also precluded any free action of man. Even the minority of theoretical determinists were not able to be consistent at that point. The contradiction of free men in a determined world took an interesting form in the environmentalism that originated in the Enlightenment and continues unabated in our age. This tradition, particularly when it is concerned with the direction of a whole society, does not manage to avoid dividing humanity into the controlled and the controllers. The former are the products of the closed causal plexus; the controllers, however, are an elite group of leaders who transcend the determined world and make decisions as to the ends toward which the others should be controlled.

The question whether man is to be understood as transcendently free or determined in his actions by the ordered world of science is so far from having been resolved that it divides contemporary philosophy into the two great camps of existentialism and neo-positivism.[29] This oversimplification has to be quali-

---

[29]Cf. Caton, *Origin of Subjectivity*, 55.

fied, however, by recognizing that the empirical tradition has in the twentieth century developed a much more sophisticated philosophy of science than eighteenth-century mechanism. It is essentially an epistemology and understands scientific knowledge to be a hypothetical "saving of the appearances" in the manner of late Greek astronomy. This is the prevailing philosophy of science at the present, and alternatives to it like those of Whitehead and Polanyi do not restore an understanding of science as a literal description of an objective world. Yet the hold of mechanism on the Western imagination has not been broken.[30] Mechanism still co-exists with a consciousness of transcendent freedom and responsibility for the future, both of individuals and of society, which is, if anything, stronger than it was in the eighteenth century.

The continuity of Western cultural development from before the Enlightenment to the present time is beyond question, but what the significance of this is has been much debated. One has only to think of the history of science or technology or political institutions like the English parliament or various literary traditions to be convinced of the continuity. The very concepts of progress and secular world history, as we have seen, are understandable only against the cultural background given by a theological awareness of history as a nonrepetitive process leading through an unknown future to a better situation. The continuity here is not confined to secularizing a heavenly city but extends to the whole development of the modern sense of history. Even Hume's philosophy was less the product of current secularism than of an empirical tradition with its attendant, modified skepticism that goes back to Ockham.[31] The conti-

---

[30]See the previous chapter. A more detailed discussion of the lacunae between philosophy of science and the mechanistic imagination of modern consciousness is found in the first few chapters of Owen Barfield, *Saving the Appearances* (New York, [1965?]) especially 50-57.

[31]That Hume's skepticism is more radical than Ockham's is not inconsistent with the continuity of the empirical tradition. It might be noted in this connection that what Hume was skeptical about was philosophical demonstrations of knowledge of the world or God. He did not deny the validity of all knowledge—not even the knowledge of God proclaimed as revelation. *Dialogues concerning Natural Religion*, ed. Henry D. Aiken (New York, 1951) 94. Aiken's judgment that "Philo comes closer to representing Hume than any of the other characters" is surely right.

nuity extends in the other direction beyond the Enlightenment to the logical positivists and analytical philosophers of the twentieth century.

It is when one turns to the question of man's existential self-awareness or religious consciousness that interpretations have been most controversial. Carl Becker, who was more perceptive than most historians of the intellectual currents in his own day, went through a period of pessimism regarding the rationality of man and the viability of his highest ideals. It was in this period that Becker published his most celebrated work, *The Heavenly City of the Eighteenth-Century Philosophers*. The book aroused a storm of criticism. Thinking of the disillusionment he and others had experienced in the twentieth century, Becker declared that the eighteenth-century philosophers were closer to the thirteenth century than to the twentieth. The philosophes, he said, had simply brought the heavenly city of previous Christian generations down to earth and expected to realize it by the practice of science and the exercise of reason to remove the corruptions that had accumulated in society. The natural goodness of man would thus be freed to pursue the ideal of a society in accord with the laws of nature. There is an old Christian prayer, "thy kingdom come *on earth* as it is in heaven," which ought to caution us against too simple a distinction between "this worldly" and "other worldly" at least in Christian thought; but the secularizing of the Christian hope was, nevertheless, a major development of the Enlightenment. The crux of the matter was less a matter of cosmic geography than of whether the outcome was solely in the hands of man or chiefly in the hands of God.

Although his treatment of this significant shift of commitment was light-handed and even flippant, Becker's thesis was sound as far as it went. If his study had not been limited by a focus on the eighteenth century and thus included so much playful irony at the expense of the philosophes, Becker could have made an even stronger case. Generally speaking the intellectual elite of the eighteenth century had little use for tradition. Reason with a method derived from natural science and good, sound common sense were considered adequate guides to truth. The corrupt past was better left behind or remembered only as a warning not to go that way again. Becker's book is a needed reminder that the Enlightenment, for all its contempt of tradition, was in its major aspects a product of the European past. Yet the instincts of his critics have not been unfounded; they have not adequately defined his shortcomings, but "in their hearts they knew he was wrong."[32] Becker made two serious errors. He did not realize how great a break with the past was involved in secularizing the hope for a better future—for a heavenly city, if one likes. The Enlightenment repudiation of Christianity introduced a dichotomy into the basic religious foundation of Western culture. It is a true dichotomy because the Christian faith has continued strong and culturally effective and the new humanism retained enough of the biblical tradition to provide common ground with Christianity, at least culturally, and a strong continuity with the whole Western past. Becker does not seem to have grasped the full significance of this break. His other error was in underestimating the continuity of the humanistic tradition from the eighteenth century to our own day. He was disillusioned by the revolt against reason in much of recent Western thought and the anti-humanitarianism of much in recent political history. Later, as Leo Gershoy pointed out, Becker recovered his faith in what he considered the positive values of the Enlightenment. Gershoy's introduction to Becker's *Progress and Power* (New York, 1960) concludes: "he had returned to the fold. He had rejoined Voltaire and Condorcet and Wells and all the goodly company who wished humanity well."[33] His return had been as much an act of faith as he had accused the philosophes of. Becker never solved the common modern dilemma which he reveals so succinctly in the conclusion of *Progress and Power*: Without God and with the world now known to be dead and meaningless, man is on his own in a hostile universe. Becker's ability to find spiritual peace in this situation was certainly a triumph of faith equal to anything in the eighteenth century.

---

[32]See the convenient collection of publications debating the Becker thesis: Raymond O. Rockford, ed., *Carl Becker's Heavenly City Revisited* (Ithaca NY, 1958).

[33]Gershoy's introduction was republished in the *American Historical Review* 55 (1949): 22-35. *Progress and Power* was first published in 1936.

Becker's failure to appreciate properly the continuity of the Enlightenment with the twentieth century was a result of his having defined the historical results of the Enlightenment in so narrow a manner as to include only those aspects of it which he approved and saw threatened in recent times. He was sad that the rationality of man, at least in the Enlightenment sense, was no longer tenable; that natural law, if it has any validity at all, is certainly not so easily known as the Enlightened had believed. He was committed to the humanitarianism of the philosophes and to the egalitarianism which, though not universal even then, did produce by the last decades of the century that "democratic revolution" which R. R. Palmer later described in two brilliant volumes.[34] But that was not the only heritage we were to receive from the Enlightenment. Even before the end of the century there was the Terror, and Napoleon has been not unreasonably described as the enlightened despot par excellence. Emancipation from God led in one form or another to the deification of man, and the forms that it has taken have not always been consistent with those ideals to which Becker was committed. Deification has usually taken the form of some historical cause or community. The secular religions that have resulted and that range from Jacobinism to various forms of nationalism or socialism or even scientific humanism are historical consequences of that great initial emancipation from God which was so hopefully heralded in the eighteenth century, and many of these secular religions are or have been serious threats to those humane values which are another important heritage from the Enlightenment. The significance of this differentiation of modern humanism will be discussed in the next chapter. Even the irrationalism that threatened Becker had some of its roots in the secularizing of empirical philosophy, psychology, and the existential dimension of Pascal. Becker's critics, so far as I am aware of them, have shared his identification of the Enlightenment with humane and liberal values and no more than he have pointed out the continuity of the Enlightenment with much more in twentieth-century culture. That the spiritual crisis of the eighteenth century was more significant than even its protagonists have claimed will, it is hoped, be made clear in the present study.

---

[34]R. R. Palmer, *The Age of the Democratic Revolution*, 2 vols. (Princeton, 1959).

There is probably no period in Western history about which it is more tempting to generalize than the Enlightenment; and yet the age was full of serious contradictions, the most important of which are still unresolved. It would be unfair to hold the philosophes responsible for all these contradictions; they resulted in considerable measure from the irreconcilable differences between the various earlier cultures and traditions that have nourished the West and contributed to its richness, its unique awareness of the range of possibilities open to human experience. What the philosophes may be held responsible for is ending that basic unity of faith which even the Reformation had hardly more than shaken. It was the Judaeo-Christian tradition that had produced enough integration of the disparate cultural elements of European society to allow us to speak of a Western civilization easily distinguishable from the Islamic world or even from Byzantium. The reconciliation of alien cultural influences was not, of course, ever fully accomplished; but with all its contradictions there was a West. The philosophical, the scientific, the historical, and the literary traditions of Europe were subject through the seventeenth century to the unifying influence of the biblical tradition with its transcendent God.

With the Enlightenment this integrating process was reversed. Science achieved the autonomy for which Christian theology had provided a basis, but now it was independent even of that basis and no longer had any effective relationship with philosophy; and if it still had much to learn in geology and biology and cosmology from the historical sense of the biblical tradition, it learned blindly without recognizing the source of its inspiration. Philosophy became increasingly dissociated from other intellectual concerns. Developing isolated elements of the great inherited tradition the philosophers became isolated from each other. What had Hegel to say to Mill or Nietzsche to Ernst Mach? Even when philosophy became most influential on politics, the effect was not integration except on a narrow scale that denied or ignored much of the great Western inheritance and tended toward the narrow, culturally impoverishing unity of the totalitarian state. But these aspects of our recent cultural disintegration can be better discussed at a later stage of our study. The new humanism retained enough of the old unifying faith to preserve continuity with the Western past and provide a basis for a continuing and developing Western tradition despite serious disjunctions and contradictions. It is still what Christian and humanist share from their common Judaeo-Christian heritage that has prevented complete disintegration.

The term "Enlightenment" is unavoidably ambiguous. Peter Gay practically identifies it with anti-Christianity; but the intellectual and spiritual phenomena associated with the new non-Christian humanism were effective throughout the culture. It is hard to say whether the nadir of Christian thought that characterized the eighteenth century was cause or effect of the denial of sin or of the hold which mechanism got on the Western imagination. Perhaps it is best not to think of the relationship as causal; perhaps we are concerned only with various aspects of the same developing spiritual and cultural phenomena. The branches of the religious dichotomy have not split into utterly disparate cultures; but the distinction between them continued through the romantic revolt against the oversimplifications of the Enlightenment and still continues to our own day. Contradictions in the inherited culture and other contradictions that developed in the period of Enlightenment have posed a growing threat of cultural disintegration. Radical divergence of the Christian and humanist bases of culture with regard to the nature of man and to man's relation to the world have made the resolution of other conflicts difficult and have thus greatly increased the threat of disintegration.

One problem that since the Enlightenment has become increasingly divisive is the relation of history and nature. As pointed out above in the discussion of Descartes, the Enlightenment on this subject was hopelessly confused. The consciousness of a freedom transcending nature and involving the capacity to know and control nature in the interest of a better and unprecedented future was deeper than any rational thought about it. Yet nature was understood as a closed system of causal order, and it was further assumed that man was a part of this closed system. Only a minority of the Enlightened seem to have been much troubled by this contradiction, and no one was able to resolve it, though Kant certainly made a valiant effort. Some of the Encyclopaedists were enthusiastic in their efforts to convince men of determinism in order to build a better world! The deification of man was not as explicit among the deists of the eighteenth century as it came to be later but it was, nevertheless, the spiritual reality of the age insofar as the age was not Christian. The exaltation of reason and science—sometimes philosophy—as the source of meaning and value indicates the spirit of the Enlightened far more than lip service to the watchmaker God. Here was the real seedbed of the better defined humanistic faiths of later times. Roland Stromberg says of Robespierre, "He believed in the worship of a Supreme Being; . . . but his true God was a kind of abstract embodiment of the People."[35]

From the beginning, however, the consciousness of transcendent freedom in the new humanism was compromised by naturalism. The use of "reason" and "nature" as, in most contexts, practically synonymous terms indicates the confusion. If reason simply followed a closed system of natural law, it could hardly be the instrument of that creative and continuous improvement which was called progress. Even later when romantics, and still later existentialists, tended to absolutize the transcendent freedom of man the compromises with nature were not avoided. Sartre declaims the freedom of man in unqualified terms and denies the existence of any human nature; but his generalizations about human existence do in fact define a kind of nature.

Repudiation of the mechanistic world view by idealists, romantics, and existentialists has not captured the imagination of the general culture. The eighteenth-century contradiction between man as a part of a closed system of causal order and man as historically free and responsible is still very much a part of the mind of the West. When the transcendent God is eliminated, there is a strong tendency to absolutize both the world and transcendently free man; hence the contradiction. Within the traditional Christian understanding both human freedom and the contingent world are subject to the sovereignty of God. Since they are not absolutized, the contradiction is not generated.[36]

---

[35]Roland N.Stromberg, *An Intellectual History of Modern Europe*, 2d ed. (Englewood Cliffs NJ, 1975) 204.

[36]This is not to say that there are not problems with the Christian view—the problem of evil, for example—but they are different problems, and neither before nor after the Enlightenment have they threatened the same kind or degree of cultural disintegration.

The same pattern may be discerned with regard to other issues. Cultural elements taken out of the context in which they were produced have led to contradictions that were obviated by their mutual relationships in the original context. In ancient Greece, as in other cosmological societies, man had a place within the natural order. In the biblical tradition man is seen as transcending the natural order in such a way that as a sub-creator he can modify it to suit his purposes. In the original biblical context nature was good, given of God for man to know and control and use. No contradiction was involved. With God eliminated, modern man has had difficulty arriving at any consistent attitude toward nature. Attempts to retreat back into a cosmological view are futile because we are inescapably aware of our responsibility for modifications of the natural world; our sense of history cannot be simply discarded. In the new situation nature is seen on the one hand as benign and the basis for the efficacy of reason and science. On the other hand nature is seen as the obstacle to be overcome in the creative achievement of human ends. The contradiction is easily documented in a scientific humanist like H. G. Wells and is widely pervasive in modern attitudes.[37] The seeds of the problem were present in the Enlightenment; but as long as deism was a useful intellectual crutch, a God-given nature could be postulated as the ultimate standard of truth and goodness, and the full force of the problems involved in seeing man as the only source of meaning and purpose in an otherwise purposeless universe could be avoided. Appeals to nature as the arbiter between conflicting human purposes were even in the eighteenth century nothing more than appeals to inherited cultural values. At the end of the century, in the controversies that produced the French Revolution and those produced by it, there was a radical disagreement as to what cultural values were to prevail; in this situation appeals to Nature and Reason were revealed as so much empty rhetoric without any power to resolve the conflicts.

From the eighteenth century until now an enervating relativity has threatened moral disintegration of Western culture as a whole. Within a given cultural context where certain traditional values are

---

[37]Willis B. Glover, "Religious Orientations of H. G. Wells: A Case Study in Scientific Humanism," *Harvard Theological Review* 65 (1972): 124-26.

generally accepted, various human purposes can be judged. But between widely divergent social schemes and historical causes communication on a profound moral level breaks down. This was seen a few decades ago between fascist countries and traditional democracies; it is seen now between those democracies and the communist societies. Of course, one can and does make a personal commitment to certain traditional values as Carl Becker finally did; but this does not establish a common basis for the entire civilization. Attempts to reestablish a natural-law basis of morality such as Walter Lippmann advocated in his "Public Philosophy" have not been successful.[38] Efforts to find a basis for morality in science and the contradictions they have led to are discussed in the next chapter.

It is not here argued that no solution to these problems is conceivable, but merely that the problems exist in the present world situation as a result of the loss of the common ground from which various now isolated cultural components derived.

Another example of cultural fragmentation as a result of loss of the historical ground of a tradition is found in the history of empiricism. As long as the empirical tradition developed within the theological context in which it originated, its skeptical implications were qualified by belief in the good creation as the ontological ground of science and by confidence in human reason as a means of at least a limited understanding of man's experience of God and the world. The skeptical implications of the biblical revelation were stated explicitly by Paul in the first chapter of 1 Corinthians, developed by Augustine, restated by Anselm, and developed into the empirical philosophy of the fourteenth-century nominalists. Even Hume saw the relationship.[39] But Hume approached the epistemological problem in independence of theological considerations. The result was a radical skepticism. The philosophy of science that eventually developed on this basis in the nineteenth and twentieth centuries is an epistemology that denies all meaning to any discussion of the ontological ground of science.

---

[38]Walter Lippmann, *Essays in the Public Philosophy* (Boston, 1955).

[39]David Hume, *Dialogues Concerning Natural Religion*, 94.

Science, itself a product of the empirical tradition, achieved, as we have seen in the previous chapter, an autonomy of its theological ground and saw its method harden into the naive mechanistic metaphysics of the eighteenth century. Although it lacks any significant philosophical support, this naive mechanism still serves the scientific community generally as its ontological assumption. Efforts like those of Bergson or Whitehead to provide a more adequate ontology have not been widely accepted. Few things are more striking about the present intellectual situation than that philosophy of science does not comprehend all that is involved in the continuingly successful pursuit of science itself. Efforts to remedy this situation have been mostly epistemological. Even scientists who are too sophisticated to be mechanists do, however, make ontological assumptions; at least they believe that the object of their investigations is really there and that it is worth their efforts. The scientist's mode of being aware of the world has roots in both classical and biblical traditions but overwhelmingly in the biblical; failure of contemporary philosophy to incorporate this aspect of experience illustrates the lack of an adequate integrating principle.

Men of the Enlightenment seem to have felt little tension between rationalism and empiricism. This was largely because they had reduced reason to the discursive reason that traces efficient causation. Reason simply ordered empirical data. This, however, was too simple. Earlier thinkers—Mersenne, for example, and Hobbes—had aready pointed out the distinction between the truths of reason and the never quite certain knowledge of the world, which could come only through the senses. After Hume the development of the empirical philosophical tradition sharpened this distinction into the logical truths and empirical information of logical positivism. Linguistic analysis can hardly be expected to bridge that gap. Since the famous theorem of Kurt Gödel one may, indeed, wonder what the status of the heretofore certain truths of logic may be. The Enlightenment cannot be blamed for a tension between rationalism and empiricism that long antedated it; but the overly simple resolution of that tension let an indefensible mechanistic analogy of reality fix itself—until now, at least, irrevocably—in the Western imagination.[40]

---

[40]The origin of mechanistic metaphysics is discussed in chapter 4.

The humanistic faith of the Enlightenment posed a new problem of evil. The old question of how there could be evil in the world
of a good and all-powerful God was still discussed;[41] but the new
faith in man generated a new problem: How could good and rational men have created so corrupt a society? The problem can
hardly be said to have found any solution. In face of the corruption
itself, however, two opposing attitudes developed: primitivism and
the efficacy of education. The tension between them reflected the
opposition between nature and history, or the question whether
man in his historical existence transcends nature. If the natural
man was good and rational, then primitive men must be closer to
truth and goodness than those more under the influence of social
corruption. To act on this principle, however, would run counter to
the general belief in progress. More in line with that belief was the
alternate approach of education. This was one way of manipulating
the environment to modify human behavior, a historical effort at
improvement.

Both belief in education and primitivism helped promote that
egalitarianism that was the essence of the Democratic Revolution in
the last decades of the century.[42] Both were congenial with a new
sense of justice as equality which had begun to challenge the older
conception of justice as the distribution of prescriptive rights well
before the Enlightenment. The uniformitarian assumption that
truth is the same in all places and at all times and is available to any
man through reason enabled Rousseau to bring much of this together both in *Emile* and in *The Social Contract*, but at the expense of
compromising the age's strong faith in progress.[43] Despite the nonhistorical bias of Rousseau the new sense of justice gave a moral
force to the egalitarian movement that made it historically effective.

---

[41]Lovejoy, *Great Chain of Being*, chapter 7.

[42]I take the phrase "Democratic Revolution" from the R. R. Palmer's *Age of the Democratic Revolution* previously cited. I am much indebted to Palmer for a clearer conception of the political movements of the century.

[43]Uniformitarianism as the "fundamental principle" of the Enlightenment is convincingly presented in Arthur O. Lovejoy, "The Parallel of Deism and Classicism," *Essays in the History of Ideas* (Baltimore, 1948).

Egalitarianism produced two political ideals that from a twentieth-century point of view seem antithetical, but which seemed much less so when uniformitarianism was a general assumption. One of these was, of course, the Democratic Revolution, which had its most significant results in the founding of the new American republic and in the French Revolution. The other was enlightened despotism. As long as the right goals for society were assumed to be easily available through reason and reason to be the same in all men, enlightened despotism might well seem a more effective means to a good society than an effort to educate back to primitive virtue masses of men who had been misled by centuries of corruption. When Rousseau published *The Social Contract* (1762), he presented the good political society as a small city state and allowed for larger political entities only as federations of such small states. He was uncompromisingly opposed to representative government, which he understandably identified with aristocracy. That representative institutions were the means by which his democratic ideas would be made effective in large states was completely missing from his thought. There was no hope, he thought, for Europe. In all Europe the only country still capable of achieving legitimate government was Corsica.[44] In 1755, however, Rousseau had seen enlightened despotism as a means to a just society.[45] The monarchies of Europe had long had an interest in reducing the power of the powerful and thus making all equal under the monarchy. Enlightened despotism had a natural affinity with the new egalitarianism. Napoleon has been called the enlightened despot par excellence; and his claim to be a "son of the Revolution" was not mere sophistry.

Both the ideal of enlightened despotism and the tendencies that eventually produced democracy developed in the eighteenth century in a society which was predominantly aristocratic. There was, as Palmer has pointed out, an aristocratic resurgence which opposed both despotism and egalitarianism. Herbert Butterfield

---

[44]Jean-Jacques Rousseau, *The Social Contract and Discourses*, trans. G. D. H. Cole, Everyman edition (New York, 1950) 49, 89-96.

[45]Ibid., 296-97.

identified a "Whig interpretation of history" which evaluates everything in the past in terms of its contribution to modern liberal democracy.[46] This bias and the Marxist dogma of class conflict have obscured the positive and aggressive role which aristocracy played in the age of Enlightenment. Actually the eighteenth century has some claim to be the most aristocratic period in Western history. In the Middle Ages and early modern times powerful aristocrats had been a threat to developing monarchies in a direct military sense. That situation had ended in the major states of Europe before the eighteenth century. Aristocrats in the eighteenth century exercised political power *within* the structure of monarchy itself and were effective in limiting autocratic power, which they called despotism. The results were strikingly different in different states.

In England after the Revolution of 1688-1689 the Parliament was clearly predominant in the English constitution. The legal aristocracy was, to be sure, confined to the House of Lords; but the Lords had effective control of many seats in the House of Commons and the other seats in the Commons were held by members of what the British call "the ruling class." Legalities aside, Parliament was in both houses an aristocratic body. It was in this aristocratic government that the institutions of cabinet administration were gradually developed. The later democratizing of the English constitution should not blind us to the fact that cabinet government was a product of aristocracy. The British government was not democratic before the Second Reform Bill in 1867. Cabinet government, or as the English call it, "responsible government," was the product of a long political tradition that owed little to the new ideas and attitudes commonly included in the concept of Enlightenment.

The French aristocracy had a medieval background similar to that of the English; but since the end of the Middle Ages the development of political institutions in the two countries had been different. After the civil wars of the sixteenth century and some fear of their recurrence in the seventeenth, Louis XIV adopted a policy of deliberately excluding the more powerful of the nobles from politics although he identified himself with them in the social life at

[46]Herbert Butterfield, *The Whig Interpretation of History* (New York, 1951).

Versailles. After his death in 1715 the Regent for Louis XV reversed this policy and from then until 1789 the highest positions in government, army, and the church went with rare exceptions to the aristocracy. Thus power and leadership in eighteenth-century France were in the hands of individual aristocrats, and on the whole, they performed quite well; but the aspiration of the French aristocracy was to exercise a corporate power in French government comparable to the power of the House of Lords in England. In the third quarter of the century their efforts were to expand the role of the parlements. They claimed to be the representatives of the nation against despotism, and though they did not realize their own ambitions, they did achieve a kind of standoff with the monarch which had as its principal effect the blocking of the efforts of the monarchy to make needed reforms through a series of very able ministers. In the period just before the Revolution the strategy of the aristocrats was to demand the calling of the Estates General as the only legal way to change the tax structure. They assumed that the reinstitution of the Estates General as a vital part of French government would give them the position of leadership which they thought was naturally and rightfully theirs. The calling of the Estates General, which met in 1789 for the first time in 175 years, was the occasion that brought into direct conflict the two most powerful political movements of the age: the aristocratic resurgence and that egalitarianism to which Palmer has given the name "the Democratic Revolution." In this conflict the aristocrats were decisively defeated, and a new age in European politics began.[47]

The great political innovation of the Enlightenment was the development of a democratic polity suitable for large states. In this the French Revolution must share the honors with the new American republic, which, in fact, narrowly antedated it. In both cases what had formerly been considered obviously impossible was achieved by the simple process of grafting on to old traditions of representation the selection of representatives by democratic constituencies. There is no use to quibble about the existence of a few democratic constituencies earlier or about restrictions on the suffrage in both

---

[47]Palmer, *The Age of the Democratic Revolution*, vol. 1, especially 3-99 and 439-88.

the United States and the First French Republic. The fact is that before no one had conceived of democratizing a large state and after the French Revolution, despite the failure of the First French Republic, democracy became a potent force in European politics. The importance of old traditions of representation in the development of democratic institutions is indicated by the viability of the American republic where the stronger and more continuous experience with representative institutions in England and the colonies gave a support that was lacking in France. France did not achieve a lasting democracy until the 1870s.

Traditions of representation were not, however, the only difference between the American and the French experiences. More relevant to this study's concern with the humanistic faith of the Enlightenment were the different attitudes toward human nature. In the case of the Americans the Enlightenment faith in the goodness and rationality of the common man was qualified by a strong traditional belief in human stupidity and greed and in the corrupting influence of political power on even good men. If the orthodox doctrine of sin was too much for most of them, they yet retained commonsense cultural derivatives from it.

Jefferson had no illusions about "the corruptibility, the fickleness, the ignorance, and the crudity of the popular mass"; but he believed that in some important sense men are equal and capable of self-government; he also believed an aristocracy of talent was necessary to furnish leadership and that the chief role of the common man in a self-governing political community was to be sensitive to abuses of power and to keep a watchful eye on his leaders. In 1787 Jefferson wrote to Edward Carrington:

> Cherish, therefore, the spirit of our people, and keep alive their attention. Do not be too severe upon their errors, but reclaim them by enlightening them. If once they become inattentive to the public affairs, you and I, and Congress and Assemblies, Judges and Governors, shall all become wolves.

In 1798 he wrote in the Kentucky Resolutions:

> Free government is founded in jealousy and not in confidence. . . .
> In questions of power, then, let no more be said of confidence in

man, but bind him down from mischief, by the chains of the constitution.

Jefferson's view of man was not merely a secularization of the Christian idea of man as an essentially good creature corrupted by sin. Jefferson saw the greed and perversity of man as a part of his essential nature provided by the Creator for ultimately beneficial purposes.[48] Other Americans, of course, held a wide variety of opinions in this matter; but the practical result was an ambiguity in the conception of man which was similar to that of traditional Christianity and offered the same practical basis for politics by its affirmation of man's capacity for both good and evil. The formulation of Reinhold Niebuhr, a twentieth-century theologian, would have been acceptable to the founding fathers: "Man's capacity for justice makes democracy possible; but man's inclination to injustice makes democracy necessary."[49]

In Revolutionary France the distribution of good and evil was conceived to be less uniform. The Jacobins were much less inclined to see the ambiguity in every man and more inclined to divide men into good patriots and the bad people who opposed them. The myth of the wise and good common people has dominated the development of the democratic tradition and has been more and more effective in American politics—so much so that the United States is probably the chief proponent of it at the present time. (Niebuhr's is a Christian opinion that is typical of American opinion now only if it is misinterpreted as imputing the justice to the people and reserving the injustice to political leaders.) The confusion that results in a society influenced by both Enlightenment humanism and the Christian doctrine of sin has prevented any stable view of human nature. As the framers of the American constitution understood, it is essential to a viable democracy that it produce effective leaders and let them lead. Recent democratic experience is that the leaders

---

[48]This understanding of Jefferson is derived mostly from Richard Hofstadter, *The American Political Tradition* (New York, 1948); Merrill D. Peterson, *Adams and Jefferson* (Athens GA, 1976); and Daniel J. Boorstin, *The Lost World of Thomas Jefferson* (New York, 1948). The quotations are from Boorstin, 177, 190.

[49]Reinhold Niebuhr, *The Children of Light and the Children of Darkness* (New York, 1944; "New Foreword," 1960) xiii.

are found and put in office but their capacity to lead is seriously handicapped by an overly suspicious public. News media have exploited the lacuna between the good people and the suspect leaders to the point of suggesting the solution of complex political problems by opinion polls. When democratic leaders are ineffective in critical situations, the way is opened for demagogues to seize power and maintain public support by propaganda and repression. That, of course, is the end of democracy.

Illusions about the unfailing virtues of common people have also made for unrealistic approaches to foreign affairs. There is a tendency in democratic countries, and again this is especially evident in the United States, to assume that political communities everywhere want the same things that the people of Western democracies want. This has created illusions about Germany during the Nazi regime, about Communist countries, and about the Third World.

Another aspect of modern democracy that has paradoxically become less realistic as it has been more effectively realized is the ideal of equality. The practical egalitarianism of the eighteenth century has been absolutized and hardened into dogma. The dispute over heredity and environment is currently used to obscure the existence of actual differences, which have to be dealt with whatever their origins.

It is one of the ironies of modern politics that totalitarianism should in its origins be related to democracy, and this goes back to the eighteenth century. Rousseau's political theory is a subject of great controversy; but at least in his hostility to what he called "partial associations,"[50] in his conception of the total alienation of the citizen and all his rights to the General Will of the political community, and in his refusal to put any effective limits on what the General Will might control, he was a prophet of totalitarianism. This is not to suggest that Rousseau anticipated the modern total state or that he would have approved any of the actual historical ex-

---

[50]Partial associations are what some sociologists have called "intermediate groups"; they are associations that include only part of a political community and which may attract the loyalty of their members away from the political community itself.

amples of it. He was writing in the context of assumptions (uniformitarianism, for example) that can no longer be made, and his emphasis was less on the power of the state than on the individual citizen's devotion to it. (This latter, of course, is also a characteristic of the total state.) Undoubtedly some of Rousseau's opinions as they were interpreted by those revolutionary leaders for whom he was a mentor supported an étatism which had an ominous future.[51]

Although it is not evident in the Declaration of the Rights of Man and the Citizen, by the time of the Convention the democratic tradition was not so much freedom from government as freedom by means of government. The political relationship had become dominant over all others.[52] There awaited only the development of the techniques of communication and control and a crisis situation for the total state to become a historical reality.

As has been pointed out there was an affinity between enlightened despotism and the egalitarianism of the Democratic Revolution; but the concept of enlightened despotism was based on a belief in universal reason. This kept the Enlightened in positive relationship to the traditional values shared by Europeans and understood at the time to be the dictates of reason. The enlightened despots hardly aspired to restructure the whole of society. The Jacobins of the Terror had such aspirations but were unable with the techniques at their disposal to accomplish their realization. When total states did actually come in the twentieth century, right reason had been replaced by some ideology or other and traditional values were tolerated only in so far as they were consistent with the reigning ideology. How the development of ideologies occurred may be clarified in the next chapter. Here let it suffice to say that each of them included only a part of the manifold Western tradition and that the imposition of a social order restricted to any one of them was bound to result in a great impoverishment of culture.

The political forces generated in the Enlightenment have resolved themselves into a conflict between democracy and totalitar-

---

[51]Robert A. Nisbet, *The Quest for Community* (New York, 1953; reprinted 1969) especially 140-80.

[52]Ibid., 167, 175, passim.

ianism, and in this conflict democracy is seriously compromised by the Enlightenment tradition of looking to government for the establishment of freedom. In this context a humanitarian concern for freedom can lead, and in some cases has led, to terror as a policy.

The Enlightenment was a seedbed of modern culture; whether one considers this a commendation or a reproach depends on how one evaluates our twentieth-century society. Contradictions were nothing new in the West. The Schoolmen had struggled with irreconcilable ideas in Aristotle and the biblical tradition; Ficino was less aware of the contradictions, but they abound in his effort to reconcile Christianity and Platonism; the new science contradicted much in old images of the world. What was different in the Enlightenment was a certain loss of ballast; or, to use a different nautical figure, in the turmoil no anchorage was found. The repudiation of Christianity by an influential minority eliminated that as a common ground. This was accompanied by a growing contempt for tradition as a guide to action. The eclipse of traditional elites by forces emanating from the Enlightenment was not an unmixed blessing. It paved the way for new elites whose claim to power was adherence to some ideology. The result has been confusion and conflict.

Belief in progress and an overly optimistic view of human nature built up hopes that led to disillusion and despair. The result can be seen at work in the frustrations of the French Revolution. The modern world since has been characterized by vacillations between optimistic aspirations and the pessimism that follows when they are not realized.

The deification of man proved to be a divisive rather than a unifying faith. The conflict and violence of the French Revolution and its aftermath was a portent of things to come.

VI   PROMETHEUS UNBOUND

The Age of Romanticism is the generally accepted label for the period in the history of European culture that immediately followed the Enlightenment. It would be hard to find a term so widely used that has been the subject of so much controversy and so little agreement. Even within the limited area of literary criticism definitions have been widely divergent and in some cases mutually exclusive. Jacques Barzun defines its essential characteristic as a "constructive and creative" mission, which it "conceived . . . in the light of a great contradiction concerning man . . . the contrast between man's greatness and man's wretchedness; man's power and man's misery." Passing over the fact that others have seen the romantics as wildly undisciplined, it is interesting that in this same passage Barzun alleges that the most famous expression of this contradiction in man is found in the *Thoughts* of Pascal, "historically not a romantic, but . . . a dissenter in his own time."[1] Barzun goes on to point

---

[1]Jacques Barzun, *Classic, Romantic and Modern* (Boston, 1961); revised edition of a book originally published in 1943 under the title *Romanticism and the Modern Ego*, 14, 16.

out that there was a revived appreciation of Pascal in the romantic age; he might also have cited as holding such a view of man the Apostle Paul or Saint Augustine or almost any informed Christian thinker.[2] T. S. Eliot, who shared this Christian understanding of human nature, explicitly declared himself a classicist and not a romantic![3]

As long as the term *romantic* is restricted to literary criticism, of course, the critic can say what he means by it—as Professor Barzun has done—and then proceed to use the term intelligently and meaningfully; but when the term is applied to a whole period of cultural history, arbitrary definitions which give the word a semi-technical status are judged by the historical reality as far as that can be apprehended. The difficulties are magnified exponentially. Arthur O. Lovejoy in a well-known essay has remarked on the contradictions in the intellectual culture of the early nineteenth century and the consequent impossibility of defining the romantic period in terms of some essential unifying principle.[4] Among the Romantics one finds ardent proponents of anarchistic individualism and others equally committed to a conservative insistence on the organic nature of society. The champions of authoritarian government and those who pressed the new cause of democracy have equal claims to be called romantic. Nature was seen as simple and uncomplicated by Wordsworth and many others; but there was also a revival of the sense of nature as irregular and mysterious, transcending the grasp of human reason. Wordsworth and Shelley in some of his moods saw nature as the benign source of virtue and bliss. But nature was also seen in the age of romanticism as the almost insuperable obstacle that had to be overcome. Indeed, the dark, unyielding reality against which the human will was pitted was for some overwhelming and was one source of what Mario Praz

---

[2]See, for example, John Herman Randall, Jr., "The Manifold Experience of Augustine," *The American Scholar* 38 (1969): 127-28.

[3]T. S. Eliot, *For Lancelot Andrews* (London, 1928), preface, ix.

[4]Arthur O. Lovejoy, "On the Discrimination of Romanticisms," *Essays in the History of Ideas* (New York, 1960 [c.1948]) 228-53.

has called "romantic agony".[5] This dark side of romanticism fore-shadowed the despair of later existentialists, but on the whole the prometheanism of the romantic period was heroic and optimistic. Certainly the hope and joy in so much romantic poetry is more generally identified with the spirit of the age than the pessimism and cruelty that Praz has so amply documented as also belonging to it.

It goes without saying that there was much in the age which it would clearly be inappropriate to call romantic. Benthamism and classical economics, for example, are continuations of characteristic cultural products of the Enlightenment. Historical periodization is always somewhat arbitrary and tends to distort the continuous development of human culture; but it is useful for all that. The new age did have a different tone from the preceding one. Even the French Revolutionary tradition and the Napoleonic tradition were "romanticized."

The rich and varied culture of Western Europe has many sources and embodies fundamental contradictions. To some degree the difference in cultural epochs is a matter of emphasis. The commonsense rationalism of the Enlightenment was not capable of dealing adequately with important aspects of the Western experience. The traumas of the French Revolution stimulated a recovery of those dimensions of European consciousness that had been suppressed, or at least not much attended to, in the Enlightenment. This explains the romantic nostalgia for the past and also the fact that so much that is called romantic is found to have antecedents in the eighteenth century. They had not been totally lost but were less in the mind of the previous age. No one essential principle explains romanticism because the romantic age was the recovery of contradictory elements of an immensely complex civilization.

The widespread revival of Christianity in the early nineteenth century fits nicely into the pattern of a romantic protest against the limitations of the Enlightenment. In the English-speaking world the most familiar part of the Christian resurgence was the Evangelical Revival which had begun with the preaching of the Wesleys and Whitefield, but which reached the height of its influence in the

---

[5]Mario Praz, *The Romantic Agony*, trans. Angus Davidson, 2d ed. (New York, 1956).

Church of England roughly about the time of the First Reform Bill. In the nonconformist churches its development was slower and reached its high point only some decades later. The revival as such was largely confined to the English-speaking world, but it was the most powerful Christian movement since the Reformation and its influence has extended throughout the whole culture—indeed, through its missionary efforts and the subsequent extension of Western civilization, its influence has been in the most literal sense world wide. The thesis first stated by William E. Lecky and later developed by Elie Halévy that it set the moral tone of Victorian England can hardly be gainsaid; and the reign of Victoria was when English power and influence was the greatest it has ever been. Although there has been a good deal of controversy about details, the immense social impact of evangelicalism is beyond dispute. It was the primary motivating force in the anti-slavery movement in the first third of the century and in the middle decades it was evanglical tories who led the fight for factory reform. From the Chartists to the present Labour Party the evangelical influence has given a certain tone and restraint to the English labor movement.

It is a curious thing about this movement that it had so weak an intellectual dimension. It produced no significant theology of its own. P. T. Forsyth might be cited as an exception, but he came late in the movement and his influence has not been great. During its heyday the evangelical movement made do with traditional theology, especially certain modified forms of Calvinism. Its relation to science and other secular intellectual developments was largely defensive.

The Catholic revival on the Continent had a similar weakness. It had a stronger hold on its intellectual tradition, but Catholic orthodoxy was so rigid between Trent and Vatican II that its intellectual potential could not be realized. The Catholic social influence was generally conservative and for that reason has tended to be underestimated by historians with their attention to new developments. The difficulty of establishing healthy social orders in the twentieth century may warrant a reappraisal of the positive value of preserving old traditions. In any event the church was greatly strengthened in the early nineteenth century and is still a potent force in Europe. The intellectual tumult that erupted at Vatican II in the 1960s indicates the life that still remains in the Catholic church and suggests that Catholicism may take a much more significant role in the intellectual life of future decades.

It is hard to generalize about the Protestant revival in northern Europe, especially Germany, in the early nineteenth century. There was a new vitality in traditional Lutheranism and Calvinism which is by no means adequately covered by the term *pietistic*. A conservative Protestantism similar to English evangelicalism, but with less evangelistic, missionary fervor, was strong in Germany and the Scandinavian countries throughout the century. There was, however, an intellectual leadership among German Protestants that was much more a part of the general intellectual life. Schleiermacher has been called both the father of German romanticism and the father of modern Protestant theology. The German churches also took the lead in establishing a new era in biblical studies. The development of a remarkable historical and critical study of the Bible was very disturbing to traditional Christians both within Germany and elsewhere; but it was a movement within the church and it aimed honestly, and in the long run successfully, at a better understanding of the Bible.[6] The revival of theology in Germany was unequalled anywhere else, but during the nineteenth century it did not sufficiently appropriate the great Christian intellectual tradition to establish theology again in the forefront of the intellectual life of the culture as a whole.

If the modern world is what it is because of the Enlightenment, it is also what it is by virtue of the Christian revival following the Enlightenment. The social and political effects of that revival are widespread, but hardly calculable. The direct influence of specifically and explicitly Christian thought was less significant; but the revival of Christian faith had, nevertheless, a diffusion through the intellectual life of the West which it would be hard to overestimate. The great literary figures of the nineteenth and twentieth centuries include a surprising number of people whose literary works are not conceivable apart from their Christian faith. Tennyson, Tolstoy, Dostoyevsky, Hawthorne, Volkoff, Hopkins, Auden, Eliot, Thorn-

---

[6]Willis B. Glover, *Evangelical Nonconformists and Higher Criticism in the Nineteenth Century* (London, 1954) 18ff.

ton Wilder and Walker Percy come to mind at once. There have been, of course, many others. And many whom it might be overly bold to identify as Christians have drawn heavily on Christian insights into human nature. What is possible in a society is determined more by the widely diffused convictions of the general population than by the brilliance of an intellectual elite. Even when they are not fully articulate, the ideas and values most widely accepted in a society open the way to some developments and close the gate on others. What Crane Brinton called "the whole equilibrium" of the Western world[7] is very different from what it might have been if the tendencies of the Enlightenment had not been partially reversed by the Christian revival that was so large a component of the romantic protest. In so far as any such equilibrium continues to exist in the West it is due in part to what non-Christian humanists and Christians have in common and in part to the fact that nobody in the West, not even those who oppose it, escapes the influence of Christianity.[8] The common ground between Christian and atheistic existentialists is a case in point.

Christian revival to the contrary notwithstanding, the humanistic faith that is Christianity's modern rival was not weakened but sharpened and better defined in the post-Enlightenment decades. Return to more traditional Christianity did, indeed, make its contribution to a clearer perception of the religious dichotomy that divided the West. In the eighteenth century it had been hard in many cases to distinguish deists from Enlightened Christians. As deism faded (except in popular form as a residual Christianity), the essentially atheistic nature of the new humanism was more evident. Not that this happened in one easy step. Some radical Jacobins were atheists who had only contempt for Robespierre's Supreme Being; but they were a minority even among fervent revolutionaries. Hegel's God was not the God of Wilberforce or Coleridge, but Hegel did use the name. Bentham and Shelley were still exceptional cases. Atheism was, however, bolder, and distinctions were becoming clearer.

---

[7]Crane Brinton, *Ideas and Men* (Englewood Cliffs, New Jersey, 1963) 424.

[8]Ibid., 105.

In his short life Shelley did not achieve a consistent philosophical position, but his great poem *Prometheus Unbound* expresses the spirit of the new Promethean humanism. Although there has been some controversy as to what Shelley's Prometheus symbolizes, it is clear that in some sense he is, in the words of Mary Shelley, "the emblem of the human race."[9] In Aeschylus's treatment of the ancient myth Prometheus is freed only when he makes his peace with Zeus.[10] Shelley gives the story a very modern twist. In his *Prometheus Unbound* there is none of the respectful piety toward the gods which in Aeschylus is the backdrop for the impiety of Prometheus. In Shelley's play Jupiter (or Zeus) is a phantom tyrant, a creation of the mind and will of Prometheus, who had given him all his power. The misuse of this power by Jupiter was responsible for all the evil in the world. Not only does Shelley anticipate Feuerbach's explanation of religion as a projection of human ideals; he goes further to see this as the source of evil in man and the world. Salvation was to be a Promethean rebellion against the phantom God. The title of Shelley's poem expresses a self-assertion of the human spirit in the face of whatever reality may be, an assertion which has continued to be a major ingredient of modern non-Christian humanism.

As complex as the age was, the deification of man acquired in it a new boldness and a clearer definition. The Christian revival contributed to this clarity by offering a contrasting background. The clarity must not be overemphasized. In German idealism, for example, Christian and non-Christian elements are confusedly mingled. The decline of deism and suspicion of the naive belief that the laws of nature were easily available to human reason did not result in an eclipse of the humanistic faith that had found in them its support during the eighteenth century. In the Enlightenment reason and natural law had in most contexts been identifiable with what was intellectually acceptable, what men of common sense would

---

[9]For an argument that Prometheus represents the One Mind of Shelley's metaphysics see the first chapter of Earl R. Wasserman, *Shelley's Prometheus Unbound* (Baltimore, 1965).

[10]Of the trilogy Aeschylus wrote about Prometheus the play in which the reconciliation occurs does not survive as a whole, but its general theme is known and is described by Shelley in the preface to *Prometheus Unbound*.

not deny. The content of "natural law" thus came to include a very large body of traditional ideas and values. John Locke's political theory illustrates the point. He appeals to reason and the laws of nature as his authority; but the content of his famous Second Treatise describes the English constitution as it had evolved out of the Middle Ages. Through Locke medieval political ideas were mediated to the modern world. The age of reason was far more traditional than it understood itself to be. The philosophes were on the whole not radicals or fanatics—at least not before 1789. The new humanistic faith was remarkably restrained through most of the century.

Rousseau introduced a more passionate element; but that is why Rousseau is so often identified with the succeeding romantic age. It is paradoxical that the very revival of so much of the Western tradition should in the age of romanticism have, possibly through the variety and contradiction it produced, brought to modern man an intensified awareness of himself as transcendently free. Michael Polanyi in his Eddington Lecture of 1960 contrasts the relatively calm "process of intellectual secularization" of the eighteenth century with the romantic dynamism of the succeeding age, its passionate emotions and inordinate schemes of political action and reform. Polanyi rightly describes these contrasting periods as stages in the development of the same cultural phenomenon. In his view the secularization of intellectual life that he thinks was almost complete by the time of the French Revolution released the dynamism inherent in the Christian ideal of community making it seem a feasible historical goal. Since this ideal was incapable of realization in actual societies, it led eventually to nihilistic attacks on existing institutions.[11] The Christian ideal of free persons united in community has continued to have such power in secular humanism because the humanist consciousness of transcendent freedom derives from the biblical Christian faith and implies for its full realization the kind of community Christians describe as the City of God. It was the denial of God coupled with the retention of that relationship of lordship over the world implied in man's own tran-

---

[11]Michael Polanyi, *Beyond Nihilism*, The Thirteenth Arthur Stanley Eddington Memorial Lecture (Cambridge, 1960).

scendence that produced the "sovereign individual" of romantic Prometheanism and its obverse, the absolutized political community.

With the denial of God the Christian doctrine of sin disappeared. In the Christian tradition the sinfulness of man offers an explanation of the foibles, inconsistencies, and evils in society and makes possible a patience with imperfection in the very process of improvement. The denial of his own sinfulness imposes on the modern humanist the burden of a standard of perfection which he is unable to achieve. The fact of his own unrecognized sin normally protects him from requiring perfection of himself and enables him to excuse himself because of the failure of society to achieve the ideal. The result is that secular millenarianism that characterizes modern politics.

Rousseau was the first to relate the absolutizing of individual freedom with the absolutizing of the political community.[12] His ideal was a secularizing of the City of God in which personality and community are aspects of a single reality. Persons cannot exist without community; and by definition community cannot exist without persons. Rousseau's vision entered the sphere of political action in the course of the French Revolution.

Modern man's deification of himself was not originally conceived as such. Even after Nietzsche only a few people of unusual insight have seen clearly that if there is no God, man must be his own God. Nevertheless, the deification was implicit in the new mode of human consciousness. The transcendence of God in the biblical tradition had meant the disenchantment of the world. The world known to modern science is without purpose of its own. If there is no God the only purpose is man's purpose; man becomes the only source of meaning and value. That is his deification. But the individual man is not capable of being God. Not even Nietzsche or Sartre has managed that; and if anyone ever should, his experi-

---

[12]Polanyi is mistaken to identify the individualism of Hobbes with the absolutized individualism of Rousseau (ibid., 8-9). Hobbes's works came before the great watershed in which non-Christian humanism took its rise. His individualism was still in a theistic and even Christian context. See Willis B. Glover, "Human Nature and the State in Hobbes," *Journal of the History of Philosophy* 4 (1966): 293-311.

ence would be rightly described as insanity. Man exists only in relationships. He is related to that purposeless world which is the
context of his life, and he achieves his personhood only in relation
to other persons. Sartre has argued that the essence of all fundamental human relationships is conflict;[13] but in *No Exit* he recognizes that the human predicament is precisely man's desperate
need for the community he is unable to achieve.

The universalism implied in eighteenth-century conceptions of
natural law and reason made a relationship to "mankind" seem an
adequate identity, and traditional patterns of conduct and meaning
supported the individual's life. But as those structures came under
increasing criticism at the end of the century, and as "mankind"
proved too vague and abstract to base one's life on, emancipated
modern men began to find meaning in more concrete historical
communities and causes. Each of these became for those committed to it a representative of "mankind" and gave to that concept a
concrete embodiment. The humanistic faith, which had been diffuse and only partly articulate in the eighteenth century, thus came
to be differentiated into a variety of concrete forms. The original
form, which may be called liberal progressivism, has continued
while newer forms have developed alongside of it. The first of these
was the Jacobinism of the French Revolution.

The Revolution had begun as a political conflict between the aristocracy and a new democratic egalitarianism;[14] but it soon developed into a Messianic cause that was actually the religion of the
Revolutionary leadership. This is no mere figure of speech. One's
religion is whatever serves as one's ultimate source of meaning.
The frenzies of the Terror have often been recognized as a religious
fanaticism; but the religion was more than the frenzy. The political
movement whereby a just democratic society was to be established
was the center of all meaning for the Jacobin leaders. Both Crane

---

[13]Jean-Paul Sartre, *Being and Nothingness*, trans. Hazel E. Barnes (New York,
1956) 364-430, esp. 364, 429.

[14]George V. Taylor, "Noncapitalist Wealth and the Origins of the French Revolution," *The American Historical Review* 72 (1967): 490-96.

Brinton and R. R. Palmer have emphasized the religious dimension of the Revolution. It was a form of the deification of man.[15]

The structure of the old society of Europe did not allow the absolutizing of the state. The most absolute, divine-right ruler was subject to the transcendent authority of God, an authority which might become very effective through the consciousness of the political community.[16] In the modern secular state the situation is quite otherwise. It is important at this point to recognize that secular states have originated in two disparate concepts. The first such state was the new American republic. In this case the state did not lay claim to a religious authority or oppose the existence of religious authorities within the society governed. Its secularity consisted precisely in its exclusion of religion from its legitimate concerns. This is clearly the meaning of the first amendment to the American Constitution. This kind of secular politics is consistent with a general belief in the political community that there is a transcendent moral and political authority to which the state is subject. This is a significant safeguard, perhaps ultimately the only effective safeguard, against totalitarianism. Some other countries, Britain for example, are still officially Christian states but have in fact

---

[15]Clarence Crane Brinton, *The Jacobins* (New York, 1930) 156-242; R. R. Palmer, *Twelve Who Ruled* (Princeton, 1941) 283, 323-34, passim; *The Age of the Democratic Revolution*, 2 vols. (Princeton, 1964) 2:113, 124-29, 250-54, 356-59. There are others, of course, who have seen the religious nature of Jacobinism. The fervor with which Michelet and Quinet were committed to the Revolutionary tradition in the nineteenth century got the name *La religion de le College de France*. Geoffrey Bruun's biography, *Saint-Just, Apostle of the Terror* (Boston, New York, 1932) also emphasizes the religious fanaticism of Saint-Just.

[16]Hobbes is sometimes interpreted as absolutizing the power of the sovereign; but this is a serious misunderstanding. Although for Hobbes the sovereign could not be called to account by any temporal authority, he was subject to the laws of nature which had their authority from God. It was because it was in fact in the best interest of the sovereign to abide by the laws of nature that Hobbes could have such faith in monarchy. It may also be noted that Hobbes allowed that in extreme circumstances the individual might disobey the sovereign even to the point of rebellion. See Willis B. Glover, "Human Nature and the State in Hobbes." Machiavelli's *Prince* may at first glance seem to put the ruler outside all authority. *The Prince*, however, is merely a handbook on how to get and keep power; it does not convey to the ruler any absolute moral authority.

become secular in much the same way that the United States is secular.

The other kind of secular state is radically different. Whereas the first type restricts the power of the state by distinguishing religion from politics in a way that removes it from the sphere of the state's activity, the second type is an extension of the political sphere to include religion. Rousseau ends *The Social Contract* with a chapter on "Civil Religion," wherein he declares:

> The subjects then owe the Sovereign an account of their opinions only to such an extent as they matter to the community. Now, it matters very much to the community that each citizen should have a religion.

He then proceeds to list the articles of a "purely civil profession of faith." Rousseau's ideas were deistic, but in his discussion it is already apparent that religion is for him reduced to a function of the state. With the eclipse of deism, which was already occurring during the first French Republic, devotion to the state appeared as an alternate religion to Christianity. When in all reality man alone is transcendently free and when he commits himself to the political community so as to transmit this capacity for free historical action to the community, then no authority exists to call that community to account. This conclusion was not reached immediately in the humanistic faith; it was first clearly evident in Rousseau, and found its first practical political expression in the French Revolution.[17]

Belief in human perfectibility, which was essentially a belief in the possibility of improvement through historical action, coupled as it was in humanistic faith with the denial of any radical sinfulness in man, led easily to the absolutizing of historical movements.[18] If man was free to create an ideal society, there was no excuse for the existence of an unjust one. Paradoxically the denial of sin by the very illusion it created of the natural virtue of men led by reaction to an absolutizing of the evil of those who opposed the establishment of a just society. Sinful men in Christian tradition

---

[17]Cf. J. L. Talmon, *The Origins of Totalitarian Democracy* (New York, 1970) 2, 4, 10, 12, passim.

[18]Polanyi, *Beyond Nihilism*, 19-20.

were essentially good as creatures of God and capable of redemption; but evil men in the new faith had denied the very essence of humanity and no possibility of redemption was conceived. The enemies of the Revolution were not permitted to repent or offered forgiveness.[19] From the point of view of the Jacobin leadership one might undertake to excuse the execution of Danton on pragmatic political grounds, but hardly that of Madame Roland or Condorcet. (Condorcet died in prison after his proscription and capture.) The Terror, especially in 1794, was no doubt, politically motivated;[20] but one misses its full significance who fails to realize that it was politically possible because it was a moral response of outrage at the failure of people to respond with appropriate enthusiasm to the possibility of an ideal state. Only much later did anarchists and Marxists defend it on merely instrumental grounds, justified by the worthlessness (rather than the immorality) of the victims and by the overwhelming value of the end in view.

The revolutionaries did not succeed in establishing a lasting republic in France, much less an ideal state. What they did, however, was to begin a new tradition in European politics that has been and still is a powerful force in Western culture throughout the world. In nineteenth-century France the democratic tradition was staunchly anti-Christian. The Catholic Church was forced into opposition to democracy by the religious hostility of the Revolutionary tradition. No such clearcut opposition between democracy and Christianity developed in England and the United States, where democracy was a pragmatic matter not so closely tied to an anti-Christian humanistic faith. Indeed, many Christians in the United States think that one of the chief dangers to the church is too close an identification of Christianity and democratic culture.

The tradition stemming from Rousseau and the French Revolution has become widely diffused throughout the culture, however, and its influence on the rival democratic tradition has in some contexts been overwhelming. Dogmatic egalitarianism, which is a persistent threat to education in the United States, is an example of

---

[19]Brinton, *Jacobins*, 220-21; *A Decade of Revolution* (New York, c. 1934) 159-61.

[20]Palmer, *Twelve Who Ruled*, 103, 291.

its influence. On the other hand, in France itself since World War I democracy is no longer aggressively anti-Christian and the church is no longer antidemocratic. The eclipse of monarchy was a major factor in this development; but there was also the fact that the Revolutionary tradition had become in France and elsewhere the sturdy root on which Marxism was grafted, and the dynamism of Messianic humanism was largely transferred from established democracy to the Marxist concern for a society of ideal justice in the future.

The Revolutionary tradition from the first French Revolution through the Commune was the first of the differentiated forms taken by the humanistic faith; but generally contemporaneous with it and closely allied was nationalism. During the Revolution itself the forms are not distinguishable in France. Where nationalism developed in opposition to Revolutionary France, as in Germany and Spain, it was, of course, distinguishable from the beginning as not identical with the new democratic tradition. And in France nationalism survived among the opponents of liberal democracy as strongly as among its supporters.

The great American historian of nationalism, Carlton J. H. Hayes, called nationalism a world religion and illustrated at length its cultic expression. He saw it as a rival of Christianity but recognized that it is frequently syncretized with Christianity. In such a relationship the Christian faith is likely to be seriously distorted and adulterated. On the other hand, Christianity has frequently been a moderating influence on nationalism.[21] A word of caution is needed here: nationalism is not a religion for every nationalist. Hayes's study is somewhat exaggerated; not every movement with a ritual is a religion. The religion of Carlton Hayes himself was Roman Catholic Christianity but that does not mean he was not an American nationalist. Nevertheless, not only the most virulent forms of nationalism but for some people benign nationalist movements have functioned as religions. When nationalism is a religion, it is not the abstract concept that is deified but some specific national community. There are, therefore, many nationalisms, each of

---

[21]Carlton J. H. Hayes, *Nationalism: a Religion* (New York, 1960).

which is a form of humanistic faith for those who find in it the supreme source of meaning. Nazi Germany and Fascist Italy are classic examples of nation states that became religious communities.
The religious dimension of the commitment that constituted these
communities has been generally recognized. There is a story about
a young South German boy who, having been reared in a Catholic
family, went through the confirmation ceremony as a matter of
course. His confirmation prayer was that he might die with a
French bullet in his heart. The source of meaning for his life was
obviously not the Christian faith but his devotion to the Fatherland.

It is not easy to make clear distinctions between those for whom
nationalism is a religion and those for whom it is not. The reason is
that all political loyalties from the ancient Babylonians and Egyptians to the present nation states have a religious or pseudoreligious quality. Even in cases where one's religious faith is clearly not
to be identified with one's political loyalties, the political commitment has this pseudoreligious character. However difficult it may
be to make decisions in particular cases, it is beyond question that
some individuals in most nations have made their political loyalty
the real religion in their lives. When this is the case, the religion is
a form of humanism in which the human community as a transcendent historical entity is deified. The fact that the values of Nazi
Germany were so radically opposed to those of the French Revolution or those of American liberal progressivism does not alter the
fact that all three are forms of humanistic faith in which man is
transcendently free to create his own future, though in the case of
the Nazis the transcendence may be restricted to the German community and a few kindred peoples

Generally contemporaneous with the origins of the French Revolutionary tradition and modern nationalism, humanism took a
third form which was based on a belief in the capacity of science to
shape man's future. The first person with a clear title to be called a
"scientific humanist" was the Comte de Saint-Simon (1760-1825);
but the way had been prepared in the eighteenth century. The increasing tendency to identify natural law with science led to a tendency to extend science to moral, political, and even historical
reality. F. A. Hayek and Eric Voegelin have traced this development

with emphasis on the role of d'Alembert, Turgot, and Condorcet.[22] The roots of later historicisms based on natural laws that control the course of history are to be found in both Turgot and Condorcet.

As the source of scientism Hayek gives especial emphasis to the *Ecole Polytechnique*, founded in 1794 and reflecting the French Revolution's pragmatic and utilitarian approach to science. It is in Saint-Simon, however, that the idea of a whole society based on science is first differentiated from the more general humanism of the Enlightenment. It is a point worth noting that Saint-Simon was not himself a scientist. Since his time some scientific humanists have been scientists and some have not. It should also be noted that by no means all or even most of the scientists of the past two centuries have been committed to what Hayek calls "the scientistic hübris." Faith in science as the ultimate source of meaning and hope for the future is not to be identified with the actual practice of science. Furthermore, it is not the results of scientific inquiry up to the present to which the scientific humanist is fundamentally committed, but rather science as a historical movement by which human perfectibility is to be pursued. Saint-Simon saw science as the latest and final effort of man to achieve power over nature; the drive to such power he saw as a universal human trait.

> Every man, every grouping of men, whatever its character, tends toward the increase of power. The warrior . . ., the diplomat . . ., the geometer . . ., the physiologist . . ., the hero . . ., the philosopher. . . . From different sides they scale the plateau on whose height stands the fantastic being who rules all of nature and whom every man who has a strong constitution tries to replace.[23]

Although in his last work, *The New Christianity*, Saint-Simon affirmed his belief in the existence of God and even in revelation, this earlier statement that it is the human enterprise to replace whatever

---

[22]F. A. Hayek, *The Counter-Revolution of Science* (London, 1955) 105-17; Eric Voegelin, *From Enlightenment to Revolution*, ed. John H. Hallowell (Durham NC, 1975) 74-135. The latter work is a collection of essays formerly published at various times and includes a brief but interesting "Editor's Preface" by Professor Hallowell.

[23]Quoted in Frank E. Manuel, *The New World of Henri Saint-Simon* (Cambridge MA, 1956) 305.

God may be is probably closer to his real belief. It is an attitude which scientism as a religion has shared with other atheistic humanisms.

Saint-Simon was brilliant, erratic, and eccentric. His erratic un-concern with consistency allowed free rein to the brilliance of his insights. His conviction that the leaders of the future would be the scientists, the engineers, and the entrepreneurs was a better pre-diction of the future than the later dogmatic speculations of Marx. Even if free enterprise gives away to statism, Saint-Simon will have predicted it and not Marx.[24] Frank E. Manuel's biography of Saint-Simon points up the religious dimension of his social theory.[25] Saint-Simon took it as axiomatic that no human society was con-ceivable without a religious basis. Since Christianity was no longer performing this function in his own society, there was need for a new unifying religion. In his *Lettres d'un habitant de Genève à contem-porains* (1802) he proposed a Religion of Newton. An international organization of scientific geniuses was to unify all knowledge by an extension of the principles of Newtonian physics. Temples, icon-ography, and a complex organization of councils was described. The mausoleum of Newton was given a function similar to the Mecca of Islam. A special appeal was made to Napoleon to take a lead in establishing the new faith and a new society under the lead-ership of scientists. But, as Manuel says, the Religion of Newton was stillborn. The scientists did not respond and Napoleon's own religious policy was satisfied with the Concordat of 1801.

Saint-Simon made two later attempts to found a scientific, hu-manistic religion. The second failed as badly as the first; but the third, which he launched with the *Nouveau Christianisme*, did flour-ish for a while among a small circle of his followers. *The New Chris-tianity* was published just before Saint-Simon died, and its message was the center of a religious community only after his death.

In his last years Saint-Simon had as a secretary and collaborator Auguste Comte. At the end of their relationship they were es-

---

[24]Cf. Roland N. Stromberg, *An Intellectual History of Modern Europe* 2nd ed. (En-glewood Cliffs NJ, 1975) 265, 267.

[25]Manuel, *Saint-Simon*.

tranged by Saint-Simon's turning to the mystical and religious, and Comte never admitted the extent of the debt he owed his older friend. Historians, in fact, are still in disagreement about the details of that debt because it is not possible to say how much of Saint-Simon's last works was really written by Comte. It seems likely that the debt was considerable; but the confused brilliance of Saint-Simon was systematized by Comte and implications Saint-Simon had not seen were carefully worked out.[26] Comte may, indeed, be seen as the chief prophet of the new scientistic faith. As Comte's thought developed, he became more authoritarian and, like Saint-Simon, he was contemptuously critical of individual liberty and freedom of conscience.[27] Also, like Saint-Simon toward the end of his life, he tried to found a new religion, "The Religion of Humanity."

Comte's influence was amazingly widespread in the nineteenth century. Positivism dominated French thought from 1850 to 1870, and it was a major influence on J. S. Mill, Herbert Spencer, and H. G. Wells. Marx affected a contempt for him, but owed him more of a debt than he admitted. The list could be greatly expanded. Positivism, as Comte presented it, owed its influence not to its philosophical depth but the the fact that it was presented with conviction to the mind of an age that was convinced man's surest grasp of reality was science. In many ways Comte was quite naive. His "law of the three states (or stages)"—the theological, the metaphysical, and the positivist—is an ingenuous "philosophy of history" that bears little resemblance to the actual course of history. His positivism recognized that science is merely descriptive, and he declared questions not subject to scientific investigation were nonsense. On the other hand, he absolutized the truth of scientific knowledge as beyond any question. Compared to Hume or Kant, his empiricism is simplistic, and it is, therefore, understandable that French thought after a flurry of excitement over positivism turned away from empiricism toward Bergson, a Catholic revival, and later to

---

[26]Ibid., 332-43.

[27]Hayek, *Counter-Revolution*, 135-40; Henri de Lubac, *The Drama of Atheist Humanism*, trans. Edith M. Riley (New York, 1950) 140ff.

existentialism.[28] One might almost say that Comte's greatest influence was merely as a publicist for the widely diffused faith in science that has characterized the nineteenth and twentieth centuries. In this study he is chiefly interesting for highlighting the religious dimensions of the modern faith in science. The new Religion of Humanity showed considerable vitality for a while. Societies for honoring great men who had become a part of that continuing essence of mankind that Comte deified as the Great Being were formed in France and England and even in Latin America.[29] The background for a cult of hero-worship had been laid in the eighteenth century belief in an immortality of honor by posterity.[30] Comte's religion had appeal so far as it apotheosized this aspect of the original humanistic faith; but it failed by far to measure up to the expectations of the founder.

Most of Comte's followers were repelled by his religious emphasis in his later years and took advantage of his own distinction between his first life and his second to affirm the philosophy of his "first life" and deny the religion of his second. They excused what they saw as a serious and eccentric aberration by reference to some mental disorder. J. S. Mill grieved over the "melancholy decadence of a great intellect."[31] More recent studies of Comte, however, find a continuity in his thought. Already in the 1820s he was insisting that the new society had to be founded on a "spiritual power" of which scientists were the priests. Gradually he came to distinguish religion from theology, still denouncing the latter, but affirming the necessity for religion in the new society. It is not coincidence that Comte followed Saint-Simon by ending his life in an effort to found the new society on a new religion. Comte in his latest phase was working out the implications of commitments he had made from the beginning.[32]

---

[28]Stromberg, *Intellectual History*, 296-302, gives a brief but helpful evaluation of Comte and his influence.

[29]Ibid., 299.

[30]Carl Becker, *The Heavenly City of the Eighteenth-Century Philosophers* (New Haven, 1932) 119 ff.

[31]Quoted in Voeglin, *From Enlightenment to Revolution*, 137.

[32]Ibid., 136-49. Lubac, *Drama*, 141.

As a religion with a priesthood, dogmas, and ritual, the Religion of Humanity was a fiasco; but it pointed to a dimension of modern man's faith in science that is often overlooked.

H. G. Wells and Julian Huxley also tried in separate efforts to found a religion of science. H. G. Wells published in 1917 a little book called *God the Invisible King*. In his conclusion he disclaims any effort at originality in the work.

> I have been but scribe to the spirit of my generation; I have at most assembled and put together things and thoughts that I have come upon, have transferred the statements of "science" into religious terminology.[33]

Wells recognized that only an elite few had yet grasped clearly the ideas he was expressing; but the whole society, he declared, was moving in that direction. A huge ground swell would transform the various religions of the world into one virtually unanimous worship of Wells's God. The book contains long diatribes against Trinitarian Christianity; but even Christianity, in its modern liberal form, was being transformed.

The book is a most amazing manifesto. Despite the passionate hostility to Christianity, the book is full of Christian terminology and biblical quotations; and a strong Christian influence is evident in both the ideas and the emotional overtones; yet the religion Wells announces is as anti-Christian as he says. It is, in fact, what in this study is called an atheistic humanism. God the invisible king is the Captain of Mankind, with whom men might have an intimate comradeship. God had come into existence "somewhere in the dawning of mankind" and "as mankind grows he grows."

> With our eyes he looks out upon the universe he invades; with our hands he lays hands upon it. . . . He is the undying human memory, the increasing human will.

---

[33]H. G. Wells, *God the Invisible King* (New York, 1917) 171.

God was not merely "the collective mind and purpose of the human race"; he was a "Being in himself" and he had "a consistency we call his character."[34]

Some light is shed on Wells's concept of God by a comment he makes out of his considerable knowledge of biology:

> The influence of biology upon thought in general consists essentially in diminishing the importance of the individual and developing the realization of the species, as if it were a kind of super-individual, a modifying and immortal super-individual, maintaining itself against the outer universe by the birth and death of its constituent individuals. . . . the species has its adventures, its history and drama, far exceeding in interest and importance the individual adventure. . . . it goes on steadily from newness to newness, remaining still a unity.[35]

As the state in Burke's conception transcends any generation in its history, so Wells's God transcends all the individuals that constitute mankind at any one time. "God the Invisible King" is a rhetorical device and means simply Humanity or Mankind as Wells conceived it. It was Mankind that would go on heroically to master Nature and turn it to its uses.

Saint-Simon spoke of a "fantastic being who rules all of nature." Comte had been agnostic with regard to the origin of the world; he neither denied or affirmed the existence of a Creator, and he was seriously concerned to distinguish his position from that of the atheist, who thought he knew. H. G. Wells had a similar view. He spoke of a "Veiled Being" who is somehow responsible for that external reality, Nature, in which man operates and which he has undertaken to control; but Wells denies that at this time we can know anything about that Being, not even whether it is supportive of man's efforts or hostile.

Wells was a great admirer of Comte, and yet he does not mention him in *God the Invisible King*. This is remarkable because his

---

[34]Ibid., ix, 15, 22-24, 61-63, 67-68, passim. A fuller account of Wells's religious views than can be given here is in Willis B. Glover, "Religious Orientations of H. G. Wells: A Case Study in Scientific Humanism," *Harvard Theological Review* 65 (1972): 117-35.

[35]Wells, *God the Invisible King*, 70-71.

ideas closely parallel the religious ideas of Comte, and it is hard to believe that he was not indebted to the earlier humanist for at least some of them. In any particular instance, of course, an idea may have been conceived independently by two working in the same tradition. In addition to their agnosticism concerning any Creator, there are the following similarities:

• God the Captain of Mankind is a close parallel to Comte's Great Being; both are ways of referring to humanity as an ongoing, purposeful being.
• Both are dualists. Wells is particularly insistent on this. He describes his God as a Promethean God and he proudly announces his affinities with Gnostics, Manichaeans, Catharists, Paulicians and "kindred sects." Dualism between transcendent man and the Nature he confronts is, of course, essential to all modern atheistic humanism, but it is especially evident in scientific humanists.
• Both deemphasize the individual and exalt the human species as a superior reality.
• In both there is a teleology that inheres in the human species and moves irresistibly toward a scientific world state.
• Both see immortality as the contribution of individuals to the developing humanity.
• Both think freedom of conscience and tolerance of beliefs or acts contrary to scientific truth will be anachronisms in the new world state. Science discovers truth and the truth will make men free—but free within the scientific truth. This implies the absolute truth of scientific conclusions.
• Both are ambiguous regarding the common man. Although both posit him as a full participant in the new society, both become suspicious of him as an obstacle to progress and become more and more elitist. What is demanded of the common man is devotion; the new world society will be unified in religious sentiment.
• Both see devotion, commitment, a response of the heart as the essential religious fact rather than any intellectual grasp of the new truths.

A possible reason for Wells's failure to identify his faith with that of Comte is given near the end of his book. Referring to "many religious bankruptcies" he cites as an example "Positivism . . .

which failed through its bleak abstraction and an unspiritual texture."[36] He evidently thought Comte's support would not have been an asset. His own apostleship, however, was a still more dismal failure than Comte's. Despite Wells's fame and popularity as a writer, this book was little read and attracted no following.

Julian Huxley's works on the "emergent religion" of science have been more widely read than *God the Invisible King*; but, despite the hearing that his position as the head of UNESCO gave him, his "Evolutionary Humanism" has not caught on as an historically identifiable religious movement. His lucid repudiation of previous "religious systems" as no longer adequate admits that they served a significant purpose in their time. Huxley's understanding of the history of religion is an uncritical acceptance of the views of J. G. Frazer. To criticize him for that, however, would be an unfair anachronism; and, besides, it would hardly affect his central theme. Huxley's civil concern to be fair is appealing, and his naive faith that every aspect of reality is in principle capable of scientific understanding has, no doubt, strengthened the faith of many scientific humanists who are not aware of the philosophical naiveté of such a stance. Like Saint-Simon and Comte and Wells he makes explicit the religious nature of modern man's faith in science when that faith becomes the central focus for the interpretation of human experience. Like his predecessors Sir Julian was right in his claim that scientific humanism was already the faith of many. The repeated failure of efforts to found a specific cult or body of religious beliefs on science results in part from the fact that such systems involve a great deal of speculation with no scientific (or other) foundation and partly from the failure of those who hold a scientistic faith to think of it as a religion at all. Huxley's "system of belief," as he termed it, may be convincing to some; but it has not produced any religious community.

Huxley was a friend of H. G. Wells and coauthor with him of *The Science of Life*, but his approach to the new faith was not the mythopoeic method of Wells; he sought rather to base his Evolutionary Humanism on "the firm ground of scientifically established knowl-

---

[36]Ibid., 173.

edge." Actually he bases his religious system—he does not hesitate to call it a theology although this in no way implies anything theistic—on farfetched and unsupported speculations. In order to avoid admitting any transcendence of nature he declares his system to be monistic rather than dualistic, and to support this position he posits a universal substance that he calls world-stuff or cosmic-stuff which is the ground of both matter and mind.[37] When we experience the world-stuff objectively, it is material; when we experience it subjectively, it is mind. Without any supporting evidence—or even argument—scientific or otherwise, it is impossible to take this "world-stuff" concept seriously. Even in his own thought it does not serve the purpose for which it was invented. He admits the existence of awe-inspiring experiences, which he, for want of a better word, calls "divine". He denies that such experiences are supernatural but calls them "transnatural" because they grow out of ordinary nature but transcend it.

Nor does his "world-stuff" enable him to avoid, except verbally, the dualism between nature and the transcendently human which characterizes all modern humanism. Evolutionary humanism sees the evolutionary process as becoming conscious of itself in man. "Whether he likes it or not, he [man] is responsible for the whole further evolution of our planet." Purely biological evolution reached a limit some ten million years ago. Since then evolution has been the development of mind and brain. Especially the development of truly symbolic language has made possible "the cumulative transmission of useful experience, and initiated a new phase, mode, and method of evolution, the psychosocial."

For all its garnishing with scientific information, Huxley's Evolutionary Humanism is not really grounded in science. Huxley has a real problem with teleology. He does not admit any purpose behind the evolutionary process and yet he speaks of the "real progress" it had made before man and of man's responsibility for "the achieving of true evolutionary progress in the future." "Man must not attempt to put off any of his burden of responsibility onto the shoulders of outside powers. . . . Man stands alone as the agent of

---

[37]The concept of a "world-stuff" he credits to William James. Julian Huxley, *Religion without Revelation*, new and revised ed. (New York, 1957) 190.

his fate and the trustee of progress for life." Responsible to whom? To himself one supposes. But what is "true evolutionary progress" except whatever course evolution in fact takes? Huxley's repeated suggestion that man could fail in his trust—unless he could, it is hard to see what he is responsible for—implies some standard, known or unknown, by which his decisions can be evaluated.[38]

A detailed criticism of Huxley's religious stance would hardly be profitable. His significance for this study is that he illustrates even more clearly than the previous scientific humanists a problem for all modern non-Christian humanism: humanism is continually being compromised with naturalism.[39] Modern man is aware of himself as transcendently free and responsible for his own future and even for the future of the natural world itself—at least on this planet. But at the same time he tries to understand himself as part of some order of nature which allows no explanation of his freedom. In the original biblical tradition man's relationship to the transcendent God gave a ground for his freedom and creativity while his creatureliness explained his involvement in the created world. This ground of human existence was removed with the denial of God.

The problem for freedom posed by the mechanistic world of the Enlightenment or the economic determinism of Marxism is obvious. Nationalisms have not all been concerned for freedom, but their call for commitment and devotion presupposes freedom; and yet they commonly defend the alleged superiority of their respec-

---

[38]The above summary of Huxley's Evolutionary Humanism is taken primarily from his *Essays of a Humanist* (New York, 1964), which represents his mature thought, though, in fact, his basic position had not changed much since his much earlier *Religion without Revelation*, the first edition of which was published in 1927. Some of the phrases quoted are from "Philosophy in a World at War," in Julian Huxley, *On Living in a Revolution* (New York, 1944). The reader is also referred to a brief summary of Huxley's faith in *UNESCO: Its Purpose and its Philosophy* (Washington, 1947).

[39]The people selected to illustrate scientific humanism exhibit a continuous tradition from Saint-Simon through Huxley, and they were chosen for that reason. This may have been misleading. A different selection might have better revealed the varied background of people who have found a religious faith in science. Max Otto, Erich Fromm, Phillip Frank, Richard Von Mises, B. F. Skinner come readily to mind.

tive nations by appeal to the *natural* superiority claimed for a race or a political creed.[40]

To return to scientific humanism, B. F. Skinner, a very able scientist, in his philosophical naiveté presents us with a veritable caricature of the contradiction. Athough Skinner does not think of his beliefs as a religion (this is true of most scientific humanists) they function as one in that they are for him the ultimate ground of meaning. The success of Skinner's experiments in modifying the behavior of animals by what he calls "operant conditioning" and his somewhat less success in extending this to human behavior led him to the dogmatic conclusion that all human behavior is the result of external stimuli operating on an organism the limits of which are given in its genetic structure. This is an unqualified determinism, yet Skinner is forever exhorting people to make use of this new knowledge to build a better world! Despite his determinism, Skinner shares with other Western men a sense of historical existence and of responsibility for the future which is not a mere opinion but a mode of consciousness.

Even scientific humanists with a much more sophisticated understanding of philosophy of science than Professor Skinner are caught in a dilemma. If man *finds* meaning through science, then it must be there to be found in the world the scientist investigates. If this is the case, man is reduced to a subordinate place in the cosmos and no more justified in his Promethean freedom than an ancient Greek. If any modern scientist were capable of experiencing the world in this way which is so radically different from the consciousness of modern man, he would have become a naturalist and not a humanist in the sense in which that term is used in this study. He would, furthermore, have reintroduced into science just that animism and teleology that had to be eliminated for modern science to develop. It is doubtful that this is a real possibility. If, on the other hand, man himself transcends the systems of order the scientist investigates and creates meaning by his will, then that which is of ultimate significance transcends science and is not discoverable by science. As a matter of fact, scientific humanists do lapse occasion-

---

[40]Existentialism is a special case that will be dealt with later.

ally into teleological views of the world, but they cannot live with them because only a teleology consisting of the purposes of a transcendent God or of transcendent man would be consistent with modern science and not a teleology inherent in the world itself.

Scientific humanism is far more widespread than those who have explicitly proclaimed it as a religious faith. Most of those who find in the future of science the ultimate source of meaning do not think of their position as religious at all. But such people are many in the modern world, and they are found at every level of educational achievement except the very lowest. They find a general cultural support, moreover, in many others who without deifying the scientific movement are yet optimistic about the capacity of science to solve many of the problems that perplex us. Despite misgivings about science in recent decades, scientific humanism is probably the most viable of all the humanistic faiths. Only a few of its adherents have felt any need for specifically religious cults or systems of thought; most have found adequate institutional support in the laboratory, the university, and the state. These institutions are not normally exclusive of Christians (except, of course, in Communist countries) but they are predominantly humanistic in that they avoid commitment to what is essentially and uniquely Christian. Christian and humanist can coexist in them because of considerable common ground. Scientific humanists, whether confessedly religious or not, share with other types of humanists previously discussed and with Marxism, which will be considered presently, a tendency to look for social salvation through political power. Scientific humanists anticipate a day when politics as presently practiced will be replaced by state planning on the basis of scientific knowledge.

It is important to note that the deepest roots of scientific humanism are not in what science has already achieved, but in the modern faith in man as responsible for his own destiny. The fact is that modern Western man insofar as he is atheist by his will or his cultural conditioning has little choice. He is as incurably religious as man has ever been, and the only alternative to God or man as the object of worship would be the cosmos in some form. But efforts to revive a sense of the sacredness of nature have not been successful. "The disenchantment of the world" in the biblical tradition is reinforced by its incorporation into the assumptions of modern science. Modes of consciousness are not easily changed; and religions are not born out of scholarly nostalgia for cultures of a by-gone era. As has been pointed out, modern humanism in general is continually being compromised by efforts to understand man as a part of nature; but naturalism remains nothing but a cultural nostalgia even when it is grafted on to a viable humanistic faith. The faith of the scientific humanist is in science as a historical human enterprise.

F. A. Hayek noted in his *Counter-Revolution of Science* that positivists and Hegelians in the nineteenth century came to similar historicist understandings of the human situation. The reason, of course, is that both were grounded in a faith in man as transcendently free to work out his destiny, and yet both inconsistently sought to secure that destiny by grounding it in a deterministic historicism. Prior to the ascendancy of Marx to the leadership of the socialist movement, several attempts to fuse positivism with Hegelianism were a major influence on his thought.[41] The most interesting of these from the point of view of the present study was that of Ludwig Feuerbach. Feuerbach's *Das Wesen des Christentums (The Essence of Christianity)* was published in 1841 just a few months before Comte completed the publication of his *Cours de philosophie positive*. The book was an immediate sensation. Feuerbach was a left-wing Hegelian who moved from the master's idealism to a more naturalistic approach, but Hegelian patterns still guided his thought. How close his highly speculative explanation of religion came to Comte's humanism was noted at the time. Lubac says Bakunin "marvelled at the agreement between those 'two great minds', though 'they never had heard of each other.' "[42]

The basic concept of Feuerbach was that mankind has infinite perfections, but that the individual man, though dimly aware of these perfections, did not realize them in himself. In order to become more clearly conscious of human qualities like wisdom, justice, will, and love man projected them onto fictitious gods in

---

[41]Hayek, *Counter Revolution*, "Part Three; Comte and Hegel," 189-206.

[42]Lubac, *Drama*, 12.

whom they could exist perfectly. As religions developed and more human virtues were imputed to God or gods, man himself was depleted of these virtues and experienced the depletion as guilt. The culmination of this process was Christianity, which was the highest of all religions and also the worst because in it God was most exalted and man most denigrated. Feuerbach does not denounce Christianity or previous religions; they were a necessary step in the development of human consciousness. That stage, however, had run its course in Christianity and it was now time to reverse the process. Man must take back into himself the human perfections he had alienated to God. This would be accomplished by substituting the species, Humanity, for the fictitious God. The deification of mankind had never been more explicitly affirmed.

Feuerbach's speculations made no significant contribution to the history of religion; but his deification of Humanity was an idea the non-Christian West was ready for. His theory of religion was attractive to a wide variety of intellectuals—George Eliot's translation into English in 1854 is still in print—but his strongest appeal was to those who were drawn to Hegelianism on the one hand and positivism on the other. Of these the most important was Karl Marx. Marx was high in his praise of Feuerbach, and there is no doubt that Feuerbach furnished the historical basis for his own religious theory; but he had some adverse criticisms too. Marx found Feuerbach too much the philosopher and not enough a sociologist. Marx was more hostile to religion as such and emphasized how it reflected the evils of society and was used as an instrument of exploitation.[43]

Marx was not interested in founding any abstract Religion of Humanity, or for that matter any religion at all; and yet Marxism itself as a social theory and a practical program of social reform became a humanistic faith. Roland Stromberg says of Marx: "He was the founder not, as he thought, of the social sciences but of the greatest religious movement of modern times."[44] Marxism is much more clearly defined than scientific humanism and its devotees are

---

[43]Ibid., 14-15.

[44]Stromberg, *Intellectual History*, 345.

more easily identified. Furthermore, its institutionalization in many Communist parties and states and in a world Communist movement gives it a better focus and a more direct political aim and influence than scientific humanism, which shares its institutions with many of other faiths.

There is neither space here nor need to analyze or criticize Marxism as a social theory or a political movement. That it functions as a religion for millions of people is also so well known as to require only that attention be called to the fact in this discussion of humanistic, secular faiths. Marxism has since World War II lost most of its appeal for intellectuals in the non-Communist part of Europe and the United States. There are exceptions, of course, but even in France and Italy where Communism has great political strength, it no longer has that aura of final truth that made it the "opium of the intellectuals" in the 1920s and 1930s.[45]

The varieties of humanism discussed up to this point have a good deal in common. Except for Feuerbach they all deify some historical community or movement. They have all attracted mass support. As religions they absolutize the object of their faith. Since this is in every case something less than the total Western tradition, they are all (except perhaps some of the utopian socialisms) possible bases for totalitarian societies which would result in cultural impoverishment by rejecting what could not be subsumed under the object of faith. This is true even though the various faiths are not necessarily mutually exclusive. Marxism in Russia has proved compatible with Russian nationalism and with scientific humanism. Yet the Russian Marxist state expends a great deal of energy in repressing significant parts of traditional Russian culture that are highly valued in the non-Communist West.

There is one form of atheistic humanism, however, that differs in important respects from those previously described; that is existentialism. Neither philosophical existentialism nor literary existentialism is necessarily religious. In fact, despite its origin in

---

[45]I borrow the phrase from Raymond Aron's book *The Opium of the Intellectuals*, trans. Terence Kilmartin (New York, 1962). Actually M. Aron is concerned with the post-World War II era, when the intellectual appeal of Marxism was still strong in France.

religious concerns, existentialism has probably been a religious faith for only a very small elite. The popular faddism of the 1950s and 1960s was not genuinely religious. Even in serious literary works existentialist influence has not been necessarily religious. Nevertheless, despite the fact that it has touched deeply only a comparatively few people, atheistic existentialism is preeminently important in the present study. It is important because of the persistence and clarity with which it has explored the situation of modern man without God.

It should be admitted to begin with that there is some danger in generalizing about existentialism; in fact, the term itself may be somewhat suspect. Jean-Paul Sartre in 1944 was the first self-confessed existentialist. He adopted the term from his critics and applied it retroactively to his own writings and to those of his predecessors.[46] The term has become a part of the languages of the West and is commonly applied to Kierkegaard, Nietzsche, Heidegger, Jaspers, Marcel, Sartre, Camus, and others.

There are several "lines of descent" by which twentieth-century existentialism can be put in historical perspective. The prometheanism of the atheistic existentialists obviously has something in common with romanticism, but the mood is less heroic, more inclined to pessimism and despair. Many of the existentialists have recognized this affinity with the nineteenth-century romantics, especially with that gloomier side of romanticism described and illustrated in Mario Praz's *Romantic Agony*. Even Kierkegaard, though not promethean in his stance, has something in common with the Romantics.[47]

In the history of philosophy proper there is a philosophy of subjectivity that runs from Descartes through Kant, Hegel, and Husserl to Heidegger. Paradoxically Heidegger denied that he had any concern with the subjective but his analysis is an effort to describe objectively the subjective human experience of "being in the

---

[46]Herbert Spiegelberg, "Husserl's Phenomenology and Existentialism," *Journal of Philosophy* 57 (1960): 64.

[47]William Ernest Henley's familiar poem, *Invictus*, though written late in the nineteenth century, expresses some of the ideas of existentialists, but from the more optimistic, heroic stance of earlier romantics.

world" and his philosophy is a development out of Husserl's phenomenology. Heidegger set out to discover a rigorous ontology, but
he was never able to get from the human reality to Being itself. The
second half of his projected work was never completed.

Another line of development in philosophy relates existentialism back to those late medieval thinkers who denied that the truth
of Christian faith needed to be or could be given rational demonstration. Seeing in the Christian revelation rather than in reason or
philosophy their surest grasp on reality, they suggested the possibility of a Christian philosophy founded on the implications of the
Christian understanding of God, Creation, and man.[48] This project
was never carried out. On the contrary, the empiricism and skeptical criticism of late medieval scholarship resulted during the next
two hundred years in a separation of philosophy and theology into
related but distinct traditions. In the Middle Ages the philosophers
were also the theologians, but later theologians whether orthodox
Catholics, heretics like Wyclif and Hus, or Protestants have little
place in the history of philosophy. There were no major figures in
philosophy during the Renaissance, and beginning with Descartes
philosophy has been largely in the hands of laymen. Until the eighteenth century, however, philosophers leaned heavily on theistic
assumptions. In Descartes, Hobbes, Locke, Leibniz and Bishop
Berkeley human and nonhuman realities were related to each other
through appeal to God who had arranged that mind corresponds
to the objects of empirical experience. (This formula would obviously require some qualification when applied to Berkeley; but
Berkeley's subjective idealism is saved from solipsism only by the
unifying action of God in supplying what we call empirical experience.) The skeptical implications of a thoroughly secular empiricism finally got their classic statement in Hume. Hume's skepticism
was not a disbelief in a substantive, objective world, or even a
disbelief in God, but rather a conclusion that philosophy could establish the reality of neither. Kant took Hume seriously and undertook by a critique of empirical knowledge to provide a basis for
scientific method; at the same time he sought a positive justification

---

[48]Bruno Nardi, *Studi di filosofia medievale* (Rome, 1960) 193-207.

for belief in God, immortality, and the moral law. Hegel's reaction was also an affirmation of a human reality beyond the object of empirical science. Hegel's philosophy was speculative rather than critical, and the system he constructed so absolutized a theoretical Reason as to absorb man along with God and nature into a closed rationalistic historicism. The system's emphasis on freedom and on reality as dynamic and historical made it very appealing to the romantic mind of the age; but in the long run Hegelianism was unable to deal adequately with either science or with the mode of human existence that characterized the West.

Kierkegaard and Nietzsche, the two great nineteenth-century sources of existentialism, were rebelling against both Kant and Hegel. The truths and values that Kant had sought to justify in his treatise on practical reason were not, as Kant claimed, grounded in a universal human conscience but were the historical products of Christian faith. Kierkegaard saw that these things—the existence of God, the moral law, immortality—could be preserved only by a relationship to God that was possible to man, not by rational contemplation, but only by the commitment of faith. Nietzsche saw the same fallacy in Kant, but he saw the Christian origin of Kant's values as itself a perverse thing to be left behind. The fundamental concern of Kierkegaard and Nietzsche alike was the plight of man without God. Kierkegaard sought an answer in faith and redemption by the grace of God. Nietzsche sought salvation in the will to power; since God is dead, man must be the source of meaning and value for himself. In other words, according to the definitions of this study, man must be his own God. The rejection of Hegelian rationalism in both Kierkegaard and Nietzsche was even more vehement than their rejection of Kant. The transcendently free, actual, concrete human being cannot be caught in his wholeness within any system of abstract thought, certainly not in the closed rational system of Hegel.[49]

---

[49]For a brief discussion (but fuller than can be offered here) of the relation of Kierkegaard and Nietzsche to Kant and Hegel see William Barrett's "Introduction" to "Phenomenology and Existentialism" in *Philosophy in the Twentieth Century*, ed. William Barrett and Henry D. Aiken (New York, 1962) 3:145-51; and also Barrett's *What Is Existentialism?* (New York, 1964), passim. This latter work deals primarily with Heidegger, but comments on Kierkegaard and Nietzsche.

It is not possible here to give a history of existentialism. It is hoped that the above summary of its antecedents may serve as sufficient background for an analysis that will show the place of existentialism within the conceptual framework of the present study. Particularly of interest are the religious nature of existentialism and the derivation of atheistic existentialism out of the fundamentally biblical mode of the Western experience.

Three fundamental realities have been present to the Western consciousness. The transcendent Creator God defines the other two. The created world is in the biblical tradition a contingent reality, completely dependent upon God. This is a kind of dualism between God and the world; but it avoids the problems of other ontological dualisms by the utter contingency of the world. Although the purposes of God operate in and through the created world, that world in itself has no purpose of its own and no meaning outside its relation to God. Compared to the world of the Greeks or other cosmological societies it has been "disenchanted". The third reality is man. This human reality, originally transcending the world in its relation to the transcendent God, remains, even in alienation from God, transcendently free and operates purposefully in and on the purposeless world. In the atheistic culture of modern times the disenchanted world and the human reality have remained remarkably stable. Efforts to recover a sense of the sacredness of the cosmos have been almost completely ineffectual.

The biblical tradition implied an ontology. The nominalistic world of the most influential thinkers of the fourteenth century was both real and good; and despite the pluralism implicit in nominalism the particular realities of the created world cohered in the purpose of God. The contingency of the world also had epistemological implications that introduced a critical dimension into Western philosophy. The absolute freedom of God meant that no order is binding on God, and, therefore, human knowledge of the world could not be certain. In the partially secularized philosophy of the seventeenth century the postulate of a God who guaranteed a correspondence between the human mind and the encompassing world staved off crisis. It was the thoroughly secularized empiricism of Hume that precipitated a crisis in Western thought. Hume showed that a secularized critical epistemology could produce no ontology at all; and without an ontology episte-mology was meaningless: the nature and validity of knowledge of what? Hume concluded that philosophy was useless. The development of the empirical tradition after Hume into the logical empiricism of the late nineteenth and twentieth centuries had no ontology and hence had solipsist implications. Since Hume the empirical tradition has not been able to relate sensory experience to any source outside the mind. Such a source is commonly assumed; but if such an arbitrary assumption can be called an ontology, it is an ontology outside the sphere of empirical philosophy as it has developed since Hume. Ontological assumptions that the world is there, is real, and is of worth persisted out of past tradition. These assumptions still persist and support modern scientific endeavors; but empirical epistemology has degenerated into a mere language analysis, which, divorced as it is from any supporting ontology, is a kind of "cultural solipsism" in which philosophy is confined to the mind of a culture as expressed in its language. Thus the empirical tradition is itself being thrust back into the limits of the human world; paradoxically, the tradition which spawned modern science has lost any significant relationship to it because in the absence of God it is unable to relate the other two realities that persist in the Western consciousness.

Existentialism is a much more a vigorous affirmation of the human reality. Its emphasis is on the transcendent freedom of man and the awesome responsibility for his own life that the historical existence of the individual entails. That the two great nineteenth-century fountainheads of existentialism were one a Christian and the other an atheist should not be passed over lightly as a coincidence. Both Kierkegaard and Nietzsche were concerned about the absurdity of the human situation without God in a meaningless, mysterious world. Neither finds a *place* for man in some natural order; for both the world is the disenchanted world of the biblical tradition. The effort of Nietzsche, the classical philologist, to refer his thought back to Greek sources is not convincing. Nothing like Nietzsche's philosophy existed or could have existed in the classical world. Even Nietzsche would not have had a problem with the death of God if he had been able to believe in the sacredness of the cosmos and in man as having a natural place in the cosmic order.

The cosmos he was left with after the death of God was a world without purpose or meaning of its own. Thus he was thrown back on a purely human reality for any meaning whatever. Although existentialism has not always been religious in its literary or philosophical expression and certainly not in the faddism of the post World War II decades,[50] it is instructive that the powerful impetus to it in both its modern cofounders was religious. Both of them were deeply troubled by the isolation of man in an alien world without God. Kierkegaard, though he had a very partial and inadequate understanding of the Christian faith, gave a Christian answer. Nietzsche gave the answer of an atheistic humanist who was too perceptive to accept as a surrogate for God some human historical project.

It can be argued that "Christian existentialism" is a contradictory term. It is not Christian to despair; nor is a promethean stance consistent with Christian faith. For Christians the world is not meaningless because it is informed by the benevolent purposes of God. Yet existentialists have explored more thoroughly than Christian theologians some aspects of the biblical tradition. Theologians can and have learned a great deal from atheistic existentialists concerning the radical freedom of man and the alienation he experiences when for him God is dead. Although the Christian concept of sin is meaningless to an atheist, few Christian theologians have described more strikingly than Sartre the condition of sinful man.

It is atheistic existentialism that is the uniquely modern phenomenon and consequently of greater concern for this study. The deeper the religious dimension of existentialism, the more concern there is about God. For the atheists, of course, it is the absence, or death, or non-existence of God that is significant. It is indicative of their cultural insight. Many modern secularists are simply bored with the question whether God exists. Not so Nietzsche or Sartre. When Camus wrote *The Rebel*, he was reacting against his former existentialist predisposition toward a revived Enlightenment hu-

---

[50]Professor J. S. Bixler in an address on "A Rational Faith for Our Times" tells of a student who remarked to him, "I can't tell you what satisfaction I feel in this ontological despair." See the Harvard Foundation for Advanced Study and Research *Newsletter*, 30 December 1961.

manism with some dependence on natural law, but he could not ignore the question of God. Repeatedly he resurrected God in order to blame him for the evil in the human world. To borrow a phrase used to describe another atheist: "He hated God as though He existed!"

VII THE WESTERN SENSE OF HISTORY

The term "sense of history" has been used repeatedly in this essay and the biblical origin of the modern Western sense of history pointed out. Nothing is more characteristic of modern culture—not even science or advanced technology. With the partial exception of the ancient Hebrews this sense of history is unique to the civilization of Western Europeans. It deserves, therefore, a somewhat more extended treatment than the references to it hitherto made.

All people, to be sure, exist historically; and all are to some degree aware of this. Historical change and the vicissitudes in the fortunes of individuals and societies are universal human experiences. With the exception, however, of peoples who have been fundamentally influenced by the biblical tradition, human societies have dealt with such experience by reference to some cosmic order which gives stability to life and offers relief from the awesome responsibility for the future which historical freedom imposes. As Richard R. Niebuhr once put it, man retreats from the terror of history into some nature or other.[1] The phrase "terror of history" is the title of the concluding chapter in Mircea Eliade, *Cosmos and History*. The modern sense of history has not always, or even usually, inspired terror, but that experience is real and will be discussed later.

Excellent brief statements of the biblical origin of our sense of history are given in J. H. Hexter, *The Judaeo-Christian Tradition*; Mircea Eliade, *Cosmos and History*; and Page Smith, *The Historian and History*. Fuller accounts are included in Eric Voegelin, *Israel and Revelation*, and in any number of recent theological and biblical studies.[2] The Hebrews became aware of themselves as existing under a God who transcended the world itself and who had chosen them for a special historical mission. The cosmos, far from being ultimate and sacred, had come into being by a free act of God's will and was sustained in its existence by his continuing to will it. As a continuing historical act of God nature was subsumed under history. The power and goodness of God was manifest in the natural world (the goodness of the creation is a major theme throughout the Bible), but the world was not in any way sacred in itself. How this eliminated belief in a teleology in things and opened the way for modern physics has been discussed in chapter 4. Man was not understood as merely one among other creatures but as that creature made in the image of God and transcending the rest of creation in his peculiar relationship to God.[3] In this transcendence he exercised a

---

[1]This is remembered from a lecture Professor Niebuhr delivered at Mercer University in 1959.

[2]J. H. Hexter, *The Judaeo-Christian Tradition* (New York, 1966); Mircea Eliade, *Cosmos and History: The Myth of the Eternal Return*, trans. Willard R. Trask (New York, 1959); Page Smith, *The Historian and History* (New York, 1964); Eric Voegelin, *Israel and Revelation*, vol. 1 of *Order and History* (Baton Rouge, 1956). Among biblical and theological studies, Gerhard von Rad, *Theology of the Old Testament*, trans. D. M. G. Stalker, 2 vols. (New York, 1962-1965); and Jürgen Moltmann, *Theology of Hope*, trans. James W. Leitch (New York, 1967), may be mentioned as particularly thoughtful and lucid. The works of Wolfhart Pannenberg are not as readable in English but make a major contribution to developing the insights of the biblical tradition.

[3]The role of angels in the biblical revelation is a complex one and not essential to the tradition. The word *angel* originally meant simply *messenger*. Angels were messengers of God, and sometimes, as in the story of Abraham, identified with God himself in a theophany. The prominence of angels in late Judaism and in the

creative freedom with regard to nature not conceived of in cosmological religions. This freedom and the creative possibilities that went with it constituted his historical existence. The center of reality for the Hebrews was their relationship to God in the dialectical responses of history.

Yahweh had not manifested himself in the cyclical time of cosmic myths as other gods had done. The Hebrews identified Yahweh as "he who brought us out of the land of Egypt." God had made himself known in a historical time that is irreversible and in which events are nonrecurring. It was a radical departure from the religions all around them and also from their own primitive past,[4] and the experience in its elaboration gave rise to a tradition of amazing depth and power. The doctrine of creation as we find it now in Genesis and in other parts of the Bible was a relatively late development out of the historical experience of the Hebrews. The world had a beginning and the purpose or purposes of God gave it meaning and direction toward some culmination in the future. History was a continuous, nonrecurring process. The Hebrews remembered their past as the means of orienting themselves toward the future. Gerhard von Rad points out that at every crisis in their history the Jews received a revelation that contained a judgment on them for their sins and the promise of a better future. In the light of each revelation they reinterpreted their own past.[5] This is a paradigm of the way historical events are now understood. Any event has meaning in terms of its context; but the context keeps changing as history continues. The French Revolution can never be the same since the revolutions of the nineteenth century; the context changed again with the Russian Revolution of 1917; and again with the rise of total states, and so forth. The Norman Conquest has meaning in the linguistic, religious, political history of England,

---

New Testament was due to Persian influence. If all reference to them were removed, the central themes of the Bible would hardly be affected. In any event, the place of man as the apex of creation was guaranteed by the Incarnation. Paul asserts that redeemed men are superior to angels (1 Corinthians 6:3).

[4]Mircea Eliade, *The Sacred and the Profane*, trans. Willard R. Trask (New York, 1959) 110-12.

[5]Von Rad, *Theology of the Old Testament*, 2:327-28, 358-64, 314-15, passim.

Europe, and the world, meanings of which even the most perceptive eleventh-century observer could not have been aware.

Orientation toward the future was characteristic of the Jews,
and it has become a salient quality of modern Western culture.
Other peoples have not experienced it. They have, of course,
known that changes occur, that some prosper and some lose
ground. They have had goals they were ambitious to achieve. But
by and large they have not expected the general context of such
changes and achievements to be much different from the present.
The Greeks acquired time perspective by looking back across a dark
age period to the Golden Age of Mycenaean culture; but insofar as
they had a historical perspective it was not oriented toward a future
that was expected to be different from the present. When they
thought about history in larger contexts, they gave cyclical explanations. Some Greeks and some Romans wrote excellent histories.
Their interest, however, was to penetrate beyond the vicissitudes of
history to eternal truths. The knowledge that there are vicissitudes
is universal; the question is how one deals with such knowledge.
Thucydides wrote the history of the Peloponnesian War as a lesson
to other cities. People still draw lessons from history by analogy;
but modern historians do not have such lessons as their primary
motivation to historical scholarship.[6] None of the Greek or Roman
historians undertook a serious historical inquiry into the origins of
their societies. So far as origins were concerned, the kind of truth
they were interested in was available in legends.[7] Serious inquiry
into the origins of Rome began with B. G. Niebuhr's history of
Rome, published in 1811-1832.

In recent decades there has been considerable interest in the
question whether there was a significant idea of progress in classical antiquity. A particularly strong statement of the thesis that the
idea of progress was a very significant part of the intellectual life of
the pagan Greeks and Romans was made by Ludwig Edelstein in a

---

[6]Cf. Paul Weiss, *History: Written and Lived* (Carbondale IL, 1962) 45; and Page
Smith, *The Historian and History*, 242 note.

[7]The Chinese also wrote histories, in their case for the instruction of the young
who were to rule. Their histories had the same function of moral and political instruction that legends had.

book published posthumously under the title, *The Idea of Progress in Classical Antiquity*.[8] Edelstein's work was very well received; but aside from a very thorough documentation, it is doubtful that he added a great deal to what was already understood. His contribution was a significant change in emphasis. That the Greeks and Romans were aware of improvements in technology and the arts and an increase in knowledge that many expected to continue into the future was not new. J. B. Bury, whose work, *The Idea of Progress*, is the background of the more recent controversy, was himself a classical scholar and quite aware of the kind of thing Edelstein documents at such length. He knew that the Greeks were aware of a great increase in knowledge since primitive times, and he notes that Seneca "saw clearly, and declared emphatically, that increases in knowledge must be expected in the future." The speculations of the Epicureans, he says, "might have led to the foundation of a theory of Progress, if the historical outlook of the Greeks had been larger and if their temper had been different." As it was, however, the cyclical view of time and the idea of moira so dominated Greek thought that the idea of progress could not develop.

> Moira meant a fixed order in the universe; but as a fact to which men must bow, it had enough in common with fatality to demand a philosophy of resignation and to hinder the creation of an optimistic atmosphere of hope. It was this order which kept things in their places, assigned to each its proper sphere and function, and drew a definite line, for instance, between men and gods. Human progress towards perfection—towards an ideal of omniscience, or an ideal of happiness, would have been a breaking down of the bars which divide the human from the divine. Human nature does not alter; it is fixed by Moira.[9]

The significance of Edelstein's work was to call attention to the fact that whatever the context in which they saw it, the ancients' awareness of progress did actually affect what they did. His treat-

---

[8]Ludwig Edelstein, *The Idea of Progress in Classical Antiquity* (Baltimore, 1967).

[9]J. B. Bury, *The Idea of Progress: An Inquiry into its Origin and Growth* (New York, 1932, 1920¹) 7-20. John Baillie in his *The Belief in Progress* (New York, 1950) is in substantial agreement with Bury so far as the Greeks are concerned.

ment of Hellenistic science is especially interesting in this regard. In this connection, however, it is worth noting that Hellenistic science itself made little progress after the second century B.C. One reason for this is surely an epistemology that thought of truth as eternal and unchanging and hence stood in the way of radical criticism of knowledge already accepted. The laws of motion as Aristotle had understood them long stood in the way of the development of physics despite significant empirical evidence against them. This matter is not irrelevant to the question whether the Greeks anticipated the modern conception of progress.

In a brief review of Edelstein's book in the *Review of Metaphysics* Edward A. Reno, Jr., recognizes the value of Edelstein's erudition in calling attention to the widespread interest of classical antiquity in the idea of progress; but he points out that he had fallen short of his purpose to discredit the traditional "antithesis between the pagan, cyclical notion of time and the Christian, linear and progressive notion of time." The weakness of Edelstein's work, according to Reno, was his failure to relate "the notion of progress to the notion of historical time."

> . . . when we go in search of the wider context, the conviction persists that the repeated forms and instances of progressivism in antiquity strain at but do not break free from the hegemony of *moira* and eternal return—even though it be not eternal return of the same.[10]

However one may differ from Edelstein's conclusions, his scholarly integrity is never in doubt. In the midst of a discussion of Seneca's emphasis on progress he notes:

> Seneca remains equally undisturbed by the prospect of the annihilation of the world and all the progress it has seen. This end, he believes, has been prepared from the beginning (*Naturales Quaestiones*, III, 30, 1) and cannot be far off. . . . Not after a period of decay but in its full flowering the world will be destroyed. and there will

---

[10]Edward A. Reno, Jr., Review of *The Idea of Progress in Classical Antiquity* by Ludwig Edelstein, *Review of Metaphysics* 21 (1968): 748.

arise another destined to witness the same greatness and the same doom.[11]

The major weakness of Bury's study is not his interpretation of Greek thought, which is substantially correct, but his failure to recognize the fundamental contributions of the biblical-Christian tradition to the modern idea of progress. This is partly due to his having defined the idea of progress so narrowly. A part of his definition is as follows:

> The idea of human Progress . . . is based on an interpretation of history . . . as slowly advancing . . . in a definite and desirable direction, and infers that this progress will continue indefinitely. And it implies that, as "The issue of the earth's great business," a condition of general happiness will ultimately be enjoyed, which will justify the whole process of civilization; for otherwise the direction would not be desirable. There is also a further implication. The process must be the necessary outcome of the psychical and social nature of man; it must not be at the mercy of any external will; otherwise there would be no guarantee of its continuance and its issue, and the idea of Progress would lapse into the idea of Providence.
>
> As time is the very condition of the possibility of Progress, it is obvious that the idea would be valueless if there were any cogent reasons for supposing that the time at the disposal of humanity is likely to reach a limit in the near future.[12]

According to this no informed Christian or Jew (in the religious sense) could believe in progress. In recent times, he allowed, some have believed in both Providence and progress, "but the fundamental assumptions were incongruous, and so long as the doctrine of Providence was undisputedly in the ascendant, a doctrine of Progress could not arise."[13] Moreover, Bury identified the idea of progress with rationalism and belief in natural law as a closed system that guaranteed the human future: "The process must be the

---

[11]Edelstein, *The Idea of Progress*, 172-73.

[12]Bury, *The Idea of Progress*, 5.

[13]Ibid., 21-22.

necessary outcome of the . . . nature of man."[14] The assumption that belief in Providence would make the future too uncertain to be consistent with a belief in progress is not tenable. There is a sense, of course, in which the absolute freedom of God makes knowledge of the future unpredictable; but for fervent Christians the psychological certainly produced by trust in the free and sovereign God to keep his promises of a perfect blessedness in community is unsurpassed by the certainty of those who believe in deterministic naturalism

The restrictions implicit in Bury's definition are hardly consistent with the pervasiveness of belief in progress in the modern world. Many have believed progress likely, even highly probable, who have thought it depended on human decisions. Indeed, Bury to the contrary notwithstanding, voluntarism is more fundamental to the idea of progress than rationalism—certainly more so than a deterministic rationalism.

Bury does note that Christian Europe made some contribution to the background of progress; but he devotes a very few pages to it. It was important, he points out, that the Middle Ages definitely abandoned the Greek cyclical concept of history. Even more important in his view was the fact that Christian theology had for the first time given a distinct meaning to the course of human events as a whole and saw it as leading to a desirable goal in the future. He treats the idea of the human race as one—the *ecumene*—as a separate contribution and sees it as something Christianity took over from the Greeks and Romans. There is no indication he is aware of the universal dimension of biblical religion in both Old and New Testaments. As early as the tradition of God's covenant with Abraham, God's promise concludes: "and in thee shall all families of the earth be blessed" (Genesis 12:3, KJV). Many passages could be cited showing the universality of God's sovereignty over human history. Among the most striking from the Old Testament are Amos 9:7 and Isaiah 19:23-25; 45:20-23; 49:6; 56:7. The whole discussion in

---

[14]The emphasis on rationalism is throughout the book and could hardly be put more forcefully than in the last sentence before the "Epilogue."

Bury, most of which is devoted to Greeks and Romans, takes less than three pages.[15]

The biblical orientation toward the future deserves much more consideration. The seven cardinal virtues were divided by medieval men into four natural virtues, which they took from classical antiquity, and three theological virtues known through the Christian revelation. The latter were faith, hope, and charity. It is interesting that the theological virtues were considered peculiar to the biblical-Christian tradition and not accessible to the Greeks by natural reason. Hope has been a major ingredient in Christian faith from the beginning.[16] And the hopeful attitude toward the future has not been confined to the afterlife. Until the post-exilic period the Jews did not believe in any afterlife except that of "shades"; but they were oriented hopefully toward the future. Christian eschatology, or the doctrine of last things, has always had a dual character. Christians look to a personal life in community after death; but they also participate in a meaningful historical process over which God is sovereign and which will continue after they are gone. At times when the immediate situation seemed hopeless, as in times of severe persecution, the hope became apocalyptic as it had from time to time among the ancient Jews. More often, however, it was a hope of improvement in the ordinary processes of history guaranteed by the promises of a benevolent and sovereign God who would see to it that history would culminate in a perfect society. Christ taught his disciples to pray "Thy kingdom come. Thy will be done, On earth as it is in heaven" (Matthew 6:10). In one of his parables he likened his kingdom to a grain of mustard seed that would grow into a great tree. And in another he said it was like leaven that would leaven three loaves. In other parables, however, he indicated clearly that at the end of "the age" there would be a judgment in which the good would be separated from the wicked (Matthew 13). The implication of this would be that the historical process would

---

[15]Ibid., 22-24. Cf. C. A. Patriades, *The Grand Design of God* (London, Toronto, 1972) 4-9, 126: "Always implicit within the Christian view of history, the idea of progress was now [early Enlightenment] secularized."

[16]The three theological virtues are mentioned together by the apostle Paul in 1 Corinthians 13.

not improve indefinitely. With varying emphases all of these ideas have been incorporated into Christian views of history. Christian eschatology has been complex and confused and there has been no consensus about it; but there is agreement that God is sovereign over the whole historical process and will in the end bring good out of it.

At first the historical mission of the church was largely confined to spreading the good news and making converts. There was little interest in the reform of secular institutions. Social evils were considered to be an obvious result of sin; and in the first few generations the end of history was expected so soon that social reform could hardly have occurred to the Christians. Perhaps equally important was the fact that the political influence needed for such reforms was not available to Christians. With the formal conversion of the Empire, however, the situation was radically different. Eusebius in his *Ecclesiastical History* presents a universal history based upon his interpretation of both Old and New Testaments. He was so enthusiastic about the triumph of Christianity in the Roman Empire that he saw Constantine as a new Moses; and he was so convinced that the promises of God had been fulfilled that he did not think much about the future. His understanding of history had no eschatology.[17] His view of God's purpose in history did, however, introduce into Christian historiography the principle of progress.[18]

Almost a century later when the Empire was reeling under German invasions, Augustine gave a very different interpretation. God had used Rome and might use Rome still as he had other great empires in the past, but Augustine is much more cautious about incorporating the Empire into *Heilsgeschichte*. He does not pretend to know the future of Rome. In his doctrine of the two cities, however, Rome is definitely a part of or an instance of the earthly city. The City of God, which is the ultimate meaning of history, is not to be identified with Rome. On the other hand, the earthly city is at once

---

[17]Patriades, *The Grand Design*, 16.

[18]The element of progress in Eusebius is emphasized by Robert W. Hanning, who cites in support of his interpretation Mommsen, D. S. Wallace-Hadrill, and Norman Cantor. *The Vision of History in Early Britain* (New York, London, 1966) 23-32.

a gift of God and a creation of sinful human wills. As a gift of God it is to be accepted as good, a good relative to the sinful human condition. Like any individual man who is good as a creature of God, but marred throughout by sin, the earthly city was sinful to its very foundation and was not redeemable by any efforts of social reform.

With this as his background Augustine does not put limits on what God may do in history. Human history he divided into epochs corresponding to the days of the week. The sixth day began with the birth of Christ and would continue for a time known only to God. This period of indefinite length Augustine identified with the biblical thousand years in which Christ would reign with his saints. (The thousand years, he said, should be understood figuratively, not literally.) At the end of this period there would be a brief period, three and a half years, of conflict with Antichrist followed by a general resurrection and judgment. The end of history would be a seventh day, a Sabbath, of "full, certain, secure felicity." Although Augustine calls the seventh day a "perpetual Sabbath," at the end of the last book of *The City of God* he writes "suffice it to say that the seventh shall be our Sabbath, which shall be brought to a close, not by an evening, but by the Lord's day [a reference, perhaps, to the Christian Sunday, which is the day upon which Christ arose], as an eighth and eternal day, consecrated by the resurrection of Christ, and prefiguring the eternal response not only of the spirit, but also of the body. There we shall rest and see, see and love, love and praise."[19]

Augustine's treatment of the seven epochs followed by the eternal eighth is so brief that interpretation of it is hazardous. He was certainly aware of the kind of progress in arts, techniques, and knowledge that some of the Greeks had recognized. He cited such as an example of the graciousness of God and the goodness of the creation. These increased human resources, however, could be used for evil as well as for good. He recognized that pagans could achieve very great virtues, but since they were achieved in independence of God, they were virtues only relative to our sinful state and not "true" virtues at all. There is no reason to think Augustine

---

[19]Saint Augustine, *The City of God*, trans. Marcus Dods (New York, 1950) 725-28, 730-32, 846-47.

expected any moral improvement in the earthly city. The true meaning of history was in the development of the City of God, and that was largely a matter of recruiting the elect. In Augustine's own day, however, there were impressive assertions of a Christian belief in historical progress. In the dispute between pagans and Christians over the altar of Victory in the Roman Senate the pagan Symmachus argued that the rights of ancestors ought to be respected. Ambrose replied, "Why should we do so? Has not everything made advances in the course of time toward what is better." In two memoranda addressed to the emperor, Ambrose "made it clear that he shared the current belief that Christianity was a progressive factor in history."[20] As the argument continued, Prudentius (c. 403) presented the Christian side in a poem entitled *Against Symmachus*, which T. E. Mommsen calls "the greatest poetical expression the Christian idea of progress ever found in early Western Christendom."[21]

Augustine's theology dominated the Middle Ages and the Renaissance and Reformation; but as Robert Hanning has pointed out, medieval historiography followed the example of Eusebius. The lacuna between the two may be part of the explanation for the failure of Christian thought for so long to develop its sense of history into a continuously developing historical scholarship. Nevertheless many elements in the thought of Augustine laid a foundation for the secular conception of progress in the Enlightenment and the development of historical scholarship in the nineteenth century and since.

It is important to remember that the idea of progress is only one aspect of the uniquely Western sense of history. The too simple conception of progress whose history Bury traced and which Robert A. Nisbet credits with virtually all human creativity—at least in the West[22]—has been seriously called into question by some of the most sensitive minds in the modern West, and, indeed, by events

---

[20]T. E. Mommsen, "St. Augustine and the Christian Idea of Progress: The Background of *The City of God*", *Journal of the History of Ideas* 12 (1951): 366-67.

[21]Ibid., 367.

[22]Robert Nisbet, *History of the Idea of Progress* (New York, 1980) 8-9.

themselves. It needs to be radically modified, and the most promising modifications come also out of the biblical tradition. Skepticism about progress as well as the idea of progress itself is an expression of our sense of history. Oriented toward the future we are aware of opportunities for the improvement of the human condition; eighteenth-century philosophes were optimistic about indefinite improvement. At the same time we know that the future will be created by our historical decisions and actions. We are responsible, and the difficulty of the problems facing us sometimes overwhelms us. Just when scientific advances were giving promise of a greater control over our natural environment than previous ages dreamed of, problems of human origin, products of that historical process that had been expected to bring progress, have loomed up before us, and we have not found solutions. Some of the problems were unexpected until they were upon us. World wars have occurred and another threatens. Horrible totalitarian tyrannies have arisen in advanced nations. Marxian communism, which many in the West looked to for the elimination of social injustice, has instead produced the most enduring, at least to this point, of such tyrannies. While most countries were still proud of their growth, it became almost suddenly apparent that overpopulation is the most serious and intractable problem faced by the human race. Resources are being consumed at an unprecedented rate, and there are more hungry people in the world than in any previous age. Many fear that atomic power may, because of human historical decisions, be a curse rather than a blessing.

Yet science continues to advance. The production of economic goods is at an all time high. Our concern for social justice is real even if adulterated with self-serving motives, and it makes some progress. Is it any wonder that modern man vacillates between optimism and despair? The culture as a whole has not learned to live comfortably with the sense of historical existence which has been sharpened and intensified by its secularization in the eighteenth century. In this situation Christians have the advantage of a ballast that can prevent such wide fluctuations between hope and despair. Reinhold Niebuhr declared in 1942 "The errors and illusions of our culture . . . are, almost without exception, . . . expressions of too great an optimism about the goodness of human nature."[23] In 1942 this was a better generalization than it would be today when the number of nay-sayers has greatly increased. Niebuhr himself, of course, had an antidote for too optimistic an opinion of human nature in his understanding of sin. The swing of the pendulum in the other direction Niebuhr was not much worried about, but as a Christian theologian he had the antidote for that too in his belief in the sovereignty of God over history and nature. If for many the idea of Providence had an inhibiting effect on the development of the idea of human progress, it also precluded the despair that from time to time has overtaken modern secular man. Despair for a Christian would be a denial of his faith. The biblical sense of history is the source of both optimism and pessimism about human history, but within the context of the tradition as a whole they are held within limits not provided by secular humanism.

An analysis of the Western sense of history reveals three aspects of it that are especially pertinent to this study: a linear, unidirectional sense of time; voluntarism, an emphasis on will and purpose as creative of novelty; and a faith in God's sovereign control over both nature and history. The last, of course, does not carry over into secular or atheistic experience of historical existence; but the first two are shared by Christian and secular humanist.

The linear view of time gave to history a significance it could not have in the cyclical contexts of classical culture. Events were not only unique; they shaped a novel future. The leaders of the ancient church, immersed as they were in Greco-Roman culture, were tempted to cyclical conceptions, but the uniqueness and unrepeatability of the Incarnation, Crucifixion, and Resurrection of Christ were an absolute barrier to a cyclical ontology.[24] Christian interest in history was focused on the Christ event and the early history of the church. It is interesting how much of the New Testament is history in some obvious sense; the Gospels, the Book of Acts, and considerable parts of the epistles. The further development of history in the early centuries was inhibited by belief in the imminent return

---

[23]"A Faith for History's Greatest Crisis", *Fortune* 26 (July 1942): 99-100, 122-31.

[24]Patriades, *The Grand Design*, 13-14.

of Christ. As this expectation receded from the foreground of Christian consciousness, the attention of the intellectual leaders of the church was overwhelmingly concerned with theological problems, especially those that led eventually to the formulation of the Nicaean doctrine of the Trinity.

As was noted earlier it was the conversion of Constantine that brought ecclesiastical and secular interests together and stimulated Eusebius to write the first universal history from a Christian point of view. By the time of Augustine a century later the situation did not look so promising. Although Augustine had a very highly developed sense of history—his great *City of God* is essentially a theology of history—he attached much less significance to Roman civilization than Eusebius had done. Robert Hanning says that insofar as the combination of sacred and secular history was concerned Augustine's work was "the negation" of Eusebius.[25] Despite Augustine's domination of medieval thought generally, however, it was Eusebius who prevailed in medieval historiography. Even Augustine's disciple Orosius in his immensely influential *History Against the Pagans* is more like Eusebius than his master and presents Rome and her empire as monuments to God's sovereignty over history.

It is not possible here to trace even in abbreviated form the history of historiography in Western Europe. Attention must be restricted to certain problems and results. One such problem is why history in this historically-minded culture should have been so slow developing into a serious discipline pursued cumulatively by professional historians in schools and universities. There is truth in the conception that the modern Age of History began with Friedrich A. Wolf's *Prolegomena* to Homer in 1795 and B. G. Niebuhr's three-volume history of Rome in the early nineteenth century. This, however, plus the negative attitude toward history that characterized the immediately preceding period of Enlightenment, has often obscured the very great interest in history and the impressive output of historical writing in Europe from the very early Middle Ages on. Considering the general condition of society the amount and

---

[25]Hanning, *The Vision of History*, 33.

variety of early medieval historical writing is astounding. Although the range of quality in these histories is very great, taken as a whole they evidence a sense of historical existence that cannot be denied; and the best of them are very good indeed. Compared to the long, complex histories of various Germanic peoples—Goths, Lombards, Franks, Anglo-Saxons—Einhard set for himself a simple task in his *Life of the Emperor Charles*, yet it compares quite favorably with the biographies of Suetonius that he took as a model. Beryl Smalley in her *Historians in the Middle Ages* also credits Adam of Bremen, Jocelyn of Brakelonde, William of Malmesbury, and William of Tyre with having surpassed Suetonius in the portrayal of character.[26]

The histories of peoples, families, reigns, wars, and crusades vary greatly in quality, but they have a linear sense of time and an interest in origins and development that put them closer in approach to modern historians than to the great pagan histories of Greece and Rome. In this regard as in others Bede is outstanding. His linear sense of history that pushed his research back to the continental origin of the pagan Angles and Saxons, his critical use of sources, his care to indicate what his sources are have all been duly praised. Also it is noteworthy that it was the wide influence of Bede's work that established the method of dating events backward and forward from the birth of Christ.[27]

If the British and Carolingian revivals of learning had been able to continue, there might have developed in Europe an intellectual culture around the biblical-Christian sense of history, but the destructive raids of the Vikings cut it short. When the Viking disruption was over, history like the rest of the culture revived; and historiography advanced in the period of the early Crusades. History was not, however, the most exciting part of scholarly life. The sudden vigor with which the highest levels of theological and philosophical thought emerged in the period beginning with Anslem is one of the most astonishing phenomena in intellectual history. The

---

[26]Beryl Smalley, *Historians in the Middle Ages* (London, 1974) 188.

[27]A Scythian monk living in Rome invented this scheme of dating in 525. It caught on slowly and was common in Spain in the last half of the seventh century; but Bede was the first influential authority to use it. It was not adopted at the Vatican until 963. Patriades, *The Grand Design*, 21.

method of the new learning was based in Aristotelian logic as learning had never been before. With its assumption that reality is governed by unchanging laws, Aristotelian logic is not congenial to historical interest. Historiography, nevertheless, held its own until the rest of Aristotle's logic and those of his other works that are now known became available to European scholars in the late twelfth century. The ensuing crisis in European thought turned attention away from history. Beryl Smalley says of the historians of the thirteenth century: "These writers are shallow compared with William of Malmesbury, Otto of Freising or William of Tyre."[28]

Historiography revived in the fourteenth century and was actively pursued in the Renaissance. History was one of the five disciplines (along with grammar, rhetoric, poetry, and moral philosophy) that were included in "the humanities." The voluntarist, activist anthropology of the Renaissance was an aspect of the Christian sense of historical existence, and with that as a basis Renaissance historiography might have had a much more creative development if Renaissance historians had not been even more inclined than their medieval predecessors to follow classical models. Even so history made real progress. The linguistic scholarship of the period introduced new techniques in historical method. The most famous examples are Lorenzo Valla's proofs that the Donation of Constantine was a forgery and that the apostles could not have written the Apostles' Creed in the form received. The method itself was utilizing a knowledge of the history of language and other historical information.

The development of better critical methods of analysis continued on into the nineteenth-century Age of History despite the skeptical attitude toward history in the Enlightenment. Jean Bodin wrote the first treatise on modern historical method (1566) and the monks of St. Maur developed the practice. Their work is a landmark in the history of historiography.[29] The Reformation also stimulated historical criticism as both Catholics and Protestants

---

[28]Smalley, *Historians in the Middle Ages*, 191. See also 179-81. Cf. A. G. Molland, "Medieval Ideas of Scientific Progress", *Journal of the History of Ideas* 39 (1978): 563.

[29]Edward Gordon Simmons, *Histoire générale de languedoc: A Study of Maurist Historiography*, an unpublished dissertation at Vanderbilt University.

undertook to justify their historical claims and discredit their opponents.

The Enlightenment was contemptuous of tradition and generally skeptical of the validity of historical knowledge; yet it was extremely significant in the history of the modern sense of history. Its critical and cosmopolitan spirit was a major contribution, and even more its secularizing of the Western sense of history.

Christian belief in the purposeful providence of God in history moving toward the eventual redemption and perfection of man had been restrained by a sense of human sin, which prevented undue optimism about the immediate future and made God, not man, the chief agent of improvement. Deism denied the sinfulness of man, at least it denied that what was bad in man was too fundamental to be dealt with by human reason, and thus removed the chief inhibition to the development of the progressiveness inherent in linear time and the ultimate optimism of the biblical faith. The mechanistic world order which the deists affirmed was not consistent with the free historical action of either God or man; and the deists did, indeed, deny providence, but they made an exception of man. The overwhelming majority of the philosophes still considered man free to follow reason—which it was his nature to do—or unnaturally to deviate from it. Deists were, of course, a minority in Europe; but these aspects of their thought were widely believed by professing Christians, especially among those whose intellectual leadership was shaping the Western mind.

The secularizing of history was ultimately to stimulate historical scholarship; immediately, however, the Enlightenment provided its own inhibitions to such scholarship. History did not provide the "clear and distinct ideas" Descartes had insisted on; nor was the knowledge it offered empirically verifiable. The success of the new physics not only contributed to this skepticism by its emphasis on empirical verification but its metaphysical influence was an even greater obstacle to historical interest. The success of Newtonian physics was so impressive that the hypothetical nature of all knowledge of the world, which had been so important a principle in the origins of modern science, was eclipsed by the conviction that at last the truth was known. There was a tendency not only to absolutize mechanistic physics but to extend mechanism to the whole of reality as a metaphysics not recognized as such. A mechanistic metaphysics of eternal laws had implications of an underlying reality as changeless as the cosmos of the ancient Greeks. The Enlightened found very congenial the Greek attitude toward history as "philosophy teaching by example."[30] Hume, who wrote an excellent *History of England* and who understood the inadequacy of the current mechanistic metaphysics, might have been expected to escape such an anti-historical concept; but he said in his *Inquiry*:

> Mankind are so much the same, in all times and places, that history informs us of nothing new or strange in this particular. Its chief use is only to discover the constant and universal principles of human nature by showing men in all varieties of circumstances and situations. . . . [31]

Mechanism has kept its hold on the Western imagination and still functions as a metaphysics even though it has no ground in either recent science or philosophy. But there have been significant revolts against it; and with the important exception of scientific advances in directions not anticipated in the Enlightenment they have been recoveries of some aspects of the Western sense of history. The first of these was the development of a new pattern of explanation in the Romantic revolt against the Enlightenment. For mechanists the favorite pattern of explanation had been analysis into components or causes and effects and rational reconstruction. The new pattern explained things in terms of how they came to be that way, their development or evolution in time. The Greeks and Romans had been content with legends and myths to explain their origins that the historians of the nineteenth century could not accept. The Bible, although so largely a book of history itself, had been understood by a variety of hermeneutical devices with little concern about the history of its composition.[32] The nineteenth-cen-

---

[30]The phrase is the subtitle of a chapter on history in Carl Becker's *The Heavenly City of the Eighteenth-Century Philosophers* (New Haven, 1932).

[31]David Hume, *An Inquiry Concerning Human Understanding*, ed. Charles W. Hendel (New York, 1955), 93.

[32]Except, of course, for a concern to know which of early Christian writings were by the apostles.

tury "higher critics" of the Bible did not think they could understand a book until they had discovered its date, its authorship, and
its composition. If it was a composite work, of course, other problems of date and authorship were involved. Various linguistic and
historical techniques were needed, but higher criticism of the Bible
was essentially historical scholarship.

The new pattern of explanation had its influence in science also,
and it may yet be the source of a scientific revolution. Certainly at
this point the implications of a conception of time as linear and not
reversible, leading into a future of novelties, have not yet been fully
explored. The concept, however, has already had a major impact.
In the early nineteenth century geology became a rationally organized science by means of the concept of an earth's crust developing through various stages in a chronological sequence.[33] The same
can be said of that branch of biology that deals with the differentiation of species. Although it now seems incredible, Thomas Jefferson did not think the extinction of a species possible. Since the
bones of mastodons had been discovered in North America, Jefferson was sure that members of the species were still to be found.
That was eighteenth-century thinking of a "plenary universe" in
which everything needed for its completeness was provided. It
was, in other words, an essentially static universe. Yet even before
Jefferson died in 1826, the idea that the variety of species had been
produced by an evolutionary process had been advanced, and half
a century later Darwin's theory was gaining acceptance in the scientific community. One could go on to mention the influence of the
pattern of development in time on cosmological speculation: the origin of the solar system, the natural history of stars and galaxies,
the expanding universe, the big bang theory. If the Greeks had had
the data of Sir Charles Lyell or Darwin, it is very unlikely they
would have constructed evolutionary explanations of it; their mind-
set would not have oriented them in that direction.

The scientific examples are common knowledge to anyone
whose reading has taken him as far as *The Reader's Digest*; the influ-

---

[33]Charles Coulston Gillispie, *Genesis and Geology* (New York, 1959). This book is
naive in its treatment of theological and philosophical issues, but as a useful narrative it has won its place in most relevant bibliographies.

ence of historical patterns of explanation on philosophy is less well known, but in some respects more interesting. Scientists are aware that novelties occur—the evolution of higher species of animals is, perhaps, the most obvious example—but the uncritical assumption of a mechanistic metaphysics leads them to reductionist explanations in terms of so-called "laws of nature," which are assumed to be eternal. Only a few sophisticated people have been much bothered by the fact that the laws are generalizations or constructs of the human mind from its limited sensory data. The "laws of nature" are, indeed, changing with the advance of science.[34] Philosophers have been more aware of the fallacy of mechanistic assumptions and some of them have developed process philosophies that conceive reality itself as changing fundamentally in some teleological direction. Of these Hegel, through his relationship to the wider movement of German idealism, has probably been the most influential. Henri Bergson and Alfred North Whitehead are easier for a twentieth-century reader and more palatable; but none of the process philosophers can be said to have a wide following today. Two reasons for this may be advanced. One is the hold of mechanism on the Western imagination; and another is the preoccupation of modern philosophy with epistemology and its deep and general suspicion of metaphysical speculation. Process philosophies are, nevertheless, of significance to this study because they are so obviously, if unconsciously, developments of an important facet of the biblical-Christian intellectual tradition. Their conception of time as linear and not cyclical as well as their understanding of the most fundamental reality as a teleologically directed but nonrecurring process would have been most unlikely in a culture not shaped by biblical influences. They are, in short, products of the uniquely biblical and Western sense of history.

Process philosophy, and this is especially evident in Whitehead, is also an attempt to develop an ontology that would provide a

---

[34]Einstein is an interesting example of a very eminent scientist whose own work contributed to the undermining of the mechanistic world view but who was very uncomfortable with the still more radical implications of quantum physics. There are many others, including some of the significant figures in the development of quantum mechanics. See, for example, P. A. M. Dirac, "The Physicist's Picture of Nature," *Scientific American* 208 (1963): 47-48.

ground for human experience in a meaningful cosmos. If the attempt had succeeded, there would be an alternative to Christianity
and non-Christian humanism; but the attempt did not succeed.

If neither God nor the cosmos is experienced as a source of
meaning, the modern humanist has only the human reality to re-
sort to. Man must deify himself as the ultimate source of meaning.
This is what has brought about what Karl Löwith refers to as "the
boundless intensity of modern history."[35] It is boundless because it
is no longer limited by God or nature. Secularization has intensified man's sense of historical existence. The modern sense of history is the very essence of modern humanism. As discussed in
chapter 6, it takes two forms: various historicisms on the one hand
and existentialism on the other.[36] The historicisms find in history a
substitute for nature. The individual can thus find in the deified
historical process a place to retreat from the terror of history. The
existentialists face the godless, meaningless world more boldly. The
individual must create his own values by his own will and historical
decision and action. In existentialism the Western sense of history
finds its most extreme atheistic expression. Paradoxically, this extreme interpretation of historical existence may nullify history itself. If each individual is nothing but what he makes himself, as
Sartre has asserted, if there is complete discontinuity between individuals, or alternately, if the only possible relationship between
humans is conflict, then there can be no common humanity and no
history.[37]

Not all who can be called existentialists have reached this conclusion. The existentialism of Ortega y Gasset, who was much influenced by Dilthey, was less individualistic. Man, he said, does not
have a nature but a history. This lack of nature, he thought, gives

---

[35]Karl Löwith, *Nature, History, and Existentialism* (Evanston, 1966) 29.

[36]Ibid. Löwith by a somewhat different analysis came to this same conclusion.

[37]Jean-Paul Sartre, *Being and Nothingness*, trans. Hazel E. Barnes (New York,
1956) 364, 410-12, 423. This idea is expressed with great clarity and force in *No Exit*.
Cf. Emmanual Mounier, *Personalism* trans. Philip Mairet (New York, 1952) 30; and
Page Smith, *Historian and History* 240. James M. Robinson says of existential theology that it "dissolves history into the historicness of existence." *Theology as History*, James M. Robinson and John B. Cobb, Jr., eds. (New York, 1967) 14.

mankind possibilities toward the future that are limited only by the past.[38] Karl Jaspers also recognized history as the uniquely human product of man's transcendent freedom. Historical man should be the first concern of philosophy.[39]

Despite Jaspers, however, and a few others of like mind, philosophy of history has not been equal to the task of interpreting the Western sense of history. Historians explain and evaluate events by placing them in some context and there are contexts within contexts. The career of Robespierre, for example, may be understood in the context of the Jacobin movement, which is in the context of the French Revolution, which is in the context of the history of democracy in France, and so on. Or the same event may have various meanings in a variety of contexts. The Norman Conquest may be understood in the context of the history of the English monarchy, or of the development of the English language, or of ecclesiastical history, or of the history of feudalism, and so forth. This is what professional historians concern themselves with. But if we raise the question of the meaning of the historical process as a whole or try to understand historical experience in relation to the whole of reality, we are outside the province of the professional historian. These questions can be answered only in terms of some ultimate faith or some speculative system. In the absence of any common ground in such a faith or system, historical scholarship has developed as an autonomous discipline analogous to the development of science. Historians, of course, draw on other disciplines, such as economics, sociology, political theory, and the various natural sciences. They also in some measure support other disciplines. What is lacking is any basis for a coherent integration into other salient aspects of the Western experience. To provide such an integration is surely the most important practical contribution to be hoped for from the philosophy of history.

It must be said, however, that at present there is little ground for such hope. Philosophy of history is a recent concern of a few his-

---

[38]Ortega y Gasset, *History as a System* (New York, 1961) 212-18. The essays in this volume were first published under the title *Toward a Philosophy of History* (1941).

[39]Karl Jaspers, *The Origin and Goal of History* (New Haven, 1953). For a concise statement of the basic importance of history see 275.

torians and philosophers and its achievements have not been impressive. Three approaches to philosophy of history have been made. Labels for them have reached no consensus; but for this comment they may be called: (1) speculative, (2) epistemological, and (3) analytical.

The speculative philosophies of history would include Hegel, Marx, some of the scientific humanists, Spengler, and Toynbee. At present only Marx has any considerable following and that has significantly diminished in the last few decades. How Marxist China and the Communist European countries now are is problematical. Marx still has a considerable following in Western Europe and the future of his influence there cannot be anticipated. In the United States in scholarly circles Marxism is strangely enough strongest among students of American history, where the argument for it would seem to be weakest. The history of the United States is a de facto refutation of virtually every prediction Marx made.

Hegel's influence has been less on historiography than on philosophy of history. Probably all idealist philosophers of history, of whom Benedetto Croce is the outstanding representative, owe some debt to Hegel, though many would certainly not want to be called Hegelians.

Page Smith describes Spengler, Toynbee, and Eric Voegelin as "meta-historians." Of the three Voegelin would seem to be less inclined to impose on history a pattern of interpretation that would enable him to predict its future course.

It is the speculative philosophies which have made historians suspicious of philosophy of history. Laws of history are not the aim of historians and they get in the way of the honest interpretation of available data.

Studies of the nature and validity of our knowledge of history have mostly reflected some epistemology developed independently of any concern about history. They do not contribute much to our understanding of history or of our strong sense of historical existence. Some of the positivists have even denied the possibility of any knowledge of the past.[40] The best approach to an epistemology

---

[40]Arthur C. Danto, *Analytical Philosophy of History* (Cambridge, 1965) 29-30, 34-62. Danto describes this position and offers a refutation of it. For a brief summary of Danto's discussion see Leon J. Goldstein, *Historical Knowing* (Austin TX, London, 1976) 5-20.

of history will probably be a study of how historians actually proceed. Leon Goldstein's *Historical Knowing* (cited above) is such a study.

Goldstein's approach to an epistemology of history is an example of what is here called analytical philosophy of history. Analytical philosophy of history needs to be expanded, however, from the analysis of historiography to a study of our sense of historical existence. As this kind of study is pursued, there will probably develop a definite bifurcation between those with Christian theological assumptions and those with atheistic humanistic presuppostitions. At this point the theologians seem to have advanced further. Jürgen Moltmann and Wolfhart Pannenberg in Germany and Richard R. Niebuhr in this country have made significant contributions. It must be said, however, that their work has had very little impact on Western scholarship as a whole.

A discussion of the Western sense of history must necessarily be somewhat disconnected because the study of it has not been pursued far enough to relate to each other its various ramifications. One problem associated with it that has not received adequate attention is the question of teleology. In the originating biblical conception the teleology immanent in the cyclical reality of cosmological cultures was abandoned; and both nature and history were informed by the purposes of a transcendent God, purposes that were partially revealed and partially inscrutable. With God eliminated in modern secular humanism teleology became a problem—although frequently an unrecognized problem.

Except for existentialism all of the culturally significant humanistic faiths are historicisms. In them the deification of man takes the form of deifying some cause or community the destiny of which is the ultimate source of meaning and value. Marxism and scientism are typical examples of the deification of a historical process. Each of them posits a direction and a goal in history that transcend the conscious purposes of individuals and carry history to a predetermined end that has only recently become known. Focused as they are upon history itself, the historicisms are inclined to be vague and unimplicit about any ground in nature; but whether such ground is alleged or not, the historicism is itself a teleology and one which restricts the consciousness of radical historical freedom. In fact, one of the attractions of historicism is the relief it gives from the terror of history. Existentialists, who find no source of meaning in either nature or history, experience their individual historical existences as absurd and speak of the human situation as one of nausea, anxiety, despair.

Friedrick Hayek has revealed the fundamental fallacy in attempting to plan a whole society and, by an obvious extension, one of the fundamental weaknesses of historicism. Hayek is himself a Nobel prize winner in economics, but he is sharply critical of social scientists for attempting to use the same methods that have been successful in the physical sciences. The difference, he says, is that the social sciences are dealing with purposeful objects. The knowledge and purposes of individual men interacting with each other produce social wholes beyond the intention of any. The planing of a complete society is impossible because no mind can grasp all the knowledge and purposes that exist in the individuals composing the society and because individuals respond in unpredicted ways to the efforts of the planners. One may make specific plans within a society and achieve specific objectives; but the total result will always be more than and different from what was planned due to the interaction with other purposers.[41]

The way in which the human will produces action in the observable physical world is not known. Scientists can study the results and relate them on the level of physics with the situation before the purposer intervened; but the purposing itself and its relation to physical action eludes scientific methods. The scientist is dealing with abstractions from a whole some aspects of which escape him. The elusiveness of the human will may by analogy aid in conceiving a transcendent teleology observable only through its effects. We can return to this analogy when we have called attention to evidence of teleology in science.

The possibility of science is evidence of unity and continuity in the world process; but science is an abstraction from the total process. Scientific "laws" can describe certain aspects of the process as we experience it; what they cannot do is account for the unity and continuity of the process from which they are abstracted. The very

---

[41]F. A. Hayek, *The Counter-Revolution of Science* (London, 1955).

existence of order in the world led some classical philosophers to posit a cosmic Reason as explanation. In Christian thought it has been taken as the design of a transcendent Purposer. Modern secular man has seen no problem since it is as logically possible to posit the existing cosmos to be ultimate reality as to see a principle of Reason or a Creator as ultimate. This question, however, may be relevant to the evidence of teleology in nature. There is not space here for an extensive discussion, but a few examples from biological evolution will call attention to the problem.

Evolution as a whole appears to be in direct contradiction to the law of entropy which specifies that in any closed system the organization is becoming simpler and the amount of energy is declining.[42] If there exists a system in which a physical explanation of evolution can be given and the application of the law of entropy explained, our science is not capable of describing it. One may if one likes assume on faith that such a system exists; but it has no other status. In the light of what is known about evolution, it might be more plausible to remember that biological reality transcends the abstractions upon which the law of entropy is constructed. A teleology may exist which transcends the methods of science in the way that the human will transcends the physics of bodily movement.

Arthur Koestler, citing a number of eminent scientists, furnishes us in *Janus* with a convenient discussion of deficiencies in the current explanations of biological evolution. Most of the problems involve data pointing toward a teleology that biologists are reluctant to accept. One of the oldest of such problems is the evolution of the eye. Some parts of the eye including the optic nerve developed out of brain tissue moving outward. Other parts developed from skin tissue. The evolution continued through thousands of generations and, according to current theory, a multitude of mutations which had to occur in just the right order. During this long development the eye had no survival value. Pierre Grassé, who held the chair for evolution at the Sorbonne, was well aware of how incredible the theory of evolution by random mutation and natural selection is:

---

[42]Pierre-P. Grassé, *Evolution of Living Organisms*, trans. Grassé himself (New York, San Francisco, London, 1977) 2.

The probability of dust carried by the wind reproducing Dürer's "Melancholia" is less infinitesimal than the probability of copy errors in the DNA molecule leading to the formation of the eye; besides, these errors had *no relationship whatsoever* with the function that the eye would have to perform or was starting to perform. There is no law against daydreaming, but science must not indulge in it.[43]

Many other examples as impressive as the eye can be found. One of the most interesting is the human brain. Its evolution had presumably equipped homo sapiens some hundred thousand years ago with a brain essentially the same as that of modern man. Its capacity for twentieth-century mathematics, quantum physics, and the technology that put a man on the moon had no survival value whatever during the thousands of generations through which it had evolved. Paleolithic man, who had not even invented the bow and arrow, could have done as well with a brain not much better than an ape's. Obviously something more was involved than "natural selection" even in its most sophisticated recent development.[44]

Another kind of evidence is given in the parallel development of mammals in Australia and in the rest of the world. There are two sub-classes of mammalia; marsupials and placentals. Both sub-classes appeared from a common ancestor just before Australia separated from the Asian mainland. Only the marsupials got into Australia. The two lines then evolved in complete independence for about one hundred million years. What is remarkable is that so many of the Australian species are in appearance strikingly like placental counterparts. Koestler illustrates with pictures of marsupial jerboa, flying phalanger, and Tasmanian wolf (skull only) paired with the placental jerboa, flying squirrel, and wolf. That this parallelism could have resulted from two independent successions of blind, random mutations is incredible. Some biologists have suggested that there are a limited number of viable organic forms. If

---

[43]Ibid., p. 104; italics are in the original. See also pp. 9, 56, 92, 97-98, 102, 107, 128, 152, 193.

[44]Arthur Koestler, *Janus, a Summing Up* (New York, 1979) 274-77.

so, the limitation is not severe; there are more than two million existing animal species. In any event the conclusion would seem to be inevitable that nature is in some manner *aimed* at the production of certain forms. According to Koestler, who mentions several by name, an increasing number of neo-Darwinians have come to recognize this.[45] Certainly there has been a more general recognition that teleological concepts are a legitimate part of biological method.[46]

There is no intention here of entering into biological controversies; but some of the attitudes revealed in the discussion of teleology are relevant to this study. There is a tendency to treat human purpose as absolutely unique and to deny that there exists any other *conscious* purpose in nature without offering any scientific grounds for the denial.

> Dr. [Julian] Huxley himself calls it "a glorious paradox" that "this purposeless mechanism, after a thousand million years of its blind and automatic operations, has finally generated purpose" now that "Man the conscious microcosm has been thrown up by the blind and automatic forces of the unconscious macrocosm."[47]

Huxley avoids using the word "purpose" in this passage to describe the evolutionary process, but as discussed in the previous chapter he does include a teleological element in his understanding of that process which he never reconciles with its "blind and automatic" character.

The strongest bias revealed in the discussion of teleology in evolution is the concern to avoid giving any foothold for theism. This concern has sometimes led to the indefensible assumption that in principle the total reality (sometimes human consciousness is tacitly and irrationally excepted) is subject to scientific explanation. This, or course, contradicts the well-established principle that scientific generalizations are *always* abstractions and *never* capture the

---

[45]Ibid., 206-13.

[46]See, for example, Francisco J. Ayala, "Teleological Explanations in Evolutionary Biology," *Philosophy of Science* 37 (1970): 1-15.

[47]Stephen Toulmin, *The Return to Cosmology* (Berkeley, London, 1982) 67.

whole of reality. Anti-theistic bias has also produced a partiality for locating teleology in nature itself. Herbert Muller, who had a Guggenheim Fellowship to study the relation of science to literary criticism, expresses a commonly held view:

> "Purpose" is not imported into nature, and need not be puzzled over as a strange or divine something else that gets inside and makes life go; it is no more an added force than mind is something in addition to brain. It is simply implicit in the fact of organization.[48]

In his concern to avoid recognition of a divine Purposer Muller introduces into nature that inherent teleology that for so long hindered the advancement of science. Koestler is also concerned to avoid any divine Purposer. He takes advantage of his neo-Lamarckianism to argue:

> The Purposer is each and every individual organism from the inception of life, which struggled and strove to make the best of its limited possibilities; and the sum total of these ontogenies reflects the active striving of living matter towards the optimal realization of the planet's evolutionary potential.[49]

This could hardly be called a solution to the problem. "The active striving of living matter towards the optimal realization" surely transcends the purposes of each individual organism. And how are we to understand "optimal realization of . . . evolutionary potential"?

It is interesting that so many scientists and other informed people should find it easier to believe teleology to be inherent in nature than to attribute it to Whitehead's immanent God or to the transcendent God of the biblical tradition; the former would, indeed, call for a more drastic modification of our conception of the world. If it led to something like Greek cosmology, it might also run counter to modern man's awareness of a radical historical freedom.

---

[48]Herbert J[oseph] Muller, *Science and Criticism*, (New Haven, 1954) 109. Koestler, who quotes this same passage, confused the literary critic with the Nobel prize-winning geneticist Hermann Joseph Muller. *Janus*, 213.

[49]Ibid.

The analogy of the human will may help us at this point to avoid the fear that recognition of an external teleology in the world would undermine science. Early modern scientists through Newton believed that the purposes of God operated in nature; yet they could exclude consideration of purpose from their method.[50] The way in which God's will effected the creation of the world and the way his will exercises sovereignty over it remained inscrutable; but the resulting order could be studied. It was precisely the transcendence of the Purposer that freed scientific method from a teleology inherent in things themselves or in the cosmos. (See chapter 4.)

Scientific method is not something fixed for all time. Biologists have included teleological considerations in their method. There is no reason they should be so embarrassed about it. Teleological explanations have a validity in their own right; certainly they are more valuable than empty explanations in terms of efficient causes that cannot be specified. The unity and continuity of nature is accepted by atheistic scientists as an ultimate reality requiring no explanation. Perhaps the teleology that has become increasingly evident in nature might be treated in the same way. The trouble is that it much more strongly suggests, if it does not strictly imply, a purposer. Perhaps the medieval distinction between the *potentia absoluta* and the *potentia ordinata* of God might find some application here. Recognition of a transcendent Purposer need no more interfere with the autonomy of biology than it did with the autonomy of seventeenth-century physics. Denial of the transcendent Purposer might saddle biology with a return to that teleology immanent in a noncontingent world which for so long stood in the way of the development of science. If such a denial also involved a denial of the transcendence of human purpose, it would compromise on the level of theory, but not eradicate in fact, the historical consciousness of modern man which is basic to belief in the scientific enterprise itself. Professor Grassé points to the possiblity of suspending

---

[50]The commonly held view that Newton restricted God's governance of the world to the correction of certain aberrations in the planetary system is a gross misunderstanding. He is, in fact, explicit and emphatic about God's complete and active sovereignty over nature. See the "General Scholium" which he added to his *Principia*. Isaac Newton, *Mathematical Principles*, trans. Florian Cajori (Berkeley, 1960) 543-47. On this point Newton's theology is quite sophisticated.

judgment on what transcends science without commiting oneself
to any particular metaphysics [or theology]:

> The united efforts of paleontology and molecular biology, the
> latter stripped of its dogmas, should lead to the discovery of the ex-
> act mechanism of evolution, possibly without revealing to us the
> causes of the orientations of lineages, of the finalities of structures,
> of living functions, and of cycles. Perhaps in this area biology can
> go no farther: the rest is metaphysics.[51]

It is interesting that Kant, for whom the problem arose in a somewhat different context, came to conclusions quite similar to those
expressed above:

> Mechanism, then, and the teleological (designed) technique of
> nature, in respect of the same product and its possibility, may
> stand under a common supreme principle of nature in particular
> laws. But since this principle is *transcendent*, we cannot, because of
> the limitation of our understanding, unite both principles *in the ex-
> planation* of the same production of nature, even if the inner pos-
> sibility of this product is only intelligible [*verstandlich*] through a
> causality according to purposes (as is the case with organized mat-
> ter). We revert then to the above fundamental proposition of tele-
> ology. According to the constitution of the human understanding
> no other than designedly working causes can be assumed for the
> possibility of organized beings in nature; and the mere mechanism
> of nature cannot be adequate to the explanation of these its
> products.
> . . . .
> But since the ground of this compatibility lies in that which is nei-
> ther one nor the other (neither mechanism nor purposive combi-
> nation), but is the supersensible substrate of nature of which we
> know nothing, the two ways of representing the possibility of such
> objects are not to be blended together by our (human) reason.
> However, we canot judge of their possibility otherwise than by
> judging them as ultimately resting on a supreme understanding by

---

[51]Grassé, *Evolution of Living Organisms*, 246. Grassé uses the term "finality" to
refer to end, purpose, or teleology. See 165-67, 170.

the connection of final causes, and thus the teleological method of explanation is not eliminated.[52]

"Absolutely no human reason," said Kant, "can hope to understand the production of even a blade of grass by mere mechanical causes."[53]

Summary

The Western sense of history is a product of the biblical-Christian tradition that was secularized during the Enlightenment. Since that time some of the salient characteristics of modern culture are due to it. These would include modern faith in progress; a new pattern of explanation in history and science; professional historiography, beginning about 1800; new ontologies of process; humanistic historicism; and existentialism.

There is a serious "problem of history" in modern culture. It is generated by the conflict between a strong sense of historical existence and the compulsion to understand human experience in the context of a concept of nature still heavily mechanistic in its overtones and assumptions.[54] Most historians write for a community of scholarship that includes both Christians and humanists of various persuasions. They, therefore, tend to avoid the broad and profound questions that divide the community of historians. Generally speaking, Western historiography has tacitly assumed that history operates in and does not transcend the natural order associated with science. On the other hand, historians have been very much on guard against any alleged "laws of history." Their caution at this point has caused them to be suspicious of *any* philosophy of history, even those that do not involve or imply such laws. Despite some attraction to universal history, the best work of historians has been the piecemeal investigation of past events.

---

[52]Immanuel Kant, *Critique of Judgment*, trans. J. H. Bernard (New York, 1951) 262-63, section 78.

[53]Ibid., 258, section 77.

[54]See, for example, William A. Galston, *Kant and the Problem of History* (Chicago, 1975) esp. 4-38, 210-15.

The mechanistic imagination of the West contradicts but has by no means obliterated the Western sense of history. It has, however, stood in the way of its adequate development. Although mechanism will always be a fundamental element in scientific method, developments in science itself have undermined it as a metaphysical assumption and thus opened the way for new developments in method. One new development is an increasing recognition of teleology in nature. The revival of teleology may eventually come to support the theological concept of reality as basically historical, that is, as ultimately a product of God's will and as involving human will in a dialectical process.

Inability to find a generally acceptable relationship between the modern concept of progress, process philosophies, existentialism, humanistic historicisms, chronologically based sciences like geology, biology, and cosmology, problems of teleology, and the more prosaic study of human history is a major instance of cultural disintegration in the West.

For the development of our sense of history beyond the badly fragmented experience of it that now exists there may need to be some frank divergence between Christian and atheistic approaches to the subject.

VIII THE NEW HUMANISM: FAITH AND CULTURE

The passionate religious intensity with which some have been committed to a humanistic faith has been obscured by the fact that the humanists rarely identify their faiths as religions. Comte and Huxley are exceptions; H. G. Wells is a partial exception. The term *religion* is generally taken in the West to refer to Christianity or Judaism or perhaps as a generic term to include all the traditional religions. The overwhelming majority of humanists think of themselves as without religion, and many, the Marxists, for example, are militantly antireligious. Most humanists, like most confessing Christians, including highly intelligent individuals in both cases, have simply not thought much about their fundamental commitments. This is not remarkable. In any large human society the general run of people share in the common ground that unites the society simply by participating in the culture that the religious basis of the society has to a large degree shaped.[1]

In totalitarian countries the popular culture may be focused and homogenized by the political imposition of an ideology on the so-

---

[1]Cf. T. S. Eliot, *Notes towards the Definition of Culture* (London, 1948).

ciety. In this case there exists a continuum from fanatical devotion to the ideology on the one hand to passive acceptance on the other. Serious dissidents, as long as the total regime is successful, are a small and powerless minority. In nontotalitarian societies the situation is more complex. Some groups, whether Christian or humanistic, may be fanatically devoted to their own faith and passionately opposed to others. But in non-totalitarian countries of the West the lack of passion and incisive criticism in most of the population has resulted in a confused blend of Christianity and humanism that is sustained by the considerable heritage of ideas and values that are common to both. The very fact that both faiths in their various concrete manifestations are compromised in this important section of the population provides a ballast that goes far to enable the society to continue to function with some degree of integration. It also obscures the very real differences between atheistic humanists and Christians that are a major source of confusion and contradiction in Western civilization.

One can learn something about the religious basis of a society by studying its popular culture; but it is important to proceed cautiously. Judgments about Buddhism, Islam, Hinduism, or Christianity that are based on popular beliefs and practices may be very misleading and contradict the best ideas and values of the religious leaders of such societies. If one wants to get at the essentials of a faith it is important to consider the best products of the best minds that have been committed to it. This is true of modern humanism. The atheism of most non-Christian humanists—including most of those who are well educated—is unreflective and dispassionate disbelief. The belief of most theists, of course, is equally passive and uncritical. It is when one turns to the most original and creative humanists that the relation between atheism and the deification of man becomes evident and the passionate attacks on God and those who believe in him become understandable.

The Enlightenment was more than a "climate of opinion"; it was a powerful movement of the human spirit, and its essentially religious nature can be seen in the attitude of many of the philosophes toward Christianity. Theirs was not a calm, rational decision that certain tenets of the Christian faith were false. There was a virulent hatred of Christianity.[2] Under cover of deism Man was deified, and he has proved to be as jealous a God as Yahweh himself. The Christian doctrine of the sovereignty of God over nature and history as well as the doctrine of original sin were anathema to those whose faith was in the fundamental goodness of man and his capacity to perfect himself and his institutions. Penfield Roberts says that what Queen Caroline and her bishops wanted was "freedom from 'prone submission to the heavenly will.' "[3] It was not by chance that the most serious religious persecution of the eighteenth-century West was the persecution of Catholics by the Jacobins. In this regard the spririt of the Enlightenment has outlived many of its ideas.

In previous chapters several cases were cited as examples of the virulent hostility to Christianity in various humanisms. Saint-Simon was quoted (and H. G. Wells might have been) to the effect that man's fundamental desire is to replace God. Some of the existentialists, though less sanguine about the possibility, have made the same affirmation. Nietzsche said: "If there were gods, how could I endure not to be a god! Hence, there are no gods."[4] And he has the madman say regarding the murder of God: "Must we ourselves not become gods just to appear worthy of it?"[5] Sartre gives a rational argument for his atheism. According to him if the "Being-for-itself" (that is, the human reality) could become "Being-in-itself" without ceasing to be Being-for-itself, that would be God. But that is impossible because the for-itself is precisely a nihilation of being, a nothingness, a kind of hole in Being. Man can become a

---

[2]It is true that many ideas of the Enlightenment were widely espoused by Christians as well as non-Christians. In some cases—humanitarian concern, for example, or the concept of natural law—this is explainable in terms of the biblical heritage common to both. In other cases the position of the Christians was seriously compromised. The eighteenth century was the weakest period of Christian theology since the second.

[3]Penfield Roberts, *The Quest for Security, 1715-1740* (New York, 1947) 153.

[4]Friedrich Nietzsche, *Thus Spoke Zarathustra*, trans. Walter Kaufmann (New York, 1954) 86.

[5]Friedrich Nietzsche, *The Gay Science*, trans. Walter Kaufmann (New York, 1974) 181.

Being-in-itself only in death; but then he is not a for-itself. Nevertheless, it is the fundamental desire of every man to become God. There is no escape from this frustration.[6] In another context Sartre defines God as that Other who would know the for-itself completely as an in-itself. Fortunately, from Sartre's point of view, no such other exists; for Sartre sees every human other as a threat and an embarrassment. The only possible relationship between humans, he says, is conflict. Thus if God did exist, we could only hate him.[7]

Albert Camus in that strangely confused book, *The Rebel*, is deeply distressed over the failure of modern humanism to produce a just society, and comes to the despairing conclusion that the only moral stance possible, now or in the future, is rebellion. Repeatedly he refers to the deification of man and the death of God. One chapter is entitled "The Deicides." "Nothing," he says "can discourage the appetite for divinity in the heart of man."[8] And this appetite for divinity he relates to the hostility to God:

> The deicides of the twentieth century . . . draw the ultimate conclusions from the logic of rebellion and want to make the earth a kingdom where man is God. The reign of history begins and, identifying himself only with his history, man, unfaithful to his real rebellion, will henceforth devote himself to the nihilistic revolution of the twentieth century, which denies all forms of morality and desperately attempts to achieve the unity of the human race by means of a ruinous series of crimes and wars. The Jacobin Revolution, which tried to institute the religion of virtue in order to establish unity upon it, will be followed by the cynical revolutions . . . of the right or of the left . . . which will try to achieve the unity of the world so as to found, at last, the religion of man. All that was God's will henceforth be rendered to Caesar.[9]

---

[6]Jean-Paul Sartre, *Being and Nothingness*, trans. Hazel E. Barnes (New York, 1956) 540, 566, 575-76, 581, 592, 615, 620-23, 626.

[7]Ibid., 364, 410-12, 423.

[8]*The Rebel*, trans. Anthony Bower (New York, 1956) 147.

[9]Ibid., 132.

As has been shown, what Camus sees in the twentieth century began much earlier. Voegelin quotes Marx's doctoral dissertation of 1840-41:

> The confession of Prometheus, "In a word, I hate all the gods," is [also philosophy's] . . . confession, its own verdict against all gods heavenly and earthly who do not acknowledge human self-consciousness as the supreme deity. There shall be none beside it.[10]

That writers from such disparate points of view should exhibit such similar attitudes toward God and concern for the deification of man suggests that these experiences are not the product of their philosophies, but are the prerational context within which their thought developed.

As Camus pointed out in the passage quoted above, once a community or historical cause has been deified into the absolute source of meaning and value, there is no moral authority to guide its decisions. This was not immediately apparent. As long as non-Christian humanists were deists, they could believe in traditional values as natural laws imposed by the watchmaker God. The Jacobins were sincere about their Republic of Virtue. They did not liquidate people any more than the traditional states before and since. They were self-righteous and tyrannical; but they were not amoral. More recent atheistic humanists have derived moral systems out of their respective historical movements, but these moralities are not binding on the movements themselves or on those who act in their name. Traditional values do, however, still influence judgment even in zealous devotees of totalitarian ideologies and are, indeed, strong enough to bring disillusionment to many of the faithful when they are flagrantly breached as they were in the liquidation of the kulaks.

The lack of any adequate ground for ethics has led not only to atrocities but to a kind of hyper-morality in which values like equality or nonviolence are absolutized. This has added to the confusion. Violence continues and the inevitable inequalities in society lead to recrimination and a search for scapegoats. Camus's effort in *The Rebel* to return to a natural law basis of ethics, like the efforts of Wal-

---

[10]Eric Voegelin, *Science, Politics, and Gnosticism* (Chicago, 1968) 35.

ter Lippmann and others, was bound to failure.[11] In a meaningless cosmos and in the absence of God, natural law could only mean what is. An empirical examination of human nature offers no criterion to distinguish good from evil. Camus faced the problem of evil in a new form. If man is the only source of meaning and value, then whatever human evil there is must be laid at his door—if, indeed, it would make any sense to call it evil. Camus, needless to say, did not come to such conclusions; but neither did he find any solution. Rather than blame man, he repeatedly blames evil on a God who does not exist!

Eric Voegelin, deeply disturbed by the absence in the modern world of a moral and metaphysical basis of social order, has described atheistic humanism as a modern gnosticism.[12] The analogy between the two great spiritual movements can be enlightening; but Voegelin goes beyond comparing the two analogically. He argues that the modern faith developed historically out of the ancient faith. This is not acceptable because there are crucial and irreconcilable differences between the two. Further, the historical roots of modern atheistic humanism are in the largely Christian society of early modern Europe. The roots of ancient gnosticism are in Persian dualism; the gnostics are close kin to the Manichaeans, who incorporated the dualism of gnosticism into their syncretic faith. The roots of modern humanism are not in gnosticism but in the biblical tradition and especially in the unique biblical doctrine of creation.

Voegelin's interpretation is rooted in his identification of gnosticism with seeking salvation not in a reality transcending history but within secular history itself. As will be shown later, this is not true of ancient gnosticism, but it is true of modern humanism, and

---

[11]Walter Lippmann, *Essays in the Public Philosophy* (Boston, 1955).

[12]Voegelin first published his interpretation of modern atheistic humanism as gnosticism in *The New Science of Politics* (Chicago, 1952). He continued this theme in *Wissenschaft, Politik und Gnosis* (Munich, 1959); this work was published in English along with an essay entitled "Ersatz Religion" as *Science, Politics and Gnosticism*. In 1975 John H. Halloway edited and published a collection of Voegelin's hitherto unpublished writings from the 1940s and early 1950s under the title *From Enlightenment to Revolution* (Durham NC). Some of these essays also deal with the gnostic question.

Voegelin is right to see the Christian faith as the source of modern man's faith in history. His concern to link the modern phenomenon to ancient gnosticism led him, however, seriously to overrate the influence of Jewish apocalyptic and Christian chiliasm or the belief in a millennium when Christ will rule for a thousand years. Jewish apocalyptic was a retreat from the historical nature of the Hebrew faith. When situations got so bad that there seemed no possibility of effective historical action, some people took refuge in the hope and belief that God would intervene catastrophically to destroy the forces of evil and save his people. The immediate effect of such belief was likely to be quietistic.[13] Christian apocalypticism expects deliverance to come with the second coming of Christ and a final Battle of Armageddon between the forces of good and the forces of evil. The social dualism involved here is not a metaphysical dualism like that of ancient gnostics; but the resemblance offers some plausibility to identifying them.[14]

The emphasis Voegelin gives to chiliasm is misleading. Chiliasm, especially of the violent sort, has been a minor theme in Christian history. Furthermore, Christian chiliasts, for all their interest in a social salvation at the culmination of history on earth, have not given up their hope of individual salvation into a kingdom of God transcending history. Christian chiliasm has not been at all the kind of secularism that characterizes atheistic humanism. In a well-known history of millenarianism Norman Cohn concludes with an emphasis on the resemblances between earlier Christian chiliasts and the Nazi and Communist movements of the twentieth century.[15] It is not necessary to suppose any significant causal relationship in order to account for certain patterns of thought and action being available in the traditional culture. Rather than a direct continuity between chiliasm and certain humanist movements, it is more probable that similar convictions of the absolute rightness of a cause, similar frustrations with intractable situations, and similar

---

[13]Paul D. Hanson, *The Dawn of Apocalyptic* (Philadelphia, 1975), 11-12, 17-19, 21-23, 26, 28.

[14]H. H. Rowley, *The Relevance of Apocalyptic*, 2d ed, (London, 1947), 158-63.

[15]Norman Cohn, *The Pursuit of the Millennium*, 2d ed. (New York, 1961) 308-319.

confrontations with the enemies of righteousness have produced similar patterns of response. There is, after all, nothing remarkable about a secular utopian movement taking on some of the characteristics of chiliasm. It is also important at this point to remember that not all humanisms are utopian.

Voegelin himself has pointed out that belief in the perfectibility of man has taken two forms: progressivism and utopianism.[16] An adequate explanation of the source of modern humanism must include both. The secularizing of the biblical tradition in the Enlightenment was, as has been previously discussed, the origin of atheistic humanism. The transcendent God was abandoned; but the biblical understanding of man and of the world that had derived out of belief in such a God was retained. How this has produced problems for recent humanism will be discussed later in this chapter. Now it will be useful to see how the historical sense of the biblical tradition was developed into a drive for human perfectibility.

From the time of Christ a tension has existed in Christian thought between the sinful societies of this world and the kingdom of God, which transcends history and which ultimately will be brought to fulfillment not by human effort but by the redemptive powers of God. With the significant exception of the Book of Revelation, written during a time of persecution, the New Testament is generally positive in its attitude toward existing political authority. Christ said "Render unto Caesar the things that are Caesar's"; Paul said, "The powers that be are ordained of God."[17] But nothing was further from Christian thought than the idea that human effort could achieve in history the perfections of the kingdom of God. Whether the redemptive power of God would achieve the perfection of humanity within history or in some transcendent realm is not a question on which there has been a Christian consensus; but

---

[16]Voegelin, *The New Science of Politics*, 120-21. On 175-77 Voegelin identifies progressivism and utopianism as "right wing Gnosticism" and identifies a left wing of violent activism. In this discussion he says that "the only Gnostic activist movement that achieved a noteworthy measure of success was the National Socialist movement on a limited national basis." Communism, he says, is a development of liberalism and has nothing to do with Soviet expansionism.

[17]For a full discussion see Oscar Cullmann, *The State in the New Testament* (New York, 1956).

there is a consensus that such achievement would be the end of history as it is presently known. Saint Augustine in his remarkable synthesis of Christian thought at the end of the ancient world took essentially the position just stated. The City of God is the end toward which all history moves; but the earthly city, though sinful to its core, must be accepted and supported by Christians as a gift of God necessary to the earthly peace of sinful humanity until the end is achieved.[18]

Despite the enthusiastic optimism of Eusebius over the conversion of the Roman Empire, no serious program to reform society in accord with Christian ideals was generated before the end of the ancient world. In the centuries immediately following the fall of Rome the general confusion and lack of political order prevented any such project developing in the West.[19] The first Western ruler to make a significant effort to create a Christian society in history was Charlemagne. Since that time with more or less concern and more or less effectiveness the church has not abandoned its sense of responsibility to guide the general society in the direction of Christian ideas and ideals. With what degree of intelligence and moral consistency it has sought to discharge this responsibility is not here in question. Voegelin dates the beginning of modern gnosticism with John Scotus Erigena in the ninth century but saw it surfacing in the twelfth century with Joachim of Flora. The Reformation, he says, gave rise to numerous gnostic movements. Until its secularizing in the Enlightenment he identifies gnosticism with efforts at establishing Christian societies in the here and now. Calvin's *Institutes* he sees as a gnostic Koran; and he takes English Puritanism as described by Richard Hooker to be a paradigm of Christian gnosticism. He is not able, however, to show how this kind of Christian effort led to the secularism of Voltaire.

A better explanation is to show that developments among lay thinkers led to a repudiation of Christianity for deism and then show how this produced modern atheistic humanism and its belief

---

[18]Saint Augustine, *The City of God*, trans. Marcus Dods (New York, 1950) 481-82 (book 15, 4) 695-97, 707 (book 19, 17, 26).

[19]No attempt is made to assess the situation in Byzantium since that is hardly relevant to the problem discussed here.

in the perfectibility of man by human efforts. That is the approach of this study. The rise of secular humanism in the Enlightenment has been described in a previous chapter. How this secularism led to the pursuit of human perfection is perhaps not too hard to see. The deep-rooted sinfulness of man, a doctrine by no means neglected by Calvin and the Puritans, was generally accepted before the Enlightenment and prevented any notion that man could perfect himself or his society. Since ancient times sin had seemed an adequate explanation for evils like war and slavery. Even vice, if not formally accepted, was expected. Sir Thomas More's *Utopia* was an effort to imagine what a sinless society might be like; neither Sir Thomas nor his readers, however, took it for a historical goal.

Denial that God is active in nature or history left the field to the transcendently free, historical man of the biblical tradition; and the denial of sin as a flaw too deep for human eradication removed the inhibition that had prevented the historical sense of the biblical tradition developing into confidence in the perfectibility of man. Over optimism about this has from time to time produced violence against those who seemed to be wayward obstructionists; and sometimes too optimistic a hope has led to disillusionment and nihilism; but the general mood of modern man has been optimistic.

In the biblical Christian faith man is related to the world through the purpose of God. Without God modern humanism is essentially a radical dualism between man and the world. Modern atheistic man is still aware of himself as free, purposeful, one who acts creatively to produce a history that transcends nature. He is aware of the world deprived of the purposes of God as a world entirely indifferent to him, a world without meaning or purpose. It is in this dualism that the analogy with gnosticism may be useful.

In ancient gnosticism the dualism was a speculative response to the experience of alienation. In modern humanism the dualism is not speculative but experiential. Prior to any thinking about it modern man is aware of himself as existing historically; that is he knows himself to be free in a way that transcends any natural necessity and makes him capable of creative action and responsible for his future. Although some of his speculations about himself (romanticism, some forms of idealism, existentialism) recognize this transcendent freedom and historical responsibility, it is so far from being a product of such speculation that it persists experientially even when man tries to understand himself in terms of forms of naturalism that deny his radical freedom. His experience of the world as indifferent to him and yet subject in some measure to his creative will is also given prior to speculation about it. Those who seek to explain the nonteleological world as a result of modern science make a historical error that misleads them in regard to the present human situation. Historically it was the nonteleological world that opened the way to modern science.[20] The first century of modern science was in a Europe still Christian, and the nonteleological world was a part of the biblical-Christian tradition. In a Christian context the lack of a cosmos in the Greek sense did not lead to alienation; though Pascal in his awe of the immensity of a world "that knew him not" certainly saw the possibility. Whether he sees the value-emptied world as opportunity for his projects or as a threat to all meaning, the modern atheistic humanist finds himself over-against the indifferent world. This provides the possibility for alienation; perhaps it even implies it strictly; but if the latter is so, the inference is not always made. The existentialists have pursued some of the implications of humanism more rigorously than other humanists, and it is in them that the experience of alienation has been given its fullest modern description. Hans Jonas added to his study of gnosticism a last chapter entitled "Epilogue: Gnosticism, Existentialism, and Nihilism" in which he discusses the analogy between ancient gnosticism and modern existentialism. The analogy can be broadened to include atheistic humanism generally. All non-Christian modern humanists exhibit a dualism between the human reality and the world man confronts. In his last paragraph, Jonas does speak of the modern mind generally and calls "the disruption of man and total reality" "a dualism without metaphysics" and points out that the illogicality of such a dualism does not make it any the less real.[21] Not all modern humanists have experienced this dualism as alienation but insofar as they have the analogy with

---

[20]See chapter 4, above.

[21]Hans Jonas, *The Gnostic Religion: the Message of the Alien God and the Beginnings of Christianity*, 2d ed. rev. (Boston, 1963) 340. In ancient gnosticism, of course, there was a dualistic metaphysics. Ibid., 335.

gnosticism is strengthened. That alienation is not confined to nihilists and existentialists is illustrated by H. G. Wells. Wells is not
consistent at this point. In *First and Last Things* and elsewhere he
finds meaning in a cosmic scheme of things; but in *God the Invisible
King* he develops a dualistic religious speculation in which a rebel,
Promethean God, the Captain of Mankind, sets out to conquer a
possibly hostile universe controlled by a "Veiled Being."[22] Wells explicitly recognized his position to be Promethean and through its
dualism akin to Manichaeism and gnosticism.

The gnostics saw nature as hostile to what is essentially human.
Modern humanism sees nature as indifferent to all human values
and aims. Jonas points out that hostility is still a relationship; an indifferent universe is more shattering; it alone "represents the absolute vacuum, the bottomless pit." This, he says, is what gives
modern nihilism more depth than gnostic nihilism and makes it
"more radical and more desperate."[23] Most humanists, to be sure,
have not faced up to the nihilist implications of a nonteleological
world. There have been repeated efforts to give naturalistic explanations of man; but there is simply no support in a meaningless
world for human concerns. Marxists find meaning in historical
structures that are themselves grounded in a physical world without meaning. Julian Huxley talks about a blind, purposeless, evolutionary process becoming conscious and acquiring purpose and
direction in man; then he worries for fear man will fail in his responsibility and not assure "true evolutionary progress"—responsible to whom? By what standard is evolutionary change judged
progress, much less true progress?[24] What modern atheism has not

---

[22]H. G. Wells, *First and Last Things* (New York, 1908); and *God the Invisible King*
(New York, 1917). For a fuller discussion of Wells's humanism see Willis B. Glover,
"Religious Orientations of H. G. Wells: A Case Study in Scientific Humanism,"
Harvard Theological Review 65 (1972): 117-35.

[23]Jonas, *The Gnostic Religion*, 339.

[24]Julian Huxley, "The Biologist Looks at Man," *Fortune* 26 (December 1942): 139-
41, 146-52. Reprinted as "Philosophy in a World at War" in Julian Huxley, *On Living
in a Revolution* (New York, 1944). This kind of thinking in which the obvious question raised by a dubious fundamental assumption in not allowed in what Eric Voegelin denounces as an intellectual swindle; Voegelin cites Marx explicitly, but not
Huxley. Eric Voegelin, *Science, Politics, and Gnosticism*, 22-28.

been able to do is to relate the human reality to the world it is aware of confronting. The disjunction between man and the universe, says Jonas, condemns man "to stare at isolated selfhood," and if he tries to escape into a monistic naturalism he will "abolish . . . the idea of man. Between that Scylla and this her twin Charybdis, the modern mind hovers."[25] To return to the analogy, existentialists, who have been willing to stare at isolated selfhood, are similar to the gnostics in their contempt for the concept of nature.

In both cases out of this contempt there developed an antinomianism that denies every objective rule of moral conduct. Here again the analogy fits existentialism much better than historicist forms of humanism. The latter, however, though not contemptuous of nature, do not find in the valueless world any curb on the arbitrary standards decided upon by deified communities in the pursuit of historical causes. The totalitarian state is frightening because there is no moral authority to which it is subject.

It might seem that the most obvious analogy between gnosticism and humanism would be that both seek salvation through knowledge. This, however, would be a misleading play on the word knowledge. It is true that some forms of humanism expect to pursue perfectibility through scientific knowledge and subdue the indifferent world through technology. Others depend on their special knowledge of the pattern and end of history. Even the existentialists, though they do not offer much in the way of salvation, do seem to think that understanding the human situation will help men live authentic lives. Ancient gnosis was radically different from any of this. It was not knowledge of the world or of history or even knowledge of the human situation, but knowledge of the alien God.

That is one of the places where the analogy breaks down. It is interesting that Voegelin, who makes "the murder of God" a prominent part of his analysis of what he calls modern gnosticism, should have paid so little attention to the fact that ancient gnosticism was theistic.[26] The fact is that modern atheistic humanism is a very different religion from gnosticism. For the gnostic salvation

---

[25]Jonas, *The Gnostic Religion*, 340.

[26]Chapter two of *Science, Politics and Gnosticism* is entitled "The Murder of God."

was escape from this world, an escape that was possible only through the power of the God who was alien to the whole of creation—not merely other than the creation but in the most fundamental way hostile to it. The most obvious thing about atheistic humanism is its freedom from any kind of otherworldliness. All but the existentialists and possibly some proto-existentialist romantics offer a salvation, but it is a social salvation to be achieved by man himself in this world. Every major form of humanism except existentialism has been a historicism. In them it is not the individual who is deified but mankind or some community or cause; and salvation is to come through human effort in history. In most cases, as in Marxism, it is to be the inevitable result of a historical process. Gnostic salvation, on the other hand, was the escape of the individual human spirit into another world; it was as far as could be from secular. It is true that Jonas points out that the gnostic myth was a kind of nonrecurring cosmic history; but the cosmic history of the gnostics, in which effective action was in the hands of the alien God, was a very different thing from the mundane history in which the modern humanist has his hope.[27]

It is hard to understand how so learned a scholar as Voegelin could have ignored these very real differences and identified as the same two such different religions. Voegelin may have been so concerned with the denial of a Platonic view of reality by both gnostics and modern humanists and the consequent failure of either, in his judgment, to establish a viable order of society that other aspects of the two faiths may have seemed of secondary importance; but that is hardly an adequate explanation.

The analogy with gnosticism tends to call attention to the less positive and productive aspects of modern humanism. It is important to remember that nihilism has not been the dominant mood or idea of the modern West, and yet atheistic humanism in various forms has been the strongest spiritual force for more than two centuries. In those centuries the sometimes bewildering confusion has been overshadowed by an amazing creativity in a wide variety of areas. Those who like to compare our situation with the declining

---

[27]Jonas, *Gnostic Religion*, 334-35, passim.

Roman Empire would be hard pressed to find in the last two centuries of classical paganism anything to compare with the achievements of the recent West. To be sure, these achievements have not all been those of non-Christian humanism. Beginning with the Enlightenment the West has exhibited a genuine religious or spiritual dichotomy. Non-Christian humanism split off from the Christian past; but Christianity has continued a potent spiritual basis of cultural creativity. Furthermore, humanism did not merely continue much of the biblical-Christian tradition; as this study has been concerned to show, it is in its essence the development of some fundamental elements of that tradition while repudiating others. It is the common ground between Christianity and non-Christian humanism that has allowed the continued existence of Western culture as a viably integrated historical entity.

A good deal of what has been of value in the last two centuries must be credited to Christianity and a good deal to anti-Christian humanistic efforts; but it is important to note that much of our common culture can be positively related to both—that is the significance of those elements of the biblical tradition that are shared by both. Even where the differences beween Christian and atheist are sharp, there has been considerable influence of each on the other. The Christian doctrine of sin has had a general influence on social attitudes and has even strengthened the tendency of some forms of humanism to divide people into the good guys and the bad guys. Also Christian concepts of forgiveness, grace, and redemption have had an influence beyond those who believe in them in the Christian sense. On the other hand, the optimism of many humanists about the achievement of a just society in history has been very stimulating in some Christian circles, especially in liberal Protestantism.[28] A long list of such examples could, no doubt, be drawn up.

One problem of interpretation in this study is that emphasis on the biblical roots of modern humanism might lead one to think of

[28]For a brief discussion of this influence see Glover, "Religious Orientations of H. G. Wells," 133-35.

it as a Christian heresy. That would be a very serious mistake.[29] The differences with Christianity are at least as important as the common ground. It is better to consider humanism in its varied non-Christian forms as a fourth biblical religion alongside Judaism, Christianity, and Islam. This way of thinking about it should prevent us from underestimating the power of atheistic humanism as a spiritual movement.

An opposite error and one more common at the present time is to underestimate the continuing vitality of Christianity. This is perhaps inherent in the situation. Unless one is a very passionate atheist, the denial of God and the ignoring of God come to much the same thing. But if Christian scholars or publicists (on any level of education) seek the widest common ground, they have to play down what distinguishes them from humanists and base their cases as far as possible on the common ground between themselves and atheistic humanists. This has given an enormous advantage to humanists in Western universities and the Western press. An example is seen in the way we talk about antisocial attitudes and behavior. In Christian theology sin is basically a relationship to God; and for that very reason it is hard to introduce into discussions of human injustice and malice except in restricted circles. This despite the fact that Christian insights in this particular matter are of considerable value.[30] Christians who assert distinctively Christian opinions are more likely to be thrown on the defensive in contemporary intellectual circles than humanists who deny them.

Yet the Christian faith in the last two hundred years has proved to be continuingly creative. The most obvious example of this, Christian belles lettres, was commented on in a previous chapter. Many of the greatest modern writers in both poetry and prose have written from a Christian point of view. The significance of this is

---

[29]The World Council of Churches in 1948 declared Marxism to be a Christian heresy.

[30]R. H. S. Crossman writing of the need for a philosophy of socialism declared: "*The evolutionary and the revolutionary philosophies of progress have both proved false* [italics his]. Judging by the facts, there is far more to be said for the Christian doctrine of original sin than for Rousseau's fantasy of the noble savage, or Marx's vision of the classless society." *New Fabian Essays*, ed. R. H. S. Crossman (New York, 1952) 8.

not that some individuals who happened to be Christians have had extraordinary literary talent, but that their Christian perspective gave them unusual insight into human experience in the modern West. The Christian influence on literature has not, of course, been limited to authors committed to the Christian faith.

The influence of Christianity on modern scholarship is harder to detect and evaluate. The primary reason is the difficulty of distinguishing distinctively Christian influence from the continuing development of elements in the biblical tradition that are basic to both Christian and humanist traditions. Certainly there have been Christians in every field of scholarship and science. The degree to which their thinking is actually influenced by a Christian perspective does, however, vary widely. The relevance of a Christian perspective depends in large part on the field—little or none in mathematics, very much in history or literary criticism. In some fields—sociology, for instance—non-Christian presuppositions and biases have inhibited the development of Christian perspectives. It has not been without effect that Comte was the father of modern sociology and that Marx is seen by many to be the most influential single figure in the field.

One very significant field of scholarship which has been predominantly Christian is the study of the Bible itself—a fact often overlooked. The critical study of the Bible was controversial among Christians in the nineteenth century, and to some degree still is; but not only were the people in the field almost all Christian, they were also motivated by and guided by the historical nature of the Hebrew-Christian faith.

A list of Christian scholars like Lord Acton, Douglas Bush, C. S. Lewis, Jacques Ellul, J. H. Hexter, and Henri-Iréné Marrou would mean little. Everybody knows there are some; but opinion as to their significance or the significance of their faith to their scholarship would vary widely with the perspectives and information of readers. Certainly it is fair to say that the Christian influence is not insignificant.

This study is primarily concerned with intellectual culture; but ideas affect actions and institutions. It is relevant, therefore, to mention a few examples of modern Christian influence of this kind. An obvious instance is the antislavery movement, in which the En-

glish evangelicals played so prominent a part. Somewhat more controversial is the evangelical influence on social reform in
nineteenth-century England or the cultural effects pro and con of
the modern missionary movement. On the continent the Roman
Church, which has taken on new vitality since Vatican II, is still a
major political and cultural influence. The Christian element in
Christian democratic parties is hard to assess but not to be denied.
When Churchill in World War II called upon the West to defend
"Christian civilization," his were not thoughtless words nor those
of one ignorant of the sensibilities of those he led.

It is not necessary to the thesis of this essay that the point be
belabored. Christianity has obviously proved more viable than Voltaire supposed. There is even some evidence of a revival of Christian concern in intellectual circles,[31] but that has not reached
proportions that make it very significant for the present study.

Some areas of remarkable achievement have become so nearly
independent of either Christianity or humanism that they do not
divide one from the other. Science has historical roots in the Christian intellectual tradition, but except for historians of the origins of
modern science, the fact is little known. It makes little difference to
science what the faith stance of an individual scientist is.[32] Even in
the case of science, however, cultural orientations derived from the
biblical tradition still function. Early in the development of empirical philosophy it became a commonplace that we cannot know
things in themselves but only their effects on us. Hume went so far
as to demonstrate that empirical philosophy cannot know that the
thing-in-itself exists. Nevertheless, Western scientists, most of
whom are closer to empiricism than to any other philosophy, do not

---

[31]Cf. Roland N. Stromberg, *An Intellectual History of Modern Europe* 2d ed. (Englewood Cliffs, New Jersey, 1975) 501-502.

[32]The conflict between science and religion in the nineteenth century was mis-
guided and even to some degree spurious. Sometimes it was a conflict between
Christianity and scientific humanism, but it assumed the proportions it did because some scientific conclusions contradicted an interpretation of the Bible that
was already being rendered obsolete by biblical scholarship. It is ironic that the two
areas of greatest concern to Christians, geology and biological evolution, were
both developments that would hardly be conceivable in a culture not impregnated
with a biblical conception of reality as a nonrecurring process.

doubt the reality and worth of what they investigate. They are rarely alienated; they believe in the "good creation" whatever they may think about the Creator. It will be interesting to see if an autonomous science does not eventually undermine the faith of those Japanese scientists who are Buddhists and as such believe that nothing exists except "Only-Mind."

The biblical world in which things do not have purposes of their own is what banished teleological explanations from science. That orientation toward the world still prevails, and the avoidance of teleology has become a dogma of scientific method. Perhaps it is a dogma too rigidly held. The Christian intellectual tradition has not held that no purpose exists in the world, but rather that it is God and man, not physical objects that have purpose. In fact, a major emphasis on the will is characteristic of the tradition. It is interesting that biologists, most of whom deny a teleology in nature, yet make use of the concept in their actual approach to nature. The development of a Christian philosophy of biological science might make this legitimate by admitting that God's purposes operate in nature while yet insisting that the only way to discover them is empirical. Maybe the insect *does* look like a piece of bark so that it can avoid its enemies!

The case of technology is much the same as that of science. The concept that the world is for man to control and use is a part of the story of creation in Genesis and is the prevailing attitude in the modern West; yet technological advance has become autonomous of any religious ground, and, indeed, was never a conscious derivative from such.

No one would argue that every bit of culture is a direct product of the religious-philosophical outlook of the society that produces it. But the sense of what is ultimately real and important will open the way to some developments and inhibit others. Furthermore, as the society faces and attempts to solve its problems, the solutions will reflect the worldview of the problem solvers. Sometimes as in art this may be a conscious expression of faith. The twentieth century is one of the really great periods in architecture. New materials have been used to develop new forms; and the impressive results are sometimes used to express Christian faith and sometimes the ideal of some non-Christian humanism.

The same can be said of music. It has an inner history of its own; but it can be made to express various human values and commitments. The development of Western music since the early Enlightenment is one of the greatest human achievements. This is one of the areas in which Christian inspiration has been particularly strong.

Two of the greatest fields of creative achievement in modern history have been mathematics and logic, and both would seem to be completely independent of any other intellectual traditions whatever. It would be difficult to imagine the twentieth century without the science and technology which advances in mathematics and logic have made possible.

It is highly pertinent to this study, however, that with the exception of highly technical fields like logic every major philosophical movement of modern times shows a fundamental influence from the biblical tradition. This is not just the influence of one idea upon another. All philosophy begins in a context that is prior to philosophizing. The context varies, of course, from person to person, and an individual may deny this or that attitude or awareness that is characteristic of his general cultural milieu; but anyone whose sense of his own existence and awareness of the world contained no biblical elements would hardly be a Western man or be convincing to others in the West. This admittedly sounds a bit tautological; but an examination of major philosophers of modern times would reveal the presence in all of them of strong biblical elements.

Empiricism, voluntarism, and a sense of reality as a nonrecurring process are salient features of the biblical intellectual tradition, and they are equally prominent in modern philosophy. Since they all derive historically from belief in a transcendent God, in the absence of such a God it has been hard to hold all of them together, and that has given rise to some of the most persistent problems in philosophy.

Some recent empiricists have thought of philosophy as beginning with Hume. In fact, of course, Hume belongs in an empirical tradition that extends back at least as far as Ockham and that derives out of medieval theological considerations as was discussed in chapter 2. Hume is, nevertheless, a pivotal figure. Up until Hume philosophy since the Middle Ages had been theistic. What Hume did was to secularize the empirical tradition by refraining from positing the transcendent God. The result was a radical philosophical skepticism. Hume showed that there are no philosophical grounds for belief in the existence of God, causal relationships, or even the existence of any substantive ground in an external world for our empirical experience. Hume never said these things were unbelievable; his point was that there is no rational basis for believing them. If Hume's skepticism does not in the strict sense imply solipsism, it left no philosophical argument against it. The Western sense of a material world that is both real and significant is as strong as ever, but philosophy became less relevant to this reality; and atheistic (in the sense of nontheistic) empiricism has not succeeded in adequately relating the human reality to the purposeless world.[33] As the empirical tradition has developed into linguistic analysis, its relationship to the biblical-Christian tradition is less obvious. The problem of relating the human reality to the world is, nonetheless, still a problem for the analysts; and that problem is a result of the essentially biblical way of being aware of the world which is the context of empirical philosophy.

Ernest A. Moody has pointed out that it was the impact of medieval theology which has made the mainstream of modern philosophy quite different from the mainstream of ancient classical philosophy. The latter was rationalistic and speculative, he says, and the former is empirical and critical.[34] It is interesting that the empirical tradition has retained that critical quality throughout its history. Whereas the emphasis of ancient philosophy was on metaphysics, the emphasis of modern philosophy has been on epistemology. There are exceptions, of course, but highly speculative systems have not proved viable in the long run. The most successful of these, Hegelianism, has less direct influence today than He-

---

[33]It may be noted that Bishop Berkeley did not have this problem or any tendency toward solipsism because he posited both the transcendent God and other minds.

[34]Ernest A. Moody, "Empiricism and Metaphysics in Medieval Philosophy," *Philosophical Review* 67 (1958): 146-50, 161, 163.

gel's opponents and those who have developed their ideas.[35] If by critical we mean skeptical or partially skeptical, this characteristic is not in modern philosophy confined to empiricism for it is an element in the thought of Kant, Husserl, the existentialists, and, I would say, Whitehead.

Another characteristic of modern philosophy that dates from the Middle Ages is voluntarism. Emphasis on the will is one source of the widespread distrust of rationalism. The primacy of the will was central to the thought of Augustine and was given a new philosophical relevance by the nominalists of the late Middle Ages. Voluntarism is a corollary of modern man's awareness of himself existing historically as one who is transcendently free and responsible for his own future. Rationalism as a way of knowing the world presupposes a fixed order to which the mind corresponds; but if man, as in the biblical tradition, transcends the orders of nature in his historical freedom, his will transcends his reason and guides it. Hume said, "Reason is, and ought only to be the slave of the passions, and can never pretend to any other office than to serve and obey them."[36]

Kant, in his effort to save reason from Hume's devastating skepticism, divided the experience of reality into the phenomenal and the noumenal. In his epistemology of pure reason Kant is clearly not a voluntarist; but in his analysis of the noumenal aspect of experience his emphasis on will and motive is an example of the voluntarism that pervades Western culture.

In the case of Hegel, despite his conception of reality as the working out of the will of God to the end of human freedom, his philosophy is essentially rationalistic and speculative; it is thus an exception to Moody's analysis of the difference between modern and ancient philosophy. It is remarkable that such a speculative system should have had so much influence. The explanation is undoubtedly in other aspects of his thought which gave it affinities

---

[35]Marxism won an amazing following in the twentieth century but as a philosophy it is already losing its appeal except where it is supported by political motives.

[36]David Hume, *A Treatise of Human Nature*, ed. L. A. Selbe-Bigge (Oxford, 1888) 415 [Book II, Part III, Section III].

with the romanticism of the nineteenth century. In the long run, of course, Hegel's critics carried the day against him.

It is in these critics and their successors that voluntarism has been strongest in modern thought. Both Kierkegaard and Nietzsche understood the primacy of will over reason. Indeed, the much discussed antirationalism of the late nineteenth and twentieth centuries is not a merely negative or pessimistic attitude but a recognition that human experience cannot be reduced to a more or less rational response to reality and that there is truth in Hume's famous dictum even if one admits a greater validity to human thought than Hume thought philosophically defensible.

The pragmatists subordinated reason to immediate, intuitive experience; and Husserl's intentionality introduced a voluntarist element into his epistemology. The existentialists, who were heirs of Husserl as well as the heirs of Kierkegaard and Nietzsche, are the most voluntaristic of all. In the recent epistemologies of Michael Polanyi and Owen Barfield the voluntarism is not only basic but it has a conscious and explicit Christian reference.

There remains to be considered those philosophers that present reality as nonrecurring process. Most famous of such philosophers is Hegel; but Alfred N. Whitehead and Henri Bergson, both with strong voluntarist elements in their philosophies, also emphasize the unidirectional and evolutionary nature of the world. It is impossible to imagine any of these philosophies developing in a cosmological culture in which reality is believed to be fundamentally eternal and unchanging. The biblical tradition in which reality is presented as a drama moving toward a culmination which has never hitherto existed made it easy for evolutionary philosophies to be credible as, indeed, it opened the way to patterns of scientific thought like the geologic column, biological evolution, and the infinitely expanding universe. It may be wondered why, if these philosophies are so congenial to the Western mind, they have not attracted more adherents. Actually, of course, Hegelianism was a dominant influence on much of European culture for several decades, and there have been revivals of it since. In the long run, however, the philosophy of Hegel, like that of Whitehead, proves too rationalistic and speculative to be more than a minority movement in the empirical, critical atmosphere of modern thought. Anyone familiar with it would admit that Whitehead's philosophy is an impressive and fascinating intellectual construction; but there is no convincing reason to think it is literally true. Whitehead himself presents his philosophy as a cosmological hypothesis; and even though he says that such a cosmology should not be accepted unless it offers an explanation of all items of experience, he recognizes that no philosophical system is final. "In its turn every philosophy will suffer a deposition."[37]

Bergson is, in the context of this study, an even more interesting case. His emphasis on teleology in biological evolution as evidence of the organic nature of reality cuts across the grain of two important elements of the contemporary mind. There is a very strong prejudice in the scientific community against the recognition of any purpose in nature itself. Modern science did not begin its spectacular career until physics divested itself of all explanations in terms of a teleology inherent in things. The method that was so successful in physics has been adopted in the other physical and biological sciences where it has had a comparable success. Biologists in fact make more use of teleological considerations than most of them like to admit. Some birds migrate over thousands of miles of open water to avoid winter temperatures and find winter feeding ground; ducks have webbed feet so that they can swim—such explanations are common. The confusion of method with metaphysics, however, makes such explanations suspect. To avoid the teleological heresy, explanations involving purpose or final causes have to be transposed into nonteleological efficient causation even though the latter, in most cases, cannot be specifically identified.

More to the point, perhaps, if teleology is allowed in biological evolution, which is a nonrecurring process, it could hardly be like the unchanging teleology in things that characterized the animism of cosmological cultures. Purpose in evolution would imply a purposer that transcends the process. The ready acceptance of this in an intellectual culture that has become so largely atheistic is hardly to be expected.[38]

---

[37]Alfred North Whitehead, *Process and Reality* (New York, 1969), chapter 1. The quotation is from page 10.

[38]For a fuller discussion of the problem of teleology see the concluding pages of chapter 7, above.

Our cultural heritage is too rich to be accommodated by the common ground shared by humanist and Christian or by any of the humanistic faiths into which modern man's deification of himself has differentiated. The result is a crisis of faith which is currently more obvious in the secular faiths than in Christianity.

IX   FAITHS
IN
CRISIS

Evaluating the culture of any age in the history of a great civilization is hazardous. This is especially true of our own time. In addition to the difficulty in any age of getting the contemporary scene
in a perspective not seriously distorted, there are salient characteristics of the twentieth-century West whose relationship to each
other does not seem at this time to be definable. Amazing creativity
in a number of fields is proceeding in a society beset by a confusion
so deep that it finds no common ground for the discussion of its
basic problems. A sense of meaninglessness frustrates many sensitive and talented people. We are experiencing a crisis of faith
more complex and profound than anything known in the West
since its origin in the early Middle Ages.

The fields in which creativity is most obvious and, therefore,
best known are in science and technology. Developments in physics, biology, and chemistry have produced an increasing number of
sub-fields: quantum mechanics, bio-physics, bio-chemistry, ge-
netics, and so forth. Mathematics has developed so far in this century that the mathematicians in a good university cannot

communicate to each other the new developments in their respective fields. It would take an army of specialists to list all the achievements. For the purpose of this essay it will suffice to call attention to some of the significant advances in technology that have been made since World War II. It is hard for younger people to realize that commercial television and scheduled air transportation did not exist before that war. Much more striking has been the invention of transistors, solid state circuits, computers, laser technology, and sophisticated feedback mechanisms that make it possible to produce any material good automatically. That men have walked on the moon and returned to earth is now so commonplace that the high technology that made it possible is sometimes overlooked. The capacity to change by a very small fraction of a degree the path of a space ship hundreds of thousands of miles from earth requires a number of techniques not in existence four decades ago.

This is not to ignore that new techniques have brought social problems of a bewildering and terrifying nature that have so far eluded all efforts at solution. The most obvious of these is the danger inherent in atomic fission and fusion. But probably more dangerous still is the overpopulation resulting from so benign a thing as the reduction in infant mortality. Our social failures bring us closer to the subject of this essay; but before we explore the underlying crisis of culture, it should be recognized that recent creativity has not been confined to science, mathematics, and technology.

Achievements in architecture, literature, and music have been outstanding. Some would say that the best twentieth-century architecture surpasses aesthetically anything since thirteenth-century Gothic. New structural techniques making use of steel frames have made possible new uses of glass and chrome to create buildings of great beauty in which the aesthetic quality grows right out of the basic structure.

Twentieth-century literature, if not superior to that of earlier periods and if often reflecting a spiritual malaise peculiar to modern times, is yet worthy of the great traditions it has inherited. Solzhenitsyn may not be quite up to Dostoyevsky, nor Eliot, Auden, and Yeats quite up to Shakespeare; but such comparisons do not tell us much. This century's poets and novelists in a number of languages have made this age one of the great periods in Western literature.

Music is harder for the layman to evaluate. It is clear, however, that this century has been one of daring and brilliant innovations in rhythm and tonal combinations. There has also been a kind of dialectical movement between innovation and a concern to bring order to the new sounds. The result has been a strong development of the Western musical heritage. This development has been stimulated by an unprecedented interest in non-Western music. Music has probably been more influenced by other cultures than science, technology, mathematics, or the other arts; an exception to this may be the influence of African abstract primitivism on the visual arts.

With significant exceptions recent art has been less concerned to convey some profound meaning than has the art of various earlier periods. The absence of this concern and also the important exceptions to that absence reveal something about the fundamental crisis of contemporary culture. Art for art's sake is not a peculiarity of the last hundred years. To delight in pleasing sounds or beautiful visual images or the word play of poetry for its own sake is a human experience common in any age. The degree, however, to which modern art ignores the society at large and addresses itself to elite, esoteric groups of artists indicates a failure of the artist to find any common ground relating his deepest insights to the general culture. Many modern people, the mass men of Ortega y Gasset, have no ground for their lives beyond some superficial aspects of the culture—job, profession, material goods, sports, retirement plans, ledger sheets, and so forth. These are hardly the material for a profoundly meaningful art, though they may, of course, be the material for art of high aesthetic value. Deep commitments in our world are divisive; that is, such commitments may be the ground of a community that shares them; but such communities are in many cases mutually exclusive.

Christian artists seem to have some advantage here that is particularly evident in literature. A great deal of the very best literature of the century has been written from a self-consciously Christian perspective. Some of the authors have already been mentioned; Alan Paton, T. S. Eliot, W. H. Auden, Thornton Wilder, Robert Penn Warren, Flannery O'Connor, Charles Williams, and J. R. R. Tolkien are a few of those writing in English. The literature of secular humanism is more diffuse and harder to identify. Faulkner was certainly a kind of humanist and not an orthodox Christian, but he believed in God and his works are so much informed by the Bible that he defies classification in the categories useful to this essay. Although W. B. Yeats was also, perhaps, a humanist rather than a Christian, his retreat from modernity into occultism and ancient lore was not typical of secular humanism. Robert Frost explored the homey experiences common to us all with great sensitivity; but his poetry would not clearly identify him with any of the religious commitments that have been the concern of this study.

So far as the subject of this study is concerned, the striking thing about recent art is that the ideologies of modern humanism have been the matter of so little of it. Existentialism should, perhaps, be mentioned as an exception; but the main thrust of most existentialist literature has been nihilistic rather than the celebration of a faith. Nationalistic themes have motivated some modern art, but the best productions of it have been, like Chopin's polonaises, an old-fashioned patriotism rather than the nationalism that has functioned as a secular religion. Much of the best Russian literature has been hostile to the Communist regime. The arts are a reflection, or more accurately a paradigm, of the cultural situation. The Christian faith has only partially recovered from the crisis of the Enlightenment; but it has so deeply influenced the development of culture from the early Middle Ages that it is a powerful instrument in the interpretation of human experience in the West. The religious crisis of our time is not a crisis of Christian faith but a crisis of the humanistic faiths that have for so many replaced it.[1]

The historicisms of the nineteenth century were efforts to reorder the culture around some cultural product that was less than the whole. The weakening of traditional centers (Christianity, rationalistic naturalism) and the mutual exclusiveness of some of the new faiths bred an intolerable confusion. Totalitarianism was an effort to deal with that confusion by the use of political power to force an integration of culture around some ideology which was treated as an ultimate source of meaning. Marxism and nationalism have

---

[1]K. A. Jelenski, ed., *History and Hope* (Freeport NY, 1962), 2-3, 6-11.

been the ideologies upon which totalitarian regimes have been successfully established. Franco's Spain might be considered a kind of Christian totalitarianism; certainly it exhibited the authoritarian repressiveness that has characterized the total state; but its dependence on a universal church with an independent and international institutionalization prevented so severe a break with the traditional culture as occurred in Italy, Germany, or the Marxist countries.[2] The effort to make one element of the rich Western tradition regulatory for the whole is like trying to put a big box in a little one. In both Germany and Russia the result has been a drastic cultural impoverishment. The impoverishment would have been even greater if the governments had been successful in obliterating all the cultural traditions which could not be accommodated by the reigning ideology. No state has yet succeeded in being quite total.[3] The viability of repressive tyrannies is an interesting question that is outside the scope of this study. However that may be, it has been clearly demonstrated that the total state is not an answer to the crisis of faith that has overtaken the West. This is all the more true because the humanistic faiths upon which they were founded are, along with others, just what is in crisis.

In Russia Marxism is still the idiom of public expression much as the ideas of the Enlightenment are in the United States. The decline of Marxism in Russia is nevertheless well attested. Irving Kristol remarked recently:

> Marxist-Leninism, while it may flourish in some Western intellectual circles, is so atrophied in the Soviet Union that there has not been a single interesting work on Marxist-Leninism, of either Russian or Western origin published there during the last fifty years.[4]

---

[2]The earlier Jacobin movement in France, although it involved a strong nationalist element, was not confined to that; but it was not successful in establishing the Republic of Virtue—this was at least partly because the techniques for organizing a total state had not been developed.

[3]Friedrich Hayek has argued convincingly that it is not possible to plan a whole society: *The Counter-Revolution of Science* (London, 1955).

[4]Irving Kristol, "The Succession: Understanding the Soviet Mafia," *The Wall Street Journal* 18 November 1982, 30. See also Jelenski, *History and Hope*, 6-8, 71; Richard Lowenthal, ibid., 53-54.

As Professor Kristol indicates, there is still some adherence to Marxism among intellectuals in non-Communist countries; but its influence is greatly attenuated.

Roland Stromberg declared Marxism the most powerful religious movement in modern times.[5] The fervor of its adherents, particularly in academic circles, for long obscured from many its serious intellectual weaknesses.[6] Many sensitive people have been attracted to Marxism as offering an alternative to a culture that has lost its roots. The Russian Revolution was an exhilarating experience for many in the West who were not too close to it. In time, however, the history of the Communist tyranny proved very disillusioning. The murder of the kulaks, the purges of the 1930s, the alliance with Hitler, and after the war Russia's refusal to participate in the Marshall plan, the cold war, the oppression of Russian-occupied countries in central and eastern Europe, the Berlin Wall, among other things, have eroded the hopes of Western intellectuals in the Communist movement. Communism is at present strong in the Third World, where it offers an ideology of protest against the existing or immediately previous societies. The leaders of non-European countries whose indigenous culture has been undermined by Western technology have often found it easier to adopt Communist ideas and tactics than the more sophisticated ideas and institutions of Western democracy, for which the traditions of their societies offer little support. This, however, is outside the scope of the present study, which has to do with the spiritual and religious history of the West.

The strong Communist parties in several countries of continental Europe are more relevant, but even here Marxism is more a source of slogans and electioneering than a live and attractive faith. Their interest is pragmatic; but they say no more about Marxism as a living faith than Christian Democratic parties say about a revival of Christian faith. Other forms of socialism that functioned as religious faiths in the nineteenth century do so no more. Non-Marxist

---

[5]Roland N. Stromberg, *An Intellectual History of Modern Europe*, 2d ed. (Englewood Cliffs NJ, 1975) 345.

[6]For a brief incisive discussion of Marxism and its weaknesses see ibid., 324-59.

socialism is still a very strong option in European politics and has had a significant influence on all industrial societies; yet it can hardly be said to be any longer a religious faith. Marxism seems to be evolving in a similar way, and may, in fact, have a less lasting effect on Western society.

If one confines one's thought to the first half of this century, Stromberg's evaluation of the religious strength of Marxism is plausible enough. It is from a later perspective that we can see its staying power has not been great. It seems that both nationalism and scientism may be stronger and more influential in the long run than Marxism.[7]

The problem of Marxism is deeper than the immoralities of Communist regimes. If that were all, Marxists might simply dissociate Marxism from what could legitimately be considered gross distortions of it. Some have done so. But the problem is more fundamental. Eric Voegelin says that Marx was guilty of an intellectual swindle.[8] The alleged swindle is that Marx—and Marxists—refuse to admit questions about the ground of their system. From the point of view of Voegelin's Platonic rationalism this is particularly blameworthy because he assumes that ultimate reality is accessible to honest thought. From the point of view of this essay the fault of Marx is not essentially a swindle but a basic difficulty in humanistic faiths. No one critically examines his first principles; if he did, the basis of his criticism would supplant the principles examined as the foundation of his thought. The humanist, however, has a special problem here. The modern atheistic consciousness knows two realities—the human reality and the world. A dualism in which man as spirit confronts a materialistic world which opposes him is a common idea in the modern West, but it is not an idea with which the humanist can be comfortable. The material world for the humanist is not an evil to be forsaken but a possibility for control and the creation of a better world for himself as an individual and for society. Since the world obviously transcends his own existence and is the

---

[7]Stromberg was well aware of the decline of faith in Marxism especially after 1945; Roland N. Stromberg, *After Everything* (New York, 1975) 5-9.

[8]Eric Voegelin, *Science, Politics, and Gnosticism* (Chicago, 1968), 21-28. Voegelin makes the same charge against Hegel and Nietzsche.

context within which he exercises his freedom, he finds himself trying to relate the two realities by grounding his own existence in the order of nature. This involves him in contradiction because his historical existence is precisely a transcending of the order of nature. Humanism is continually compromised by naturalism. This is most obvious in scientific humanism. Faith in the historical scientific movement is grounded in the order of nature, which includes man himself and is assumed to be a fixed unchanging reality. Nationalism when it deifies a given people is appealing to a hierarchy of human value assumed to be given in nature. Liberal progressivism insofar as it sees progress as inevitable is appealing to a natural law of history; and when its faith in the inevitability of progress is shaken, its anxiety for fear man will fail to progress presupposes a standard independent of man's free creativity. If Marx was guilty of an intellectual swindle as Voegelin charges, it was not so much his refusal of certain questions as his unwillingness to recognize that he was caught in a contradiction between the dynamic historical movement he espoused and his claim that its inevitable success was assured by "science."

The crisis of the twentieth century is partly that the humanistic faiths of the nineteenth century and the ideologies they spawned have lost credibility. Intellectuals who turned to Marxism in the 1920s and 1930s as a way out of the emptiness they experienced have seen their new faith eroded away in disillusionment. Their experience is well described by the six former Communists who wrote the biographical essays in *The God that Failed*.[9]

The history of nationalism is more complex; but the salient features of it are so well known as to require only mention here. In the nineteenth century it was possible for people of a given nationality to believe sincerely that their nation was superior and would lead the world in civilization. Nationalism could and did in some cases have a strong moral dimension. The Boy Scout movement and the Rhodes Scholarships attest this benign side of nationalism in England. But nationalism has led to two world wars in this century, and the virulent forms it took in Italy and Germany have demon-

---

[9]Richard Crossman, *The God That Failed* (New York, c. 1949 [1950]).

strated how demonic it is. Nationalism is still a potent force. Far more than commitment to Marxism or the practice of political terrorism, it is what holds the Russian Communist state together. In those parts of the Third World in which Westernization has undermined indigenous institutions and produced an atomizing of society similar to what had resulted in Europe from industrialism and Enlightenment individualism, nationalism is sometimes a vital principle of cohesion. In Europe and the United States nationalism remains a major factor in international relations and also a foundation of political life within countries. There are even instances of increased nationalism as in Scotland and French Canada. There are two reasons that nationalistic feeling is likely to continue strong indefinitely. One is that it is supported by a kind of patriotism which is a general, if not universal, human characteristic. The patriotism Southerners feel toward the South in the United States is not nationalistic but it probably contributes to the strength in the South of loyalty to the nation-state. In Scotland a similar patriotism has recently produced a separatist movement.

The second source of nationalism's strength is the religious or pseudoreligious quality of political loyalties in general. The object of such loyalties is the political community; but the symbols by which it is apprehended vary with the type of polity—tribe, kingdom, republic, city-state, and others. In the present age the object of such commitment is the nation-state. It is interesting that since the first origin of territorial states, their health has depended upon a religious sanction for the authority they wield. There is not space here to elaborate on this obvious, and yet remarkable, dimension of politics. Christian theology does, however, offer some explanation in terms of the kingdom of God as normative for man, the fall which spoils the true community, and the earthly city as a gift of God, sinful and yet to be accepted by Christians as necessary in the present situation until the true community has been restored. In this perspective the political community becomes an imperfect and inadequate surrogate for the true meaning of life in the City of God. One Christian political tradition, influenced by Greek thought, sees the ideal state as a part of the original order of creation. The other major tradition, following Augustine, sees the state as an artificial creation made necessary by sin and eventually to be replaced when the coming of the kingdom of God has been fully realized. In either case the political life of man, because it answers to the deep need of man for meaning in community, has a pseudoreligious quality even for those for whom it is not the ultimate meaning of existence.

For many nationalism still functions as a kind of pseudofaith in a way similar to certain one-issue political causes, commitment to which may be meaningful enough to offer some relief from nihilism. Opposition to nuclear power, some form of racism, and women's liberation would be examples of the latter. Despite its continued political strength, however, nationalism has failed as a faith capable of meeting the need of modern man to find the ultimate meaning of his life or an adequate ground for the rich cultural tradition he has inherited.

The eclipse of science as a viable humanistic faith has been more surprising than that of Marxism or nationalism, but it is of comparable magnitude. The scientific enterprise is still a religion for many—Julian Huxley was not the last of them—but it has little religious appeal for the general educated public. There has been no slowing down of scientific progress; but science has proved too ambiguous in its results to appear any longer as a savior. Some authority beyond science is needed to guide its unpredictable discoveries into socially constructive uses. Economic motivations in a free-enterprise society are sure to produce abuse as well as legitimate use of scientific knowledge. Nor can political authorities, to which scientific development is to a considerable degree subject, be counted on to turn it to the good. The political communities themselves, however democratically organized, are too confused regarding any ground for ethical decision to correct those who wield the political power generated by the community. Science is potentially as demonic as Marxism or nationalism, and this is too generally recognized for science to function as the religion of the West.

In 1957 Erich Kahler published *The Tower and the Abyss*. Kahler rejected the Christian anthropology of Reinhold Niebuhr with its pessimism regarding man's capacity to perfect his society. Unanticipated advances in technology, he argued, had refuted Niebuhr and put utopia within the range of human capacity. The vision of utopia with which he concludes sounds like an empty voice from the past—warmed-over Enlightenment optimism made less, not more, credible by the advances in technology.

Existentialism has been identified in this essay as a humanistic faith. Since some of its leading proponents, notably Nietzsche and Sartre, have extolled the self-deification of the individual person, it qualifies as a humanism in the meaning of that term here. Yet it has certainly been a genuine faith for very few people. Even Sartre committed himself to Marxist Communism, and Camus in *The Rebel* retreated from existentialism to affirm a sense of justice rooted in natural law. Its vogue for two decades after World War II was far most hardly more than playful flirting with nihilism. This is not to discount it as a thoughtful intellectual venture which has made a real contribution to our self-understanding. Sartre and other literary existentialists including Camus have explored the situation of modern man without God more honestly and profoundly than any but the very greatest of Christian thinkers and have thus made a major contribution to Christian thought. Heidegger, though less interested in religious questions, did yet through his analysis of human transcendence develop further what is an essentially biblical anthropology whether he knew it or not.

Popular interest in existentialism has waned sharply, but its contribution to philosophy, theology, and related disciplines can hardly be questioned. It is not within the scope of this study to attempt an evaluation of it as a philosophical movement; concern here is simply to discuss its function as a humanistic faith. As a faith it has involved too few people and has been too radically individualistic to offer any prospect of furnishing a basis of social cohesion.

Despite its phenomenal creativity and its having produced a society which from its poorest to its richest is the most affluent the world has even dreamed of before, the modern West is experiencing a crisis of faith and is suffering from a debilitating malaise. This statement is not capable of proof because the crisis itself is a lack of the kind of common ground upon which a proof could be built. It must remain a matter of judgment. Nevertheless, there is evidence that such a crisis does exist. It is impossible now for most people to "believe in" the ideologies of the nineteenth century as offering answers to ultimate questions. The nineteenth century has been called "The Age of Ideology"; it might equally well be called an age of faith. There were competing faiths and even mutually exclusive faiths, to be sure; but nihilists were few and even fewer the sensitive, prescient figures like Matthew Arnold who realized the foundations of culture were eroding away.

Paradoxically the seriousness of our situation has been obscured by the decline of humanistic faiths. Western Europe has made a remarkable recovery since World War II. Politics and economics have been much less disturbed by passionate movements than was the case in the period after World War I. Nevertheless, the anxiety that pervades our society and is continuously revealed in the news media is not without foundation. Solutions for new problems are not found because no consensus exists which could support a solution. There is certainly not space here to catalogue, much less discuss, the problems facing the West. A few examples should suffice to make the point. Aside from the religious crisis itself, the most serious crisis facing the race today is the population explosion. Although the technical means to deal with the problem are readily available, practically nothing has been done about it except for the practice of voluntary birth control in Europe, Japan, and the English-speaking world outside of Europe. It is astounding how little public interest has been generated by this problem. Only since about 1960 has there been any general recognition that the problem exists. Various moral problems are, of course, involved, but there is no agreed-upon basis for resolving them. The secondary problems that stem, at least in large part, from population pressure are what have attracted public attention and generated passionate social movements. Examples are easily found.

Poverty in Latin America is very real and has aroused an appropriate emotional response. Concern for the poor in Central and South America has turned Catholic priests into Marxists. What is scarcely ever mentioned is that absolutely no social reorganization or redistribution of wealth will alleviate the poverty in countries where the rate of population increase will, if it persists, double the number of people in twenty-five years. If there is such a thing as moral energy, it is certainly being wasted by efforts to improve the conditions of the Latin-American poor through social reform or the increase of democratic polity.

Concern over the ecology is another case in point. Resources are being used up, wilderness areas are disappearing, large wild animals are in imminent danger of becoming extinct. None of these would be in crisis if it were not for the increase in human population. Why, then, is the root problem so seldom the primary concern of the ecologists? Related to ecology but transcending it in several directions is the problem of nuclear power.

It is doubtful that anybody wants to see nuclear war between major powers; at present the blackmailing of weaker powers by the threat of nuclear arms is prevented by the stalemate between the nuclear forces of the U.S.S.R. and the U.S.A. The problem of preventing nuclear war is essentially technical and political; at present it seems to be basically a matter of preserving the stalemate and if possible reducing its costs. Despite the anxiety of many who think a real moral issue is involved, the fact is that the issues have to do with means rather than with the end—everyone wants to avoid nuclear war. Though the choice of means might involve moral issues, the basic problem does not divide people morally or religiously. The peaceful use of nuclear power is a separate issue. It is clear from the evidence available that nuclear power is much less of a threat to human life and the ecology than power derived from organic minerals. There have been a few scares vigorously promoted by the news media; but no nuclear power disasters have occurred that are comparable to those of coal mines, burning and explosion of fossil fuels, accidents to oil tankers, collapse of off-shore oil rigs, and others. In view of all the facts the strength of the opposition to nuclear power in the United States is a remarkable case of irrational fear.[10] But it is more than that. It is a peculiarity of our time that modern man finding no ground for his free, creative, historical existence in either God or nature tends to absolutize his life and refuse in some contexts to accept his mortality. There is a subtle confusion in attitude here that is difficult to describe. Familiar sources of death hardly generate commonsense efforts at prevention. The public of the United States accepts too easily 50,000 highway deaths a year,

---

[10]My friend Dan Metts disagrees with my judgment in this. He says my position is analogous to that of a man who jumped off the Empire State Building and as he passed the thirty-fourth floor shouted, "So far, so good!"

many caused by drunken drivers. Millions still smoke cigarettes despite the recent discovery of their often lethal effects. The federal government in the United States discourages smoking while subsidizing the production of tobacco. Yet the American public will panic sometimes over a few deaths from some unexpected source and react extravagantly to close a whole industry. And in a society in which murders are reported in almost every newspaper, millions will be spent to prevent a few death penalties from being carried out. We do not have a generally accepted source of moral principles that would make possible more rational attitudes.

Sometimes the weakness of moral thought and conviction is evident in areas where moral talk is most glib. *Human rights* is a term bandied about quite loosely. In its use by the United Nations and in various international conferences and treaties it is simply a general term for the humane treatment of people. There is no agreed upon list of human rights. What may be considered a right in some countries would be an immoral offense in another. The concept, if it can be called that, has, nevertheless, had a meliorating influence. In the United States there has been a ridiculous proliferation of so-called rights. Almost anything that somebody desires and thinks important is likely to be claimed as a right. In addition to traditional civil rights that are defined in law, there are asserted the right of a woman to an abortion, the right of the fetus to live, the right of the public to know, the right of the reporter to protect his sources, the right to work, the right to strike, the right to education, the right to a comfortable standard of living, the right to marital happiness, and others.

There is nothing very seriously wrong with all this. It could be considered merely a manner of expression. The manner of expression does, however, give an undue weight to rights claims by associating them with the more meaningful ideas of Locke and Jefferson. The problem is that twentieth-century "rights" are supported by no authority except in some cases the authority of governments. The rights specified in the Declaration of Independence had behind them the will of the Creator. Whatever one may think of the inadequacy of Jefferson's deism, the rights he claimed were not left dangling intellectually. The result of the present situation is not merely the inanity of appealing to "human rights" as though the phrase itself was authority for any content we choose to give it.

It is much more important that the lack of any ground for moral opinions in some shared acceptance of what is ultimately real leads inevitably to moral relativism. This was especially evident when the Nazis were in power. Perceptive people realized that without any universal authority to which to appeal it was impossible to argue rationally that the values of the Western democracies were right and those affirmed so vigorously by the Nazis wrong. Walter Lippmann wrote *The Public Philosophy* in an effort to solve this problem by reviving a belief in natural law. Leo Strauss with the same motive published his *Natural Right and History* in 1953.[11] Strauss recounts the origin of natural rights doctrine in Greek philosophy. This doctrine, he says, was modified to some degree by Thomas Aquinas, but it continued through Richard Hooker at the end of the sixteenth century. Between Hooker and Locke there was an important watershed. The difference between classical and modern conceptions of natural right, or more generally natural law, occurs first in Thomas Hobbes. The difference resulted from "the emergence of modern natural science of *nonteleological* natural science, and therewith the destruction of the basis of traditional natural right."[12] The political theory of Hobbes was based upon a modified subjectivism. Man could have a knowledge of politics as certain as his knowledge of geometry because the state, like the figures with which geometers worked, was a construct of his own mind.[13] The subjectivism was not complete. The moral laws were the conditions of peace and were accessible to human intelligence; but they were also commands of God and as such obligatory.[14] The state still had

---

[11]Walter Lippmann, *Essays in the Public Philosophy* (Boston, 1955). Leo Strauss, *Natural Right and History* (Chicago, 1953). This volume was an expanded version of Strauss's Walgreen Foundation Lectures. In his Forward Jerome Kerwin explains the renewed interest in natural law doctrine as a reaction against totalitarianism.

[12]Ibid., 166; emphasis added.

[13]Thomas Hobbes, *Six Lessons to the Professors of the Mathematics*, E. W., 7:183-84; *De Homine, Opera . . . que latine scripsit*, ed. Sir William Molesworth, 5 vols. (London, 1839-45), 2:92-94. Hobbes claimed that civil philosophy, properly speaking, began with his *De Cive*. See also Willis B. Glover, "Human Nature and the State in Hobbes," *Journal of the History of Philosophy* 4 (1966): 306.

[14]Thomas Hobbes, *The Elements of Law*, ed. F. Tönnies (Cambridge, 1928) 72. Cf. Howard Warrender, *The Political Philosophy of Hobbes* (Oxford, 1957) 97-100; Willis B. Glover "God and Thomas Hobbes," *Hobbes Studies*, ed. Keith C. Brown (Oxford, 1965) 160-64.

an anchor point outside itself, and the moral law was not an arbitrary product of society. Strauss sees this modern natural right doctrine reaching a crisis in Rousseau and Burke and being displaced in the nineteenth century by an appeal to history. This, of course, was the end of natural law because an appeal to history was an appeal to tradition and the development of tradition without any principle to guide it could lead anywhere—sooner or later moral relativism was inevitable. Strauss hoped for a return to a classical doctrine of natural law. This has not happened and is not likely. One cannot produce fundamental belief in an ultimate reality simply by pointing out its desirability.

Strauss's analysis is very helpful, but it does not probe below the level of intellectual history. Ideas have consequences all right; but they also have sources. The concepts of natural law and natural right derived from Greek reflection on a cosmological faith. These concepts could be continued in Christian Europe because God was understood to have a purpose in nature. With God eliminated and nature disenchanted and without moral relevance, there can be no natural rights.

"Human rights" in this situation is a phrase that has considerable emotive force, but the concept is grounded only in particular and divergent historical traditions. This is a very shaky authority indeed, especially if the development of traditions is not guided by some underlying sense of meaning. T. S. Eliot's idea that traditions are the working out in history of an "orthodoxy" is a strange use of terms, but it expresses a very important truth.[15] Without some fundamental authority tradition loses its organic wholeness and elements of it can begin to grow like cancers. An example is the ridiculous degree to which American society is committed to the principle of human equality. Sound educational policies are undermined by the unwillingness to admit that, whatever their origins, important differences in human abilities, temperament, and char-

---

[15]T. S. Eliot, *Notes towards a Definition of Culture* (London, 1948) 15, 27-34; *After Strange Gods* (New York, 1934) 18-19, 21-25, 31-34; Seán Lucy, *T. S. Eliot and the Idea of Tradition* (London, 1960) 10-11, 15, 23-24. The term "orthodoxy" here is misleading because it suggests a dogmatic system of Christian belief. Eliot was using it in a more general sense.

acter exist and must have a bearing on education. Unqualified commitment to the principle of equality has also produced confusion and inanities in basic elements of political organization. The Supreme Court recently decreed that it is unconstitutional for state legislatures to be based on any principle of representation except one-man-one-vote. This is obviously and flagrantly in contradiction to the principle by which the Constitution provides for representation in the Congress of the United States and to various other constitutional limitations on majority rule. There is no question that conditions existed in state constitutions that needed correcting, but the correction imposed prohibits any state from adopting other principles of representation that might in some situations be more just. The Court itself has violated its own principle by requiring the gerrymandering of electoral districts to provide proportional representation for certain minorities. The point here is simply that the Court did not act with the kind of balanced judgment shown by those who drew up the Constitution in the first place. If egalitarianism is pushed to its logical extreme unqualified by anything else, it will contradict the incalculable worth of unique persons and produce the atomized society of mass men deplored by Ortega y Gasset.

Another example of a principle growing cancerously is the obligation of courts to protect the rights of the accused. Persons who are unquestionably guilty of violent crime are freed in the United States because some policeman or trial judge has made a technical error. This can have no beneficial effect for society except to discipline the police and the judges. Surely a more rational method of discipline and one less costly to the society could be devised. Present policies threaten to reduce criminal justice in this country to a shambles.

Since the end of the Nazi and Fascist regimes the problem of moral relativism has been obscured by the fact that the Communists have not attacked the basic values of the West but have attacked capitalistic society for having hypocritically violated them. Their claim is that in the new Communist society these values will be secured. So far as any actual Communist society is concerned, the claim has proved to be empty; indeed, it is doubtful that Communist leaders in Communist countries are even sincere in it any more.

Where established economic and political orders have continued, social inertia plus a tendency to affirm the existing order *in place of* any commitment to a fundamental reality has preserved the humane values of Judaeo-Christian and secular-liberal traditions. Whether this is in the long run a viable condition of society must remain for now an unanswered question. Where the existing order has been destroyed by revolution, the lack of adequate ground for the support of such values has been revealed. Terror became the means for establishing and maintaining structures of political and economic power. Commitment to the humane ends claimed by Communist revolutionaries has not proved strong enough to end the terror and establish order on shared commitments. The Communists have been far more guilty than the traditional societies of violating the principles they have affirmed as goals of social reform.

The decline of ideologies has removed some causes of tension but the crisis of humanistic faith has by no means been dispelled. Varying emphases on science, economic reorganization, or the need for political purification remain; but on the whole Western humanism has returned to the more general and amorphous faith of the Enlightenment. Now, however, it is without the crutches of deism or of a belief in natural law. The moral dimension and reassuring quality that natural law had in ancient cosmological civilization or in the Christian doctrine of the good Creation are not to be found by scientific study of a valueless world.

The failure of ideologies has brought spiritual malaise. An underlying nihilism has stalked the West for more than a century. In the nineteenth century it was experienced by only a few among knowledgeable and sensitive people. After World War I those who saw the West as a wasteland were more influential and constituted an intellectual community of people who felt alienated in their own culture. They had perceived an emptiness at the heart of the West and a consequent meaninglessness in the elegant and powerful superstructures that were without foundation in reality.[16] Eliot's "The

---

[16]If nihilism means utter meaninglessness, then like democracy or totalitarianism it does not exist in pure from. Any nihilists who are active, whether writing poetry or bombing laboratories, must have consciously or unconsciously some

Waste Land" and his "The Hollow Men" are striking expressions of this disillusionment with modern culture. The shock of Nazi tyranny brought back an appreciation of traditional values. This carried the Allies triumphant through World War II; but it did not relieve the fundamental weakness of the culture—its failure to find roots in reality. Economic and political recovery was amazingly swift in Japan and the democratic West, including West Germany; but in the 1960s nihilism returned, this time—for the first time—as a popular movement. The real problem, after all, was not economic nor political, but spiritual. Young adults, especially those in universities, were in the forefront of the "protest" movements of the 1960s and 1970s; but the phenomenon was by no means confined to them. Parents supported protesting students through years of nonstudy. Faculties frequently backed violent student action against university administrations trying to preserve some vestige of order. The strange attitude of the Harvard faculty toward President Pusey is a classic case.

Efforts to explain the movement as a consequence of the Vietnam War or the failure of this or that institution fail to take into consideration the international extent of the massive protests. Denmark, Holland, West Germany, France, even Japan were involved. The protesters were not opposed to violence—Ho Chi Minh and Ché Guevara were among their heroes. They adopted no ideology and produced none. Theirs was a passionate attack on what they called "the establishment" or "bourgeois society"— whatever terms of opprobrium they used, what they meant was Western Civilization. They denounced inherited standards as inauthentic, traditional morality as insincere, established institutions as bastions of injustice. They did not seek the reform of democratic institutions but denounced them in wholesale fashion. When they talked of "participatory democracy," they seem to have meant nothing more than a refusal to submit to any authority. The force of the movement was almost wholly negative. Some changes resulted—greater use of drugs and more permissive sex—but the

---

backdrop sense of values. In the case of the protest movement of the sixties there may have been for some a Rousseauistic belief that the natural goodness of man was being thwarted and corrupted by society.

movement solved no problems. Its failure to develop any program of its own reveals the lack of any adequate source of values in modern secular society. Simple life in communes without the amenities of modern civilization and without the cohesiveness of any social authority did not appeal for long. Unrelieved nihilism is, perhaps, not likely to last for long; the movement ran its course in less than two decades.

The situation out of which the protests had come did not, however, change in any fundamental way. Nihilism took another form. It hid itself in acceptance of secondary and superficial cultural values. As was suggested above there is an underlying nihilism in the stridency of one-issue political movements. Kierkegaard pointed out that people avoid questions of ultimate meaning by turning their attention to what he called frivolities. Political issues, professional careers (including scholarship), economic success, almost anything can be used to occupy the mind and ward off the essential human question of meaning. As Kierkegaard well understood, these dodges are not a solution to nihilism but an expression of it. Students of the past decade have turned to vocational concerns. Colleges have been able to tighten their general education requirements, but liberal education in the traditional sense of a concern with disciplines that introduce the student to the fundamental traditions of society, its basic ideas and values, is still in eclipse. When faith in the ultimate source of such values and ideas in reality is lost, liberal education becomes an empty thing; the pursuit of it is reduced to blind traditionalism, sentimentality, art for art's sake, or mere status seeking.[17]

The status of Christianity in this situation is hard to evaluate. It has not made significant gains against its humanistic rivals; on the other hand, it is clearly not moribund. That Christian faith is the source of much of the best twentieth-century art—especially literature—has been previously mentioned. The biblical Christian tradition is still a dominant influence in philosophy, even though the philosophers are mostly unconscious of it. The liberal theology of

---

[17]For a brief discussion of the essential meaning of liberal education see Willis B. Glover, "Liberal Education and the Christian Intellectual Tradition," *Perspectives on Liberal Education: Pioneers and Pallbearers* (Macon GA, 1982) 9-13.

the nineteenth and early twentieth centuries, though its contributions to biblical scholarship and social ethics are noteworthy, has borne little genuinely religious or theological fruit. World War II occasioned some revival of the Christian religion, but it was short-lived. Since then Vatican II has released an unexpected liveliness among Roman Catholics; and in the United States a conservative Evangelical Protestantism has attracted a large and increasing following among working and middle classes, but its obscurantism with regard to biblical scholarship and science has cut it off from the more sophisticated. What will be the long range cultural effects of such movements it is impossible to say.

As Christianity confronts modern secularism one might expect to find the creative edge in theology. There is a great biblical Christian intellectual tradition that could shed much light on many facets of modern culture and even, perhaps, offer historical grounds for the integration of many of its most important elements; but Christian theology for the past three hundred years has failed to appropriate its heritage; and despite great erudition and intellectual brilliance the theologians have had a minimal effect upon intellectual culture. Pascal marks the end of an era. He was a worthy representative of the great Augustinian tradition, and his participation in the scientific creativity of the seventeenth century might well have kept theology in a healthy relationship with the development of modern science; but Pascal had no disciples—his genius was recognized, but he initiated no intellectual movement. The spirit of the age moved in a quite different direction. The proto-deism of the seventeenth century developed into the deistic humanism of the Enlightenment. In the long history of formal Christian thought the nadir was the eighteenth century. John Wesley was an educated man and his modified Calvinism was not without depth, but he made no significant contribution to theology. The Jansenists gave a good account of themselves against the philosophes. William Law, Jonathan Edwards, and a few other individuals continued respectable traditions; but the controversies which attracted attention were exceedingly arid. The deistic controversy in England centered in the issues of revelation and providence, and neither side got to the bottom of either issue. The antagonists do not deserve to be compared with the best thought of the late Middle Ages or the Reformation.

Hume's skepticism is closer to the heart of the Christian intellectual tradition than what the theologians of his time were saying. His conclusion that philosophy, independent of revelation and faith, could not establish the reality of God would not have surprised Ockham or Luther.

Kant's response to Hume was more directly concerned with theology. In a sense he does not really answer Hume at all. Like Christian philosophers from Anselm to Berkeley he *assumes* the reality of God and then proceeds to show that on this assumption he can make sense of his experience. Kant's ethics shows a strong Christian influence, but he does not posit the Christian tradition as its source. His main influence on subsequent theology has been through neo-Kantians who seriously misunderstood him. Kant made an epistemological distinction between the phenomenal and the noumenal; some of his followers converted this into a metaphysical distinction. Kant was trying to save causality while avoiding the trap of a mechanically determined world. Many neo-Kantians derived from his philosophy a two-storied world—the mechanical, determined world of cause and effect; and the spiritual world of ethical responsibility and the knowledge of God. This subterfuge enabled them to affirm the mechanistic world they thought was implied in modern science while continuing to believe in freedom and ethical responsibility to God.[18] The *reductio ad absurdum* of this position was reached in Rudolf Bultmann's interpretation of the Resurrection of Christ as simply the *meaning* which the apostles saw in the Crucifixion. Bultmann saw history as a part of the mechanistic phenomenal world: it moves on inexorably from cause to effect; but free spirits may discern the meaning of history in a noumenal world that does not interfere with the world of observable

---

[18]In justice to them it should be said that a mechanistic metaphysics did seem to be implied in the physics of the Enlightenment because the successful methods of physics had been transmuted into a metaphysics. (See chapter 4 above.) This, however, can hardly excuse those recent theologians who have failed to take into account the anti-mechanistic implications of twentieth-century physics.

facts.[19] The fallacy of this is readily seen as soon as one raises the question whether Paul's grasp of the meaning of Crucifixion/Resurrection had anything to do with how his physical body moved about the Mediterranean area and affected observable events in history! Richard R. Niebuhr went so far as to say in 1957 that virtually all Protestant theology since Kant had been vitiated by a corrupt Kantianism.[20]

The nineteenth century saw a very significant revival of Christianity. Roman Catholicism profited from the general reaction against the Enlightenment to make a strong recovery. In the English-speaking world the evangelical revival which had begun with John Wesley and others had not been much influenced by the Enlightenment; but it continued to grow in the more congenial atmosphere of the post-Enlightenment period to reach its height in the middle third of the nineteenth century. The Catholic revival produced some interesting political and social theory, but neither it nor English Evangelicalism made any noteworthy contribution to theology. The theology of the evangelical revival was largely a modified Calvinism, and Catholic theology did not deviate much from what had been established at Trent. To this day the most vigorous Protestant churches, especially in the English-speaking world, are living in backwaters of theology nourished by old traditions that are poorly understood, obscurantist, and lacking in creative power. The intellectual life of Catholicism has been aptly described as having been in a chrysalis stage for four hundred years, from the Council of Trent to Vatican II. Since Vatican II there has been a great intellectual ferment in the Catholic Church. This may presage a significant theological awakening; but that has not yet occurred. Recent Catholic intellectual vitality has so far had minimal effects on the general intellectual culture and even on the life of the church.

Leadership in nineteenth-century Protestant theology was with the Germans. This theology developed along with the new biblical criticism that was mentioned in chapter 7 as an example of the pen-

---

[19]Rudolf Bultmann, "New Testament and Mythology" in *Kerygma and Myth*, ed. Hans Werner Bartsch, trans. Reginald H. Fuller (London, 1954).

[20]Richard R. Niebuhr, *Resurrection and Historical Reason* (New York, 1957) 74, 80-81.

chant of the age for historical explanation. The context of both theology and biblical scholarship was a kind of neo-Kantianism on one
hand and Hegelian idealism on the other. Neither was compatible
with the inherited biblical-Christian tradition. The distorted understanding of Kant encouraged a deterministic, mechanistic
worldview; and the German distinction between *historie* and *ges-
chichte* led to the inclusion of all observable history in the mechanistic system. The monistic ontology of Hegel offered no acceptable
alternative. It had no place for a transcendent God, the contingency
of the world, or even the Christian anthropology of radical historical freedom. Those elements of the Christian community that were
closest to what may be called the mainline Christian tradition were
thrown on the defensive and produced no adequate theological response to what was new in the intellectual life of the general culture. There were individual exceptions—P. T. Forsyth in England is
a notable example—but they had no significant following.

The major contribution of the nineteenth century to Christian
scholarship was the literary and historical criticism of the Bible. In
this as in theology it was continental Protestantism that took the
lead. Unfortunately this scholarship lacked an adequate theological
context with the result that many of the ablest contributors to it
were led by mechanism or idealism into positions that could only
be seen as dangerously heretical from the point of view of those
committed to the traditional faith. The new biblical scholarship offered escape from the debilitating and indefensible literalism of
what had come to be Catholic and Protestant orthodoxy. Its acceptance among the strongest Christian *religious* movements was
nevertheless slow because of distrust of the theology that accompanied it.[21] Modern biblical scholarship has done much to clarify
obscurities in the Bible and make it a far more realistic and credible
collection of writings; it should have led to a general appreciation of
the powerful tradition of which the Bible is the most important element. It has, however, not only been mostly confined to the universities; even there it has been too isolated from other fields of
study. It has not had the invigorating effect on Christian commu-

---

[21]Willis B. Glover, *Evangelical Nonconformists and Higher Criticism in the Nineteenth
Century* (London, 1954) 283-86.

nities that might have been expected. The authors of the best Christian belles lettres, for example, have written largely from a precritical Christian tradition.[22] This is not to say that they were not aware of biblical scholarship, but only that the results of higher criticism have not entered largely into the matter of their creative writing. This may be merely the result of a certain inertia in literary traditions. Modern biblical scholarship is a permanent contribution to the Christian intellectual tradition and to the Western mind generally; its limited impact up to this point is due in large part to its association with ineffective theologies.

Contemporary theology is hard to evaluate. The theological revival of the nineteenth century has been extended and deepened in the twentieth. The intellectual power and wide-ranging erudition of individual theologians is beyond question. The problem is why, in spite of this, theology has not succeeded in recovering for the church or for the general intellectual culture a proper appreciation for the biblical-Christian tradition that has done so much to shape the mind of the West. Some of the reasons are not hard to find.

German universities in the nineteenth century were institutions of the state. This had the good effect of freeing scholars from ecclesiastical authority in the pursuit of the new biblical criticism. This very freedom, however, tended to isolate the scholars from the life of the church. The communities in which they functioned were the university and the national and international communities of theological and biblical scholarship. This helps to account for the dominant influence of neo-Kantianism and Hegelianism and the relative neglect of Augustine, Luther, and Calvin. As the influence of Kant and Hegel waned in philosophical circles, theology was more isolated than ever from the general intellectual life. In other countries also, partly due to German influence, theology became a stepchild of the university. Theologians for the last century have written for each other. Some of them have been aware of a problem here and have realized that great Christian theology grows out of the life of the church. Barth and all three Niebuhrs, for example,

---

[22]This is true even of W. H. Auden.

kept in meaningful contact with local congregations. Their relationship to the church as a whole has, nevertheless, been indirect and
the full power of their thought attenuated in relation to the general
community of Christians.

Another weakness is the hold a mechanistic imagination has
had on theologians. This is a remarkable phenomenon. It results
from a defensiveness which makes many theologians overly diffident in relation to secular scholarship—especially toward anything
they regard as scientific. Although various theologians have been
attracted to a variety of modern philosophies, they have tended to
shy away from the modern empirical tradition that might have
helped them at this point. Instead they have tended to neglect
Hume for a naive mechanism that they wrongly associate with
Kant. The strange case of Rudolf Bultmann has already been mentioned. His wide following has not been due only to astuteness as
a New Testament scholar and his existentialism but also to his
freeing his disciples from having to contradict a mechanistic understanding of either nature or history.

The best theologians are not, of course, naive mechanists, but
an undue deference to secular thought and a lack of boldness in as-
serting the philosophical implications of the Christian tradition are
common. There is a general reluctance to accept the concept of a
Christian philosophy. There are exceptions. Richard R. Niebuhr
speaks unabashedly of "Christian metaphysics." Langdon Gilkey
early in his career had a positive attitude toward the philosophical
implications of the doctrine of creation.[23] Wolfhart Pannenberg in-
sists that theology, if it is to be credible to post-Enlightenment man,
must address itself to the fundamental philosophical problems; but
he sometimes speaks of the critical post-Enlightenment mind as if
it had some independent status to which theology must accom-
modate itself.[24]

---

[23]R. R. Niebuhr, *Resurrection and Historical Reason*, 168-70; Langdon Gilkey,
Maker of Heaven and Earth (New York, 1959) 74, 138.

[24]Wolfhart Pannenberg, *The Idea of God and Human Freedom* (Philadelphia, 1973)
92, 97, 120-31, 139-40; E. Frank Tupper, *The Theology of Wolfhart Pannenberg* (Philadelphia, 1973) 33-35, 55, 186.

Instead of developing a philosophy out of what is given in their own tradition, theologians have more commonly sought a congenial philosophy that they could use as the basis of theology in the hope that the credibility of the philosophy would make theology acceptable to the modern secular mind. Serious distortions of Christian tradition have resulted. That this methodology had any apparent feasibility was due to the fact that the philosophies to which theologians have been attracted were all derived in considerable part from the biblical-Christian tradition.[25] The problem with the method was twofold. For one the secular philosophies had denied or radically changed something essential in the Christian tradition. Also each of the philosophies chosen had derived from only a part of a very rich tradition.

Existentialism has been especially congenial to Christian thinkers. Few have explored so thoroughly the plight of man without God as the existentialists. But atheistic existentialism because it could not relate man to God could only describe what from a Christian point of view was the result of sin; it offered no basis for understanding what sin is or the possibility of redemption. The insistence of existentialists on the radical freedom of man is biblical in origin, but with no doctrine of God they have not been able to relate human reality to the world which it transcends but to which it also belongs. Theology has profited much from the insights of existentialists but existentialism is not an adequate ground for the total Christian tradition.

Process theology, based on the philosophy of Whitehead, is largely an American phenomenon. The affinity of Whitehead's philosophy with the historically oriented biblical tradition is obvious. The essential weakness of process theology is that the immanent theism of Whitehead is not reconcilable with the transcendent God of the Bible. On a different level it may be remarked that the philosophy of organism has not been widely enough accepted to make it an automatic entree to secular credibility. It is true, however, that the highly original concepts of Whitehead can offer new ap-

---

[25]Platonism did not, of course, originate in the biblical tradition, but elements of it have been incorporated into so much of Christian thought that it has been congenial to many modern Christians.

proaches to old theological problems. His ontology of organism not only avoids mechanism; it can be used to support the biblical understanding of the unity of man as opposed to the soul and body concept of the Greeks.

Instead of trying to understand theology in the context of some philosophy derived from it, theologians would have done better to have subsumed the philosophies in the great tradition from which they were, however unconsciously, derived. As Stanley Hopper put it, our culture needs to retrace its history possessively.[26] This is particularly true of theology; but what is needed is not just a better knowledge of theology narrowly understood—that the theologians pretty well have—what is needed is a repossessing of the rich and powerful biblical-Christian tradition as a whole. If this had been done, instead of timidity the problem of theology might be a too aggressive and prideful claim of the best of modern science and philosophy as its own.

The empirical philosophical tradition, which is dominant in the English-speaking world, might have had an emancipating effect on theology, but it attracted little attention from theologians. When William Hordern went from Union Theological Seminary to his first teaching position at Swarthmore College, he found that he could not communicate with his colleagues in philosophy. He decided that communication with analytical philosophy was a major task for theology. The result was a period of study to make up for the deficiency in his theological education and a brief but excellent book: *Speaking of God, the Nature and Purpose of Theological Language* (New York, 1964). Several other scholars have addressed themselves to this problem, but they have not had a wide influence in the international community of theological scholarship. There is need for critical study of the origins of analytical philosophy in an empirical tradition that goes back far beyond Hume to the nominalist theologians of the fourteenth century. Such a study might discover that the inanities of contemporary analytical philosophy result from its having severed its relationship to its theological origin. Another result might be to bring to theology a more sophisticated un-

---

[26]Stanley Romaine Hopper, *The Crisis of Faith* (New York, 1944) 22-24.

derstanding of science and open the way for a freer development of the implications of the Christian tradition.[27]

In pointing out some significant problems in theological methodology, one must not be too negative. Theology remains an esoteric concern in the universities, and even there has little impact on other fields. It is, nevertheless, true that there has been a theological revival in this century which has shown more depth and more awareness of the central tradition than anything since Pascal.

The theological giant of the recent era is Karl Barth. Barth's theology is sometimes called dialectical, sometimes a theology of the Word. He undertook to build his theology on the revelation of God as it is given in the Bible. God has revealed himself in historical action; the revelation is not itself propositional; but it is known to us through the biblical records. Barth was knowledgeable of recent biblical scholarship and uses it in his understanding of the Bible, but for him his grasp of the Word of God stood in judgment on the results of merely technical scholarship. Far from recognizing any philosophy as basic to Christian theology, he tended toward a radical separation between theology and philosophy. Neither Barth nor his followers have undertaken to deal with philosophical problems from the point of view of Christian theology. The Barthians criticize certain philosophical positions, but they have not recognized the Christian source of so much secular philosophy and tried to integrate it around its source.

Barth accepted the concept of a *Heilsgeschichte* or a "sacred history" that was that part of the whole of human history in which the divine revelation was made. This prevented him from seeing reality itself as historical. He was not so bold as Richard R. Niebuhr who saw the Resurrection of Christ as a paradigm of *all* historical events. Barth is included by Niebuhr among those whose theology has been distorted by Kantianism.[28] Recent eschatological theologians have accused Barth of having viewed the intervention of God in his-

---

[27]Hume himself suggested the possibility of a positive relationship between a religion based on revelation and a philosophy that recognized the limitations of reason. David Hume, *Dialogues concerning Natural Religion*, ed. Henry D. Aiken (New York, 1951) 94.

[28]R. R. Niebuhr, *Resurrection and Historical Reason*, 80-81.

tory in such a way as to remove God from any concern, much less sovereignty, over the course of world history as a whole.[29]

Barth's theology is the most thorough and comprehensive in the century and will probably be the center around which other theological developments will be integrated; yet the very thoroughness with which he recovered the great theological traditions of the past may have produced an attitude not conducive to radically new developments of the tradition. He was not really diffident in the face of the secular modern mind, but he gives the appearance of such in his failure to pursue boldly the implications of his theology for history.

The most exciting movement in contemporary theology has been the development of a conception of reality itself as historical. This concept would seem to be an obvious implication of the transcendence of God, the subordination of the whole creation to his sovereign will, and the historical nature of God's revelation of himself. That this implication is only now becoming a central theme of theology is a tribute to the strength of Greek influences on Western thought. If the ultimate reality, however, is not the cosmos as the Greeks thought but a transcendent God who wills and acts and is best understood by analogy with persons, then the cosmos itself exists as a product of the will and action of God. Instead of history being a minor drama in the context of nature, nature itself is subsumed under history and is transcended by both God and man.[30] It will take generations of scholars to work out all the implications, but the possibilities are staggering.

That modern man's orientation toward the future is a derivative of the biblical tradition was pointed out in chapter 7. Jürgen Moltmann rightly calls this fascination with the future "the unique characteristic of modern times."[31] The interface here provided be-

---

[29]Christopher Morse, *The Logic of Promise in Moltmann's Theology* (Philadelphia, 1979) 8.

[30]This is clearly implied in R. R. Niebuhr, *Resurrection and Historical Reason*, 40-41, 168-69. Cf. Helmut G. Harder and W. Taylor Stevenson, "The Continuity of History and Faith in the Theology of Wolfhart Pannenberg," *The Journal of Religion* 51 (1971): especially 47-48.

[31]Quoted in Morse, *The Logic of Promise*, 15.

tween the secular mind and a revived theology might be expected to return Christian theology to a creative role in Western culture. This has not happened—at least not yet. Even in Christian circles the new theology of history cannot be said to have generated the enthusiasm that its bold development of a major biblical theme would seem to warrant. In Germany the concept of reality itself as historical has been characteristic of what is called eschatological theology. To explain why in three decades it has had so little impact on contemporary thought even in the church would require a critique far beyond the scope of this essay. Some comments relevant to that problem will have to suffice.

Eschatological theology has developed upon much too narrow a base; it has divorced itself from much that has hitherto been considered essential to the central tradition of Christian thought.[32] Its two most prominent exponents, Jürgen Moltmann and Wolfhart Pannenberg, have offered bold and interesting speculations that are but tenuously related to a form of biblical exegesis and the eschatological teaching of the Bible. They have not dealt adequately with the central doctrine of the transcendence and sovereignty of God. Though both make the resurrection of Jesus central to their theology, neither has dealt with it in a convincing manner. Pannenberg comes closer to tradition here in his insistence that what was experienced in the resurrection appearances was objective; but his discussion of it is not convincing. Sound historical method, he contends, will independent of any religious faith lead to certainty regarding the resurrection of Jesus as a historical event. Faith is a result not a source of such certainty. Pannenberg seems to have believed his analysis of the historical evidence would bring to any honest modern man a certain knowledge of the Resurrection.[33] The fact is he did not even convince Moltmann, whose theology is close

---

[32]See, for example, Wolfhart Pannenberg, "Response to the Discussion," *Theology as History*, ed. James M. Robinson and John B. Cobb, Jr. (New York, 1967) 226-33.

[33]The most thorough attempt to present Pannenberg's numerous theological writings systematically is Elgin Frank Tupper's *Theology of Pannenberg*, cited above. A number of Pannenberg's own works are now available in English, and his theology is the central concern of a symposium called *Theology as History*, cited above. Pannenberg himself has two essays in the symposium.

to his in many ways. For Moltmann the resurrection of Jesus was the apostolic consciousness of an obligation to carry out the mission of Christ in the world.[34] Both Pannenberg and Moltmann have been much too diffident in relation to modern secular thought. Although Pannenberg accepts von Rad's understanding of history as the history of traditions, he has paid scant attention to the history since the New Testament of the great biblical-Christian tradition which is the subject of this essay. Indeed, he explicitly repudiates its authority and appeals to the "critical reason" of "post-Enlightenment man."[35] He seems unaware that there is a passionate anti-Christian religious dimension in Enlightenment and post-Enlightenment humanism. His uncritical acceptance of modernity as the norm to which Christian theology must conform cuts him off from much that is important for theology to reappropriate.

Moltmann is equally deferential. "The move from scriptural exegesis to systematic theology, in Moltmann's view, requires that 'Christian theology . . . think and speak, question and answer within the arena of present day philosophy.' "[36] A method so limited is bound to be restrictive of the great seminal tradition that has given rise to so many of the insights of various contemporary philosophies. It is again the case of trying to put the big box in the little one.

Neither Pannenberg nor Moltmann has made the mistake of trying to make a single modern philosophy the basis of theology. Both were strongly influenced by Hegel, and Moltmann in particular by the atheistic futuristic philosophy of the neo-Marxist Ernst Bloch, some of whose ideas were derived from the Bible. Neither Hegel nor Bloch, however, were followed uncritically. The resemblance beween eschatological theology and Whitehead's philosophy is obvious, but they should not be identified. Moltmann was at some pains to distinguish his "coming God" from the "becoming

---

[34]Jürgen Moltmann, *Theology of Hope* (New York, 1967) 202; Morse, *The Logic of Promise*, 36, 94-96, 104-5.

[35]Tupper, *Theology of Pannenberg*, 33-38, 54-58, 290-91, passim.

[36]Morse, *The Logic of Promise*, 59.

God" of process theology; but he later admitted significant correspondence between them.[37]

These largely negative comments do much less than justice to
two men of brilliant theological insights. Their contribution to theology will be permanent; but a different methodology is needed before their insights can have their full effect.

The work of Richard R. Niebuhr mentioned above offers a
sounder approach to this exceedingly important dimension of
Christian thought. His *Resurrection and Historical Reason* is a closely
reasoned critique of modern theology for not having developed an
adequate conception of historical reason. The book is both cautious
and bold. The analysis of various theologies in their understanding
of history is careful and convincing. Niebuhr, however, does not
merely criticize the thought of others; he comes to original conclusions of great import. The Christian revelation is historical because
our experience is historical. Nature as a systematic understanding
of the world is always a product of history and no such nature can
successfully be made the ground for understanding history itself.
Niebuhr states clearly at the beginning what he is about:

> It is the thesis of this essay that all conceptions of history and of his-
> torical reason that do not begin with the resurrection can neither
> gain from nor contribute to the resurrection faith any significant
> light.
>
> The contention of these chapters is that the hermeneutics of the
> New Testament resurrection tradition and the principles of histor-
> ical method appropriate to theology as a whole must be forged to-
> gether. It is because theologians so often try to endow a Christian
> faith born of the resurrection of Christ with a heterogeneous ep-
> istemology that their treatment of the final chapters of the gospels
> is so pale.
>
> . . . Theologians who still employ that approach have yet to
> learn what a secular historian like Burkhardt [*sic*] perceived,
> namely that history has no set of co-ordinates by which it may be
> calculated and laid out in neat patterns. The chapters which follow
> argue that history is its own interpreter, and that the resurrection
> event, as it is reflected in the New Testament, epitomizes the his-

---

[37]Ibid., 112-13, 119-20.

torical event itself while the resurrection tradition illuminates the nature of historical thought.[38]

Niebuhr's book is profound but brief. His concern was to develop a theological method appropriate to the tradition which theology seeks to elucidate; but he understood that Christian theology properly pursued would touch the whole of human experience. He opens the way for a better understanding of philosophy of science and the role of philosophy itself as well as history. This brilliant essay in theology deserves far more attention than it has received in the nearly three decades since its appearance.

Contemporary theology, despite the learning and intelligence of many theologians, does not constitute an intellectual community with clear goals and an internal discipline that could assure cumulative efforts to achieve them. There has been a significant recovery from the nadir of the Enlightenment, especially in this century; but we do not yet have the theological renaissance so needed if the church is to recover the full power of its intellectual tradition.

---

[38]R. R. Niebuhr, *Resurrection and Historical Reason*, 3-4.

EPILOGUE

A history that comes up to the present is likely to end abruptly. The story is not over and no one knows what will be in the next chapter. This study has concluded that the cultural crisis of our time is fundamentally religious—a crisis of faith. No nostrums are offered. Religious faith cannot be generated as a means to cultural renaissance. A religion created as a means to other ends, however noble, would lack that ultimacy that is essential to religion.

As always in human affairs the future is problematic. If anything that can reasonably be called Western Civilization is to continue, it would seem that its dynamic quality—a product of its unique sense of historical existence—will preclude any stable existence through centuries such as was achieved by some ancient cosmological societies. Despite our anxious utopianism with its insistence upon an unattainable perfection, it is unlikely we will escape continuing catastrophes. Population pressure is already producing catastrophe for millions. Repressive political regimes willing to inflict hideous tortures in order to silence opposition have become commonplace. Unless defenses against the delivery of nu-

clear weapons renders them obsolete, some use of them at some
time is probable. We can take some grim solace in the fact that the
limits of human suffering were reached even before the Assyrians
flayed their captives alive. New wars and new famines will be
worse only arithmetically, but the horror of these prospects is not
to be minimized.

Any effort to deal with our problems by unifying mankind
around some eclectic faith is bound to fail. What we can, perhaps,
do is understand our situation better. We can discover and affirm
what Christian faith and secular humanism have in common. We
can also define our differences and try to integrate culture by reference back to the historical origins and ground of its various elements. A pluralistic society in which there is considerable common
ground and mutual respect is quite feasible. To some degree that is
what we have now; but the cohesiveness of it needs to be greatly
strengthened.

To believe in something as ultimately real can only be to believe
in it because it is true—not because it is useful. Nothing else in history is so unpredictable as religious faith. Who could have predicted that the insights and speculations of Buddha would be
largely ignored in his native India and become the dominant religion of China, Korea, Japan, and other Far Eastern countries? Who
could have predicted that the eclectic, biblical religion of Mo-
hammed would energize the Bedouins of Arabia and within a century dominate the Near East, North Africa, and Spain? Who in the
reign of Marcus Aurelius could have predicted the triumph of
Christianity in the Roman Empire? Modern secular humanism was
implicit in the divine-human relationship postulated by Christianity—a relationship in which man continues his rebellion against
God— but nothing quite like it was anticipated before it developed
in the late seventeenth century.

There is no more a basis for predictions in the present situation.
It is *conceivable* that there could be a Christian revival in Europe and
the Americas; but opposition to Christianity is entrenched and active—this negative aspect of humanism has continued stronger
than its positive appeal. Predictions would be too uncertain to be
meaningful. The unexpected expansion of Christianity in some
Communist countries and in some countries of the Third World

suggests that Christian faith and a secular Western culture that is now worldwide may find a more healthy relationship there than is likely where an anti-Christian tradition is strong. Again no predictions are warranted.[1]

On the other hand, a revival of humanistic faith is also conceivable. The most likely possibility would seem to be a new faith in the scientific enterprise. Scientism might be greatly strengthened if it could incorporate some kind of theism that would serve to relate the human reality to the object of scientific study. Whitehead would offer a better prospect here than the naive efforts of Comte and H. G. Wells—pure speculation.

The immediate prospect is for a continuation of religious pluralism. As indigenous religions of the Third World are more thoroughly adapted to Western influence, this pluralism will likely become more complex. Eclecticism would not be an honest approach to the very real contradictions between the various faiths. More promising would be an effort at the level of the most serious scholarship to explore the history of the relations of religions and culture. It is hoped that this essay may make some contribution to that endeavor.

---

[1] In some Communist countries the ideological and official hostility to Christianity may not be as deep-rooted as the anti-Christian tradition in Western Europe and the United States.

INDEX

Abolitionist movement, 229
Acton, Lord John, 229
Adam of Bremen, 194
Aeschylus, 147
Against Symmachus, 190
Aiken, Henry D., 122n31
Alanus ab Insulis, 31
Albert of Saxony, 20, 39
Albigensians, 27, 45
Alembert, Jean d', 156
Alienation, 4, 113-14, 174, 176, 222-26,
  256. *See also* under Existentialism,
  Nihilism
Allegory of Love, 26
Ambrose of Milan, St., 190
Analytical Philosophy, 104, 131, 266-67
Andreas Capellanus, 30
Angels, 56, 75-76, 180n3
Anselm, St., 40, 130, 194, 260
Anthropology, 11-15, 21, 49-78, 195,
  248-49, 262
Antislavery movement, 229
Apocalypticism, 187, 219
Apostle's Creed, 63, 195
Apuleius, 27

Aquinas, St. Thomas, Thomism, 39-41,
  44, 48, 91, 253
Archimedes, 81, 86
Architecture, 231, 240
Aristocracy, 133-36, 150
Aristotle, Aristotelian, 36-41, 47, 49, 56-
  57, 59, 66, 67, 72-73, 78, 80-84, 87-90,
  95, 116, 140, 184, 195
Arnold, Matthew, 3-4, 250
Aron, Raymond, 170n45
Auden, W. H., 5, 31, 145, 240-41, 263n22
Augustine, St., Augustinian, 9, 35, 50,
  52-55, 59-62, 65, 68-69, 74, 91, 112-16,
  118, 130, 142, 188-90, 193, 221, 234, 247,
  259, 263
Avempace, 86
Averroes, Averroists, Averroism, 46, 67,
  82n2, 83, 87
Avicenna, 27, 82n2

Bacon, Francis, 119-20
Bakunin, Michael, 168
Barfield, Owen, 122n30, 235
Barth, Karl, Barthian, 263, 267-68
Barzun, Jacques, 141-42
Becker, Carl L., 119, 123-25

Bede, 35, 194
Belles lettres, 4-6, 145-46, 228-29, 240-42, 258, 262-63. *See also* under Courtly Love
Bentham, Benthamite, 13, 143, 146
Bergson, Henri, 105, 131, 158, 199, 235-36
Berkeley, Bishop George, 42n51, 98, 104, 111, 172, 260
Bernard, St., 27
Bible, 31, 36, 73-74, 77, 102, 111, 118, 180-81, 186, 188, 267;
  higher criticism, 102, 145, 197-98, 229, 259, 261-63, 267;
  New Testament, 22, 63, 70, 192, 220, 264, 270-71;
    Genesis, 11, 55, 231
      1, 60n32
      1:26-30, 53
      12:3, 186
    Deuteronomy
      10:17, 75
    Psalms
      136:2, 75
    Proverbs
      8:29, 91n21
    Isaiah
      19:23-25; 45:20-23; 49:6; 56:7, 186
      62:5, 31n26
    Daniel
      2:47, 75
    Hosea, 31n26
    Amos
      9:7, 186
    Matthew
      6:10; 13, 187
    John
      3:8, 111
    Romans
      8:14-21, 77n73
    1 Corinthians
      1, 130
      3:21-23; 6:3; 15:42-50, 77n73
    Galatians
      4:4-7, 77n73
    Ephesians
      3:18-19, 77n73
      5:24-29, 31n26

2 Timothy
  2:12, 77n73
2 Peter
  1:4, 77n73
1 John
  3:2, 77n73
Revelation, 220
  21:2, 9-11; 22:17, 31n26
Biblical-Christian tradition. *See* under Judaeo-Christian Tradition
Biology, 101-102, 161, 198-99, 205-12, 224, 230-31, 235-36, 239
Bixler, J. S., 176n50
Bloch, Ernst, 270
Boethius, 91
Bodin, Jean, 195
Books of Hours, 21, 45
Bradwardine, Thomas, 39, 50, 87
Brahe, Tycho, 89
Bramhall, Bishop John, 67
Brethren of the Common Life, 46
Brinton, Crane, 146, 150-51
Bruno, Giordano, 75, 90, 101, 109
Bruun, Geoffrey, 151n15
Bryan, William Jennings, 102
Buddhism, 214, 231, 274
Bultmann, Rudolf, 101, 260, 264
Burckhardt, Jacob, 60, 271
Buridan, John, 20, 39, 92, 94
Burke, Edmund, 161, 254
Burtt, Edwin A., 88
Bury, J. B., 183, 185-87, 190
Bush, Douglas, 109, 229
Butterfield, Herbert, 133-34
Byzantium, 126

Calvin, John, Calvinism, 144-45, 221-22, 259, 263
Cambridge, Platonists, 68, 71-72, 90-91
Camus, Albert, 171, 176-77, 216-18, 249
Cantor, Norman, 188n18
Caroline, Queen, 119, 215
Carrington, Edward, 136
Catholic Revival, 19th century, 144-45
Caton, Hiram, 120n26
Charlemagne, 22, 194, 221
Charles V, (H.R.E.), 26
Chartists, 144
Chartres, School of, 27, 30-31

Chaucer, Geoffrey, 32-33, 46
Chesterton, G. K., 83
Chiliasm, 219-21
Chopin, Frédéric François, 242
Chrétien, de Troyes, 30
Christ, 28, 70, 74, 109, 189, 192-94, 220, 270. *See also* under Incarnation, Resurrection
Christian Democratic Parties, 230, 244
Christianity and Classical Culture, 59
Christianization, 19-46
Churchill, Winston, 230
Cicero, 64, 74
City of God, 59, 148-49, 188, 190, 221. *See also* under Kingdom of God
The City of God, 114, 189, 193
Clagett, Marshall, 85n7
Classical culture, 12-13, 28, 34-38, 51, 53-54, 60n28, 61, 63, 73-74, 83, 116-17, 131, 175, 182-86, 192, 197, 205, 227, 268. *See also* under Philosophy, Cosmological culture, and specific names and subjects
Cochrane, C. N., 59
Cohn, Norman, 219
Coleridge, Samuel T., 146
Communism, Communist countries, 130, 138, 167, 170, 181, 220n16, 242-45, 247, 255-56, 274-75. *See also* under Russia
Comte, Auguste, 157-63, 213, 229, 275
Conciliar Movement, 46
Condorcet, Marie C., Marquis de, 124, 153, 156
Confessions (of St. Augustine), 59-60, 64
Conrad, Joseph, 4
Constantine, 188, 193
Constitution of the United States, 151, 255
Contingency of the World, 10-11, 38, 41, 47, 49, 52-53, 81n2, 83-84, 96-97, 121, 128, 174, 262
Copernicus, Nicholas, 94
Cosmological culture, world view, 14, 16, 38-39, 43, 49, 52-54, 80, 91, 119, 129, 174-75, 181, 203, 208, 235-36, 254, 256, 273
Cosmology, 198, 212, 236
Cosmos and History, 180

Council of Paris (1277), 80, 82, 92
Council of Trent, 144, 261
The Counter-Revolution of Science, 168
Cours de philosophie positive, 168
Courtenay, William J., 81n2
Courtly Love, 26-34
Creation, doctrine of, 9-12, 15, 38-43, 47-49, 52-57, 68, 72, 77-78, 82-84, 91, 96, 180-81, 205, 218, 231, 256, 264, 268
Croce, Benedetto, 202
Crombie, A. C., 39
Crossman, R. H. S., 228n30

Dante, Alighieri, 30-32, 46
Danto, Arthur C., 202n40
Danton, Georges, 153
Darrow, Clarence, 102
Darwin, Charles, 198
Darwinism, 198, 207. *See also* under Biology
Dating from the birth of Christ, 194
Dawson, Christopher, 21
Declaration of Independence, 252
Declaration of the Rights of Man and the Citizen, 139
Deism, 10, 12, 101, 109-15, 120-21, 129, 146-47, 152, 196, 215, 217, 221, 252, 256, 259
Democracy, 135-40, 142, 150, 153-54, 244, 248, 253, 257. *See also* under Democratic Revolution
"Democratic Revolution," 125, 132-33, 139
Democritus, 96
Denomy, A. J., 27-29
Descartes, René, 42n51, 95, 119-21, 127, 171-72, 196
Dialogues concerning Natural Religion, 99
Dichotomy, religious, 124, 127, 146, 227. *See also* under Humanism, non-Christian
Dijksterhuis, E. J., 90n20
Dilthey, Wilhelm, 200
Dirac, P.A.M., 103, 199n34
Ditmanson, Harold, 42n51
Divine Comedy, 31-32
Doddridge, Philip, 113
Dominicans, 45
Donation of Constantine, 63, 195

Dostoevsky, Fyodor, 145, 240
Dover Beach, 3-4
Drake, Stillman, 87
Dualism:
  epistemological, 99-100, 260;
  in non-Christian humanism, 162, 164,
    222, 245-46;
  metaphysical, 52, 100-101, 105, 162,
    174, 218-19, 222, 260;
  social, 219
Duhem, Pierre, 39, 80, 82, 85, 87
Duns Scotus, 60n32

Ecclesiastical History, 188
École polytechnique, 156
Edelstein, Ludwig, 182-85
Edwards, Jonathan, 113, 259
Egalitarianism, 125, 132-33, 138-39,
  150, 153, 254-55
Einhard, 194
Einstein, Albert, 199n34
Eliade, Mircea, 14, 54, 180
Eliot, George, 169
Eliot, T. S., 5, 142, 145, 240-41, 254, 256-
  57
Elizabeth I, 26
Ellul, Jacques, 229
Emerson, Ralph Waldo, 71
Emile, 132
Empiricism, 9, 11, 15, 40-44, 48-49, 66-
  67, 72-73, 83-85, 93, 98, 104-105, 122,
  125, 130-31, 158, 172, 174-75, 230-33,
  264, 266
Encyclopédie, Encyclopaedists, 127
Enlightened despotism, 125, 133, 139
Enlightenment, 9-10, 12-13, 64, 66, 75,
  97, 107-40, 141, 143, 146-48, 156, 190-91,
  195-98, 211, 214-17, 220-22, 227, 232,
  242-43, 247, 249, 256, 259, 260n18, 261,
  270, 272. See also under Liberal pro-
  gressivism
Environmentalism, 121, 132
Epicureanism, 62, 73-74, 183
Epistemology, 34, 38-44, 48, 60, 72, 78,
  98-100, 104-105, 122, 174-75, 184, 202-
  203, 233-35
Eratosthenes, 81
Erigena, John Scotus, 221
Errante, Guido, 27n16

The Essence of Christianity, 168-69
Eschatology, 187-89, 192-93, 269
Essays in the Public Philosophy, 130, 253
Ethics, 23-26, 62, 73-74, 106, 116, 129-30,
  216-18, 225-26, 245-46, 248-56, 259-60.
  See also under Sin, Nihilism, New Left,
  Courtly Love
Études sur Leonard de Vinci, 80, 85
Euclid, 37
The European Mind, 1680-1715, 10n5
Eusebius, 188, 190, 193, 221
Evangelical Protestantism (recent
  United States), 259
Evangelical Revival, 143-44, 261
Evangelicalism, 144-45, 230, 261
Evolution. See under Biology, Darwin,
  Darwinism
"Evolutionary Humanism," 163-65
Existentialism, 4, 9, 15, 49, 67, 106, 121,
  128, 143, 146, 158-59, 166n40, 170-77,
  200-201, 204, 211-12, 215-18, 222-26,
  234-35, 242, 249, 264-65

The Fable of the Bees, 115
The Faerie Queen, 33
Fascism, 130, 155, 255. See also under
  Nazi Germany
Faulkner, William, 4-5, 242
Fénelon, François, 117
Ferguson, Wallace K., 18n3, 55
Feudalism, 23-26
Feuerbach, Ludwig, 147, 168-70
Ficino, Marsilio, 50n7, 56-57, 59, 67-71,
  75-76, 140
First and Last Things, 224
Fleming, Caleb, 111
For the Time Being, 5
Forsyth, P. T., 144, 262
Foster, M. B., 39
Francis I, 26
Franciscans, 40, 41n46, 45-46, 47-49, 55
Frank, Phillip, 165n39
Frazer, J. G., 163
Frederick II, 26
French Revolution, 13, 18n1, 129, 133,
  135-37, 139-40, 143, 148-56, 181, 201. See
  also under Jacobins, Terror
Fromm, Eric, 165n39
Frost, Robert, 4, 242

Galen, 37
Galileo, 85-90, 94-95, 101
Gandhi, Mohandas, 2
Gay, Peter, 12-13, 116, 127
Geology, 198, 212, 230, 235
Gerbert (Sylvester II), 35-36
Gerhard, Dietrich, 18n1
Gershoy, Leo, 124
Gilkey, Langdon, 41n46, 48n4, 264
Gillispie, Charles Coulston, 198n33
Gilson, Etienne, 36, 44
Gladstone, William E., 102
The Gnostic Religion, 223n21
Gnostics, Gnosticism, 120, 162, 218-26
God. See also Creation, Christ, Incar-
  nation, Resurrection, Revelation;
  absolute freedom of, 11, 38, 41-43, 47-
  49, 52-53, 68, 78, 83-85, 92, 96-98, 119,
  121, 174, 186;
  sovereignty of, 38, 91, 96-97, 128, 186-
  87, 192, 209, 215, 268-69
The God that Failed, 246
God the Invisible King, 160-63, 224
Gödel, Kurt, 131
Goldstein, Leon, 203
Grassé, Pierre, 205-206, 209-10
Greene, Graham, 5
Gregory IX, 24
Gregory of Nyssa, 59
Gregory of Rimini, 50
Gregory of Tours, 35

Halévy, Elie, 144
Hall, A. R., 82
Hallowell, John H., 156n22
Hanning, Robert W., 188n, 190, 193
Haskins, Charles, 34
Hawes, Stephen, 33
Hawthorne, Nathaniel, 145
Hayek, Friedrich A., 155-56, 168, 204,
  243n3
Hayes, Carlton J. H., 154
Hazard, Paul, 9-10, 18n1, 97, 108, 113
The Heavenly City of the Eighteenth-Cen-
  tury Philosophers, 123-25
Hebrews, 52, 63, 70, 179-82, 187
Hegel, Hegelianism, 126, 146, 168-69,
  171-73, 199, 202, 233-35, 245n8, 261-
  63, 270

Heidegger, Martin, 171-72, 249
Henley, William Ernest, 171n47
Henry III of England, 26
Henry VIII of England, 26
Henry IV of France, 26
Heptaplus, 58
Herbert, Lord, of Cherbury, 110
Heresy, (Medieval heresies before the
  thirteenth century are not indexed by
  name), 45-46, 68, 73, 80, 228, 262
Hexter, J. H., 180, 229
Hinduism, 214
Hipparchus, 81
Hippocrates, 37
The Historian and History, 180
Historians in the Middle Ages, 194
Historical Knowing, 203
Historicism, 168-70, 200, 203-204, 211-
  12, 216-17, 225-26, 242-49
Historiography, 61, 182, 192-98, 211-12
History against the Pagans, 193
History of England (Hume), 197
History, sense of, 6, 9, 11-15, 44, 49, 52-
  54, 60-64, 78, 106, 116, 118-22, 126-29,
  132, 165-68, 179-212, 220, 222, 268-72
Hobbes, Thomas, 67, 94, 98, 112, 131,
  149n12, 151n16, 172, 253-54
"The Hollow Men," 257
Homage to Galileo, 90
Homer, 193
Hooker, Richard, 221, 253
Hopkins, Gerard Manley, 145
Hopper, Stanley R., 266
Hordern, William, 266
Howard, Donald R., 29
Human rights, 252-54
Humanism:
  Christian, 109;
  Non-Christian, 3, 4, 8, 10, 12-15, 19,
  51, 54, 65, 65n40, 66, 77, 97-98, 108-109,
  114, 118-20, 124-29, 130, 136-37, 146-77,
  200, 202, 213-37, 242-50, 256, 259, 270;
  Renaissance, 49-66, 65n40, 109, 114,
  116, 118
Hume, David, 60, 64, 72, 97-99, 104,
  111, 122, 130-31, 158, 172, 174-75, 197,
  230, 232-35, 260, 264, 266-67
Hus, Jan, 45-46, 172
Husserl, Edmund, 171, 234-35

Huxley, Julian, 15, 160, 163-65, 172, 207, 213, 224
Huxley, Thomas, 102
Hybris, 12-13, 54, 117
The Idea of Progress, 183, 185-87
The Idea of Progress in Classical Antiquity, 183-85
Idealism, 147, 199, 202, 222, 261-62
Imperialism, 2
Incarnation, 56-58, 77, 111, 192
In Our Image and Likeness, 55
An Inquiry concerning Human Understanding, 197
Institutes of the Christian Religion, 221
Invictus, 171n47
Islam, 1, 35, 37, 81, 108, 126, 214, 228, 274
Israel and Revelation, 180

Jacobins, Jacobinism, 125, 137, 139, 150, 151n15, 215-17, 243n2
James I of Scotland, 33
James, William, 164n37
Jansenists, 113, 259
Janus, a Summing Up, 205-208
Jaspers, Karl, 171, 201
Jefferson, Thomas, 136-37, 198, 252
Jeun de Meun, 31
Joachim of Flora, 221
Jocelyn of Brakelonde, 194
John of England, 26
John of Salisbury, 25
Jonas, Hans, 223-26
Judaeo-Christian tradition, 36-39, 52-53, 84, 108, 126-31, 140, 148-49, 174, 180-82, 187, 196, 211, 220, 222-23, 227-29, 232-33, 256, 258-59, 262-63, 265, 270
The Judaeo-Christian Tradition, 180
Judaism, 108, 219

Kahler, Erich, 248-49
Kant, Immanuel, Kantianism, Neo-Kantianism, 99-101, 103-105, 127, 158, 171-73, 210-11, 234, 260-64, 267
Das Kapital, 4
Kennington, Richard, 120
Kepler, Johannes, 89, 94
Kierkegaard, Søren, 171, 173, 175-76, 235, 258

Kingdom of God, 53, 114, 187, 219-21, 247-48. *See also* under City of God
Kingis Quair, 33
Kipling, Rudyard, 2, 4
Knight, Douglas M., 7n4
Koestler, Arthur, 205-208
Koyré, Alexandre, 88-89, 90n18
Kristeller, Paul Oskar, 39n43, 57, 60n28, 70n53
Kristol, Irving, 243-44

Labour Party, 144
Lactantius, 55
Law, William, 259
Lea, C. H., 28
Lecky, William E., 144
Leibnitz, Gottfried, 96, 172
Lenoble, Robert, 93, 95
Lewis, C. S., 26, 29-34, 71, 229
Liberal education, 258
Liberal progressivism, 150, 155, 220, 246
Life of the Emperor Charles, 194
Lippmann, Walter, 130, 218, 253
Locke, John, 42n51, 108, 112, 148, 172, 252-53
The Logic of William of Ockham, 82n2
Logical positivism, 103-104, 121, 131, 175, 202. *See also* under Analytical philosophy, Empiricism, Positivism
Louis XIV, 134
Louis XV, 135
Lovejoy, Arthur O., 117-42
Löwith, Karl, 200
Lubac, Henri de, 168
Lucretius, 96
Luther, Lutheranism, 145, 260, 263
Lydgate, John, 33
Lyell, Sir Charles, 198

Mach, Ernst, 126
Machiavelli, Niccolo, 151n16
MacNeill, William H., 1n1, 28n18
Maier, Anneliese, 39, 85, 87n11, 92
The Making of the Middle Ages, 35-36
Mandeville, Bernard de, 115
Manetti, Giannozzo, 56-59
Manichaeans, 45, 162, 218, 224
Manuel, Frank E., 96n33, 157
Marcel, Gabriel, 171

Marcus Aurelius, 64, 274
Marrou, Henri-Irene, 229
Marx, Karl, 4, 157, 168-70, 217, 224n24, 228n30, 229
Marxism, Marxists, 6, 13, 125, 134, 153-54, 167, 169-70, 191, 202-203, 213, 224, 226, 234n35, 242-50, 270
Mauriac, François, 5
Mechanism:
method, 93-95, 105;
metaphysics, mechanistic imagination, 16, 64, 71-72, 93-101, 110-11, 120-22, 127-28, 131, 196-97, 199, 210-12, 260, 262, 264
Medieval. See under Middle Ages
Mercurius Trismegistus, 70
Meredith, George, 33
Mersenne, Marin, 93-94, 131
Mertonians (Merton College, Oxford), 86
Metaphysical Foundations of Modern Physical Science, 88
Metaphysics, 58, 62, 65, 93-96, 196-97, 199, 210, 212, 223, 233, 236, 260, 264
Metts, Daniel L., 251n10
Michelangelo, 73
Michelet, Jules, 151n15
Middle Ages, 8, 11, 17-46, 47-50, 61, 68, 77, 80-89, 91-92, 98, 105, 109, 117-19, 121, 134, 148, 172, 174, 186-87, 190, 193-95, 209, 232-34, 239-40, 242, 259, 266
Mill, John S., 126, 158-59
Milton, John, 68, 71
Mises, Richard von, 165n39
Moira, 183-84
Molina, Luis de, 115
Moltmann, Jürgen, 203, 268-71
Mommsen, T. E., 188n18, 190
Monasticism, 21-22
Moody, Ernest A., 44, 72, 82n2, 84, 87, 233-34
More, Sir Thomas, 222
Moses, 188
Muller, Herbert Joseph, 208, 208n48
Music, 232, 240-41

Napoleon, 125, 133, 143, 157
Nardi, Bruno, 40, 47-49
Nationalism, 13, 125, 154-55, 170, 242-43, 245

"Natural religion," 99, 110
Natural Right and History, 253-54
Natural Rights, 253-54
Naturalism, 14, 75, 127-30, 132, 165-68, 224-25, 246. See also under Platonic naturalism
Nazi Germany, 2, 138, 155, 220n16, 243, 253, 255, 257
Neoplatonism, 14, 27, 56-59, 66-73, 76-77, 82n2, 87-91, 109
Nevill, William, 33
The New Christianity, 156-57
New Left, 6-8, 257-58
Newton, Isaac, 92-96, 108, 157, 209
Newtonian science, 5, 91n21, 157
Nicholas of Autrecourt, 20, 82n2, 84, 92
Nicholas of Cusa, 89
Nicholas of Oresme, 20, 39, 94
Niebuhr, B. G., 182, 193
Niebuhr, H. Richard, 263
Niebuhr, Reinhold, 137, 191-92, 248, 263
Niebuhr, Richard R., 48n4, 179-80, 203, 261, 263-64, 267, 268n30, 271-72
Nietzsche, Friedrich, 4, 126, 149-50, 171, 173, 175-76, 215, 235, 245n8, 249
Nihilism, 6-8, 216, 222-26, 248-50, 256-58, 256n16
Nisbet, Robert A., 190
No Exit, 150
Nominalism, 9, 11, 15, 38, 40-44, 47-51, 55, 60, 66, 73, 77-78, 81n2, 83-84, 90-91, 95, 130, 174, 234, 266
Norman Conquest, 201
Nuclear power, 191, 251
Nuclear war, 251, 273-74
Nygren, Anders, 70n53, 76

Oakeshott, Michael, 60
Oakley, Francis, 82n2, 91n21, 92, 96
Oberman, Heiko A., 50n7, 92, 92n22
Ockham, William of, Ockhamites, 20, 39, 41, 44n55, 47, 50, 66, 72, 82n2, 83, 92, 122, 232, 260
O'Connor, Flannery, 5, 241
Ontology, 10, 38, 41, 68, 76, 100, 104-105, 130-31, 172, 174-75, 192, 199-200, 211, 262, 265. See also under Metaphysics
The Opium of the Intellectuals, 170n45
Oration on the Dignity of Man, 56-57, 70
Orosius, 193

Ortega y Gasset, 200-201, 241, 255
Otto, Max, 165n39
Otto of Freising, 195
Padua, University of, 40, 66, 86
Pagans, paganism, 13, 20-23, 33, 35, 51, 116, 190, 227
Painter, Sidney, 23-25, 28
Palmer, R. R., 125, 133, 135, 151
Pannenberg, Wolfhart, 48n4, 203, 264, 269-71
Paracelsus, 75, 90, 109
Parker, Harold, 116
Pascal, Blaise, 16, 97, 113-15, 125, 141-42, 223, 259, 267
The Pastime of Pleasure, 33
Paton, Alan, 241
Patriades, C. A., 187n15
Patristic tradition, 21-22, 36, 55-56, 59, 77-78
Paul, The Apostle, 101, 130, 142, 220, 261
Peace of God, 22, 24
Pelagianism, 50, 58, 112-15
Percy, Walker, 5, 145
Perfectibility, Concept of, 118, 152, 156, 220, 222. *See also* under Progress, idea of
Petrarch, 46, 50, 59-60, 64, 74
Philip II, Augustus, 26
Philosophy:
  Christian, 40-41, 47-49, 231, 264, 271-72;
  classical, 43, 48, 54, 72-73, 205, 233, 253;
  modern, 43-44, 47-48, 66-67, 72, 126, 170-77, 199-202, 211-12, 232-36, 264-66, 270;
  of history, 200-203, 211;
  of science, 103-105, 122-23, 130-31, 199, 204-205, 231, 266-67, 272;
  See also under the names of specific philosophers and philosophies
Pico della Mirandola, Giovanni, 54, 57-59, 70-71, 75, 109
Plato, Platonism, 31, 35-36, 49-50, 54, 56-57, 59, 70, 71-73, 76, 80, 87-91, 110, 116, 140, 226, 265n25
Platonic naturalism, 30-31
Plotinus, 68, 76

Polanyi, Michael, 103, 105, 122, 148-49, 149n12, 235
Policraticus, 25
Pomponazzi, Pietro, 57, 60n32
Population pressure, 191, 250-51, 273
Porphyry, 91
Positivism, 103, 158-59, 162-63, 168-69, 202. *See also* under Analytical philosophy, Empiricism, and Logical positivism
Potentia absoluta, 85, 92, 209
Potentia ordinata, 43, 85, 92, 209
Pragmatists, 235
Praz, Mario, 142-43, 171
The Prince, 151n16
Process Theology, 265-66
Progress, idea of, 118-21, 128, 132, 140, 182-92, 196, 211-12
Progress and Power, 124
Progressivism. *See* under Liberal progressivism
Prometheus, Prometheanism, 143, 147, 149, 162, 166, 171, 176, 217, 224
Prometheus Unbound, 6, 147
Protagoras, 13n6
Protest movement, 1960s and 1970s. *See* under New Left
Prudentius, 190
Ptolemy, 37
Public Philosophy. See under *Essays in the Public Philosophy*
Puritanism, 221-22
Pusey, Nathan M., 7, 257
Pythagoreans, 88

Quinet, Edgar, 151n15

Rad, Gerhard von, 181, 270
Randall, John Herman, Jr., 67, 114
The Rebel, 176-77, 216-18, 249
Reformation, 10, 26, 46, 49, 74, 109, 126, 144, 190, 195, 221, 259
Religion of Humanity, 158-60
Religion of Newton, 157
Renaissance, 10n5, 17-18, 32, 39n43, 40, 49-78, 108-10, 172, 190, 195. *See also* under Humanism, Renaissance
Reno, Edward A., Jr., 184
Resurrection, 69-70, 101, 189, 192, 260-61, 267, 269, 271

Resurrection and Historical Reason, 48n4, 268n30, 271-72
Revelation, 40, 47, 83-84, 109-11, 259-60, 267
Rights. *See* under Human rights, Natural rights
The Rise of the West, 1, 28n18
Roberts, Penfield, 119, 215
Robespierre, Maximilian, 128, 146, 201
Roland, Manon, Mme., 153
Roman Empire, 1, 20n5, 188-90, 221, 227
Roman Republic, 117
Romantic Agony, 171
Romantic Love. *See* under Courtly Love
Romanticism, Romantics, 14, 128, 141-50, 154-57, 171, 173, 197, 222, 226
Roosevelt, Theodore, 2
Rousseau, Jean-Jacques, 115-17, 132-33, 138-39, 148-49, 152-53, 228n30, 254, 257n16
Russia, 2, 181, 242-44, 247, 251

Sabatier, Paul, 55
Saint-Just, Louis de, 151n15
Saint-Maur, 195
Saint-Simon, Henri, Comte de, 155-59, 161, 163, 215
Salutati, Coluccio, 50, 60
Sarton, George, 39
Sartre, Jean-Paul, 15, 128, 149, 150, 171, 176, 200, 215-16, 249
Schleiermacher, Friedrich, 145
Scholarship, modern lay Christian, 229
Scholasticism, 20, 34-44, 49, 53, 55-56, 60, 67, 140
Science:
conflict with religion, 79, 101-104;
Hellenistic, 80-81, 83, 184;
Islamic, 80-82, 81n2;
modern, origins of, 14, 34, 37, 49, 72, 78, 80-96
The Science of Life, 163
Scientism, scientific humanism, 13, 15, 39, 42n51, 43, 125, 129, 155-70, 202, 230n32, 245-46, 248, 275
Secular state, 151-53
Seneca, Lucius Annaeus, 183-85
Shakespeare, William, 33, 240
Shelley, Percy Bysshe, 6, 142, 146-47

Shideler, Mary McDermott, 31n28
Silverstein, Theodore, 27
Simmons, Edward Gordon, 195n29
Sin, 9, 11, 13, 58, 69, 73, 78, 102, 108-18, 127, 136-38, 149, 152, 176, 188-89, 192, 196, 221-22, 227-28, 247
Singer, Dorothea, 90n20
Skepticism, 11, 13n6, 15, 38, 40, 42-44, 47, 50, 72-73, 82n2, 84, 92-94, 99, 122, 172, 233-34, 260
Skinner, B. F., 14, 165n39, 166-68
Smalley, Beryl, 194-95
Smith, Page, 180, 202
The Social Contract, 132-33, 152
Social contract theories, 9
Socialism, non-Marxist, 125, 245; utopian, 4, 13
Solzhenitsyn, Alexander, 240
Southern, R. W., 35-36
Sparta, 117
Speaking of God, 266
Spencer, Herbert, 158
Spengler, Oswald, 202
Spenser, Edmund, 30-31, 33-34
Stephen, Leslie, 110-12
Stoicism, 13, 35, 62, 73-74
Strauss, Leo, 253-54
Stromberg, Roland N., 128, 169, 244-45, 245n7
Strong, Edward W., 88, 90
Suetonius, 194
Supreme Court of the United States, 255
Sylvester II. *See* under Gerbert
Symmachus, 190
Le Système du monde, 80

Tate, Allen, 5
Technology, 2-3, 5, 79, 122, 189, 225, 231-32, 239-40, 248-51
Teleology, 14, 42n51, 49, 52, 78, 84, 93, 108, 118, 162, 164-67, 180, 199, 203-12, 224, 231, 236, 253-54. *See also* under History, sense of
Tempier, Etienne, 80
The Temple of Glas, 33
Tennyson, Alfred, Lord, 6, 145
Theologia poetica, 75n66
Theologia rhetorica, 75n66
The Terror, 125, 139, 150, 153

Theology:
Catholic. *See* under Catholic Revival, Council of Trent, Patristic tradition, Scholasticism, Vatican Council II, and specific theologians and other scholars;
Protestant, 16, 48-49, 97-101, 144-45, 227, 258-72;
Eschatological theology, 267-71
Theology of Pannenberg, 269n33
Third World, 138, 244, 247, 274-75
Thode, Henry, 55
Thorndike, Lynn, 39
Thucydides, 182
Time. *See also* under Dating; cyclical, 11, 181, 183-86, 192, 203; linear, unidirectional, 181, 186, 192, 194, 196, 198-99, 232
Tolkien, J. R. R., 5, 241-42
Tolstoy, Leo, 145
Totalitarianism, 126, 130, 138-40, 170, 191, 213-14, 217, 225, 242-47, 256, 273. *See also* under Communism, Fascism, Nazi Germany
The Tower and the Abyss, 248-49
Toynbee, Arnold J., 202
Trinity, 76, 193
Trinkaus, Charles, 49, 50, 55, 59, 60n32, 61-62, 67, 70n53, 74, 75n66, 76
Troilus and Cryseide, 32, 46
Truce of God, 22, 24
Tupper, Elgin Frank, 269n33
Turgot, A. R. J., 156

UNESCO, 163
Uniformitarianism, 132-33, 139
United Nations, 252. *See also* under UNESCO
United States of America, 136, 151-52, 247, 251-55
Utopia, 222
Utopian, utopianism, 13, 220, 248, 273

Valla, Lorenzo, 58-63, 74, 76, 195
Vasoli, Cesare, 67
Vatican Council II, 144-45, 230, 259, 261
Victoria, Victorianism, 144
Vikings, 35, 194
Vives, Ludovicus, 63-64
Voegelin, Eric, 120n27, 155-56, 180, 202, 217-22, 224n24, 225-26, 245-46
Volkoff, Vladimir, 5, 145
Voltaire, 113-16, 124, 221, 230
Voluntarism, 50, 59-62, 83-84, 90-92, 186, 192, 195, 200, 204, 209, 232, 234-35

Wallace-Hadrill, D. S., 188n18
Warren, Robert Penn, 5, 241
The Waste Land, 256-57
Wasteland poets, 4, 256-57
Watts, Isaac, 113
Wells, H. G., 124, 129, 158, 160-63, 213, 215, 224, 275
Wesley, John, Wesleys, 113, 143, 159, 161
Westfall, Richard S., 96n33
Whitehead, Alfred North, 105, 122, 131, 199-200, 208, 234-36, 265, 270, 275
Wilberforce, Samuel, Bishop, 102
Wilberforce, William, 146
Wilder, Thornton, 5, 145, 241
William of Malmesbury, 194-95
William of Tyre, 194-95
Williams, Charles, 5, 31, 71, 241
Wolf, Friedrich A., 193
Wordsworth, William, 142
World Council of Churches, 228n29
World War I, 154, 191, 250
World War II, 4, 106, 170, 176, 191, 230, 240, 250, 257, 259
Wyclif, John, 45-46, 172

Yeats, William Butler, 4, 240, 242
Zoroaster, 70